Moralists and Modernizers

THE AMERICAN MOMENT

Stanley I. Kutler, Series Editor

Moralists and Modernizers

America's Pre–Civil War Reformers

STEVEN MINTZ

The Johns Hopkins University Press
Baltimore and London

© 1995 The Johns Hopkins University Press
All rights reserved. Published 1995
Printed in the United States of America on acid-free paper
04 03 02 01 00 99 98 97 96 95   5 4 3 2 1

The Johns Hopkins University Press
2715 North Charles Street
Baltimore, Maryland 21218-4319
The Johns Hopkins Press Ltd., London

ISBN 0-8018-5080-0
ISBN 0-8018-5081-9 (pbk.)

Library of Congress Cataloging-in-Publication Data
will be found at the end of this book.
A catalog record for this book is available from the British Library.

For David Brion Davis

Contents

Editor's Foreword

The decades of reform prior to the Civil War are a special moment in American history. Turbulent, yet productive, they set in motion the American reform tradition. Periodically in eclipse, always under assault from defenders of privilege and the status quo, the reformist instinct nevertheless informs and shapes public debates over public policies. Reformers have, in Steven Mintz's perceptive words, "stuck thorns in the side of indifference and dared to dream of a better world."

Reform in the antebellum period, as in others, sprang from a variety of motives, including social distress and anxiety, as well as from altruism and a millennialist sense of possibilities. The goals varied as activists emphasized different moral, humanitarian, and radical reforms. Moral reformers sought to uplift society and involved themselves in such efforts as enforcing the Sabbath, promoting alcohol prohibition, and combating prostitution. Humanitarian reformers sought meliorative prescriptions for social ills, including crime and disease, and created institutions for society's outcasts, from criminals to the mentally ill. Finally, radical reformers sought to remove sources of inequality by abolishing slavery and ensuring the rights of women.

The writing of the history of reform has an interesting history of its own. The persistent tradition is one that treats reform as progress, as a story of human improvement. Success stories abounded, whether they concerned the abolition of slavery, the triumph of women's rights, or the making of such institutions as the public schools, hospitals, or various asylums. Historical revisionism, however, inevitably reversed that optimistic story, focusing instead on the deviant role of reformers or interpreting the achievements of the era as the triumph of social control and class domination. Still others have applauded the reformers' moralism as a rallying standard against prevailing evil in the society.

Steven Mintz wisely avoids any simple explanation for understanding the motives and aims of the reformers. Finding elements of both humanitarianism and paternalism, Mintz emphasizes reform's duality, blending social and moral uplift with attempts to impose reformers' own values and new codes of conduct on the society. Rejecting any sociological symmetry for the origins of reform, Mintz stresses its complexity. He also understands that politics ultimately determined the success or failure of the reformists' efforts. Finally, Mintz's comparison of reform in pre–Civil War America with the interest group orientation of reformers today is telling and instructive.

The antebellum reformers believed that they operated from within the American revolutionary tradition, with the ideals expressed in the Declaration of Independence. All this is summed up as "liberalism," a concept certainly in retreat today. Historically in the United States, liberalism has been a rallying cry for those who believed in universal moral standards, who sought the removal of barriers that stifled individual fulfillment, and who refused to accept the dictates of an ill-defined "market," guided by a beneficent, all-wise, invisible hand, as an excuse for inaction. The notion of the "do-gooder," of those with a faith that society's ills could be cured either by moral uplift or by governmental intervention, is not fashionable at the end of the twentieth century. But it is a good bet that we have not seen the last of it.

Stanley I. Kutler
THE UNIVERSITY OF WISCONSIN

Acknowledgments

This book is a work of synthesis and interpretation, which draws upon the work of dozens of fellow scholars in the field of antebellum American culture. The bibliographical essay that concludes this volume provides a detailed record of the many debts I have acquired. To these authors, I extend a warm thanks.

Certain individuals deserve special mention. First of all, I want to thank a group of scholars that has shaped my understanding of antebellum American culture: Joel Bernard, Michael Grossberg, Karen Halttunen, Richard J. Jensen, James H. Jones, Jackson Lears, Jan Lewis, Patricia N. Limerick, Sonya Michel, Rod Olsen, Susan L. Porter, Eric C. Schneider, and Theda Skocpol. I am also grateful to Stanley I. Kutler and Henry Y. K. Tom, who offered encouragement and expert guidance in transforming my early drafts into a finished book. Charles Dellheim merits special acknowledgment. For more than twenty years, I have profited from his criticisms, comments, and suggestions. I owe a special debt of gratitude to Susan Kellogg for her love, support, insights, and endless patience. I would like to thank all these people for tangibly demonstrating that the academy can be a place of mutual assistance, not simply an arena for self-promotion.

Above all, I wish to thank a teacher who radically transformed my understanding of history. For David Brion Davis, history is an instrument of moral and psychological self-discovery. It is a way to free ourselves from deceptions embedded in our ideology and culture.

At a time when the hegemony of social history within the profession was virtually complete, Davis continued to emphasize the importance of ideas. Instead of treating them as free-floating entities, he has sought to locate ideas in social, political, and economic contexts that defined their meanings, implications, and consequences.

This book represents my attempt to engage two of Davis's key interests. These are problems of moral perception—why social evils, to which people had been blind for centuries, became recognized as moral problems at a particular time; and problems of social praxis—how abstract moral issues are translated into practical political action.

In Davis's hands, history offers a way to burrow into the tangled recesses of our historically shaped identities, to grapple with life in all its complexity and ambiguity, much as a novelist, a philosopher, or a psychoanalyst might. It is a great pleasure to dedicate this book to him.

Introduction

The late eighteenth and early nineteenth centuries witnessed the first secular efforts in history to improve society through reform. In Britain, western Europe, and the United States, reformers launched unprecedented campaigns to educate the deaf and the blind, rehabilitate criminals, extend equal rights to women, achieve world peace, and abolish slavery.

During the decades before the Civil War, the United States stood at the forefront of efforts to devise innovative and humane solutions to problems of poverty, crime, illiteracy, and mental illness. Inspired by the Declaration of Independence, the Enlightment faith in reason, and, above all, religious ideals, many early-nineteenth-century Americans joined together to curb drinking, reform prostitutes, spread the Christian gospel, and establish experimental communities to serve as models for society. Our modern systems of free public schools, prisons, and hospitals for the mentally ill are all legacies of this first age of reform.

Beyond their specific achievements, America's pre–Civil War reformers left an even more lasting gift: they reinvigorated American ideals and reinforced the nation's commitment to equality and social justice. If Americans today recognize the various forms that oppression, inequality, exploitation, and tyranny can take, this is largely on account of past reformers who stuck thorns in the side of indifference and dared to dream of a better world.

This book tells the story of America's first age of reform—a period of extraordinary spiritual, social, and cultural ferment. The volume begins by examining the roots of the reform impulse, which lay in a mixture of anxiety and hope. In part, there existed deep-seated fears of social disorder, violence, family fragmentation, and widening class divisions. The late eighteenth and early nineteenth centuries were a period of rapid and unsettling social changes: the emergence of a market economy, the beginnings of rapid urban and industrial growth, the decline of deference, the spread of democratic politics, an increasingly unequal distribution of wealth, and radical shifts in women's roles and status. The disintegration of an older patriarchal, hierarchical social order contributed to a deep sense of anxiety—that democracy would degenerate into anarchy, that self-seeking individualism would erode traditional morality, that commercialism would undermine national ideals. Chapter 1 examines the ways that these various fears contributed to the rise of reform. During the decades preceding the Civil War, a growing number of Americans believed that the only way to stabilize the social order was to internalize self-restraints within the depths of individual character through religion and moral reform.

But the roots of reform did not lie exclusively in fear and anxiety. Reform also arose out of a millennialist sense of possibilities that was both secular and religious in its origins. Chapter 2 analyzes the intellectual and spiritual sources of the reform impulse, notably, two trends in American religion—not only a humanitarian revolt against Calvinism but also an evangelical revivalism—which combined to produce an extraordinary sense of promise. At the core of antebellum reform was a religious and moral revival that pervaded many aspects of American society.

Chapters 3, 4, and 5 examine the efforts of reformers to create a new moral order. Chapter 3 focuses on moral reform, the effort to uplift the nation's morals and spread Christian values by distributing Bibles and religious tracts, establishing Sunday schools and religious missions, enforcing the Christian Sabbath, combating prostitution, and curbing alcohol. Through these campaigns, reformers sought to strengthen the country's Christian character and rescue the nation from infidelity and intemperance. Chapter 4 turns to a second line of reform, the humanitarian, which sought to alleviate such sources of human misery as crime, disease, and ignorance by building prisons, public schools, and asylums for the deaf, the blind, and the mentally ill. These "crucibles of character" were to rectify the failures of individual families, educate children, rehabilitate criminals, and provide refuges for society's outcasts. Chapter 5 analyzes radical reform, the effort to regenerate American society by removing the underlying sources of sin and inequality. Radical reformers sought to perfect society by abolishing slavery, guaranteeing women's rights, and constructing utopian communities to serve as blueprints for a better world. An epilogue, then, fits antebellum reform into America's broad liberal tradition.

Overall, I am concerned with the efforts of reformers to spread a new "middle-class" reform gospel. This gospel sought simultaneously to free individuals from various forms of bondage; to eradicate such "relics of barbarism" as chattel slavery and corporal punishment; and to create a sober, educated, self-disciplined citizenry. Advocates of the gospel of reform regarded their crusades as vehicles for progress and social betterment. Their adversaries, and many subsequent historians, have adopted a more critical perspective, stressing the class, gender, and racial limitations of the reformers' vision. That is, efforts to replace physical coercion resulted in less visible, but no less potent, psychological forms of discipline. And the reformers effectively created new instruments of social control and confinement, ranging from poorhouses and prisons to reformatories and asylums. I mean to capture the complexity of this extraordinary story, recounting the reformers' high aspirations and profound moral reflections, as well as the ironies and the ambiguities of antebellum reform, the reformers' unfulfilled visions and incomplete victories.

How historians have explained and interpreted pre–Civil War reform has gone through a series of interpretive cycles. For many years, the history of reform was treated from a liberal, progressive, Whiggish perspective. According to this view, the history of reform was essentially a story of progress: an advance from barbarism, cruelty, ignorance, and brutality to enlightenment. The early nineteenth century, so it was said, was marked by a heightened sensitivity to human suffering and a new sympathy for social outcasts. Modern hospitals and insane asylums, based on the most up-to-date medical principles, sought to cure disease and comfort the afflicted. The goal of prisons became rehabilitation, not punishment. Public schools sought to combat ignorance and illiteracy. Slavery was defeated, and women gained legal recognition of basic rights. If in the end many of these innovations failed to live up to the reformers' good intentions, this was on account of popular ignorance, legislative indifference, and the strength of entrenched interests.

If early historians of reform, such as Gilbert H. Barnes, Merle Curti, Carl Russell Fish, John Allen Krout, and Arthur M. Schlesinger, criticized the naiveté and extremism of antebellum reformers (in contrast to the more pragmatic, institutional reformers in the Progressive and New Deal eras), they nevertheless regarded those early reform crusades as the precursors of the struggles for the rights of labor, racial justice, and a modern welfare state. After World War II, however, a new generation of historians looked at reform more skeptically. Shaken by the horrors of fascism, the Holocaust, and the gulag, postwar historians adopted a critical perspective on perfectionism, utopianism, and social engineering. The antebellum reformers' optimistic convictions about human innocence and perfectibility seemed sadly out of date. The revisionists, as the postwar reform historians were known, viewed antebellum reformers as psychological deviants and fanatics and sought the basis of the movement in social and economic dislocations and religious upheaval. The revisionists focused much of their attention on the antislavery movement. Avery Craven, a pioneer in the application of psychology to ante-bellum reform, invoked the psychoanalytic concepts of frustration and com-pensation to analyze abolitionists' motives and behavior. Another important revisionist, David Donald, located abolitionism's origins in the status anxieties of a declining social elite.

One of the most influential revisionists was Stanley Elkins, who sought to place the American antislavery movement in a comparative perspective. He argued that American abolitionism had a uniquely American character—it was moralistic, rigid, and simplistic rather than pragmatic, immediatist rather than gradualistic. This was the result, Elkins said, of amorphous antebellum society, particularly its lack of highly developed social institutions. He saw the abolitionists as irresponsible agitators whose disdain for established political channels made civil war inevitable.

Beginning in the mid-1960s, historical approaches to reform shifted in two very different directions. Many New Left historians celebrated antebellum reformers as the forerunners of later struggles for social change in America. Unlike the revisionists, who criticized the reformers' moralism and fanaticism, New Left historians viewed them as models of uncompromising integrity, high moral idealism, and passionate commitment. According to the New Left argument, reformers' extremism and tactics of confrontation, far from being symptoms of a deep-seated irresponsibility, were in fact pitched to the level of evil in their society.

At the same time, another group of historians began to criticize reform as an instrument of social control and class domination. Urban missions, Sunday schools, and tract societies all, in this view, were the vehicles of cultural im-perialism. Campaigns against drinking and blood sports like cockfighting and bearbaiting came to be seen as paternalistic attempts to suppress an autono-mous working-class culture and impose bourgeois values. Public schools, those instruments of capitalist hegemony, instilled such middle-class traits as hard work, punctuality, self-discipline, and personal responsibility. Prisons, asylums, and reform schools were institutions to repress and isolate deviants. All efforts at reform, from this perspective, were parts of a vast campaign to impose order on society by increasing the power of the state.

In fact, the realities of antebellum reform are too complex to fit any one formula. Reform was not simply foisted on the country by traditional elites eager to impose discipline and moral order on a disorganized society. Neither was it merely an effort by middle-class modernizers to promote discipline, sobriety, and regular work habits in an increasingly urban and industrial society. Nor was it an attempt, in the interest of social efficiency, to hide deviance. From the start, antebellum reform combined a humanitarian impulse to redeem and rehabilitate the victims of social change and a paternalistic impulse to shape character and regulate behavior. This book charts a middle ground between those who regard reform as a means of class-based social control and those who stress reformers' benevolent intentions. It emphasizes the duality of antebellum reform, the social and moral uplift and the institutions of control. Older versions of the social control thesis were not only excessively conspiratorial, they failed to distinguish the reformers' intentions from the consequences of reform. This volume has consequently adopted a multicausal approach that stresses the importance of politics and the interactions among reformers and those they hoped to help.

The reformers' backgrounds defy simple generalization. Though almost all were deeply religious men and women, their spiritual, geographical, and social roots were remarkably diverse. Some were Quakers; others Baptist, Congregationalist, Episcopalian, and Methodist; still others liberal Unitarian. To be sure, a disproportionate share came from New England, but many came from outside that region. Some had only recently arrived in cities from rural farms and villages, and they were nostalgic for a supposedly more stable past and intensely anxious about urban disorder. Many others were longtime urban residents.

Reformers also diverged widely in their motives. Some were representatives of an old elite eager to preserve or restore traditional patterns of social order based on deference and hierarchy. Others were motivated by a religious vision of creating a godly society on earth. Still others were members of a rising business or mercantile class, who viewed reform as a way to mute class conflict and instill the values associated with the Protestant ethic. But the reform impulse also enjoyed broad-based support from northern working people, Protestant evangelicals, theological liberals, and moralistic Whigs.

Reform ranks included many conservatives, who wanted to stabilize the social order. Most were inspired by a more positive vision—a vision of human improvement. This would result from the dissemination of certain basic values—self-control, industriousness, sobriety, deferral of gratification, and self-discipline—regarded as necessary for individual advancement and social harmony.

Today, this set of values, which reform helped define and diffuse, is often described—and ridiculed—as "middle-class morality." But it is clear in retrospect that reform was one of the characteristics that came to define the emerging middle class: its social role, its set of social values that differentiated it from other classes, and its distinctive moral orientation, rather than a particular economic base. Middle-class morality—the values of hard work, self-help, thrift, sobriety, self-discipline, ambition, respectability, and the drive for self-improvement—animated criticism of slavery, racism, and sexual inequality.

My overarching argument is that a new moral perspective arose in the early nineteenth century, acutely sensitive to cruelty, drunkenness, and physical disorder. This new sensibility provided the sanction for a wide range of reform proposals, which included a "missionary" impulse to make leisure time conform to the standards of Protestant morality; a "humanitarian" impulse to establish "crucibles of character," institutions designed to nurture certain "middle-class" behavioral and character traits; and a "liberationist" impulse to free individuals from corrupt customs and coercive institutions. It is the duality of antebellum reform—the same sensibility inspired efforts to rescue and rehabilitate society's outcasts and to transform the behavior of deviants— that makes it impossible to categorize reformers simply as humanitarians or social controllers.

One of my primary goals is to locate the reform impulse in a specific social and economic context—a period of growing laissez-faire, when attitudes toward labor, individual responsibility, and property were undergoing momentous changes. Rejecting any simple teleology that would describe antebellum reform merely as a progressive force or, conversely, as an instrument of capitalist discipline and control, I seek to advance another line of interpretation. At a time when Western societies were moving toward free-market economies, a key question was what limits would be placed on acquisitiveness and exploitation. Antebellum reformers played a critical role in establishing minimum standards of human dignity and decency, imposing limits on exploitation, and creating modern institutions to rescue and rehabilitate the victims of social change.

The story of pre–Civil War reform is filled with paradoxes and ironies. First, for example, is the tension between reforms' religious roots and the secular form that reform took. The impetus for reform sprang from religious ideals and aspirations. Indeed, the goal of many reformers was nothing less than reestablishing the moral government of God on earth. And yet, they quickly adopted secular methods, helping to pioneer modern techniques of mass communications, propaganda, social work, and statistics.

Second, the conservative self-image of many reformers is at odds with the radical implications of the reforms that they created. The reform impulse tended to originate among the pious northeastern upper class—people who thought of themselves as conservative custodians of culture, as preservers of time-honored values, as the natural leaders of their society. But the impulse quickly spread to many outsider groups, and many women, artisans, shopkeepers, and racial and cultural minorities asserted themselves and challenged traditionally defined roles and constraints.

Third, there is a discrepancy between many reformers' anti-institutional outlook and their part in creating enduring social institutions and bureaucracies and strengthening the role of the state. During the years between 1810 and 1830, the primary tool of reform was the voluntary society, which sought to accomplish its goals through moral force, to persuade Americans to abstain from alcohol, observe the Sabbath, and recognize the sinfulness of slavery. Over time, however, the reform impulse became institutionalized and bureaucratized, and increasingly reformers came to believe that to be successful their programs needed the help of state and local governments. Establishment of public school systems, prisons that rehabilitated rather than punished, and asylums where treatment of the mentally ill was according to the most advanced medical principles—all required government action. By the 1840s, more and more temperance advocates called for legislation to prohibit the manufacture and sale of liquor, and a growing number of antislavery proponents believed that abolition of slavery could be achieved only through political action.

Fourth, the reformers idealized a more stable, orderly past, but the practical effect of their efforts was to modernize and rationalize society. Antebellum reformers tended to believe that the nation's problems were rooted in the breakdown of earlier patterns of life, especially the weakening of family and community ties. They were nevertheless modernizers, promoting market values and creating such modern institutions as the public school system, the prison, the reformatory, and the asylum for the mentally ill.

Perhaps the central irony of antebellum reform is that the reformers were at once religious moralists and social and cultural modernizers, a paradox to which I allude in the book's title. Many pre–Civil War reformers thought of themselves as moral conservatives striving to reorient American society in accordance with God's moral laws. Yet the reformers were also exponents of a distinctly modern set of values. For example, unlike religious traditionalists, who tended to oppose missionary activities, many reformers were spiritual egalitarians whose belief in universal moral values and whose faith that all humans were capable of salvation inspired efforts to spread the Christian gospel worldwide. Also, unlike more traditional Protestants, who placed a heavy emphasis on theology, reformers tended to de-emphasize theology, stressing deeds rather than creeds and defining sin not as a metaphysical abstraction but in terms of concrete social evils.

While many antebellum Americans were ignorant of or even hostile toward the latest currents of European thought and culture, reformers were cosmopolitans, closely attuned to foreign models, examples, and ideas (especially from England, provoking a violent Anglophobia from their opponents). As advocates of a positive form of liberalism, which sought to expand personal autonomy and foster individual fulfillment (the more negative form sought to restrain the power of the state), reformers attacked a host of "time-honored" customs, practices, and institutions that obstructed progress. At a time when many Americans viewed education in traditional terms—as a way to transmit social wisdom through repetition, rote learning, and memorization—educational reformers regarded schooling as a tool of self-discovery, social progress, and intellectual liberation. Temperance proponents struggled to free individuals from enslavement to alcohol in order to promote personal and social improvement; advocates of women's rights rejected older forms of patriarchy in favor of new notions of "separate spheres," sexual equality, and a single standard of sexual morality; and the more radical abolitionists advanced a new ideal of equal rights transcending race, a new conception of social order based not on the threat of physical coercion but on self-discipline and internal motivation. Above all, the reformers were institution builders and consolidators; they were among the first Americans to organize societies and other complex bureaucracies that went beyond sectarian and local boundaries, and thus played a pivotal role in overcoming localism and particularism.

As the twentieth century draws to a close, the cause of reform is ascendant across much of the world. In Africa, Asia, eastern Europe, and Latin America, popular protests and demonstrations resound with cries for an end to inequality, oppression, and entrenched injustice. Yet paradoxically, as reform ideals and aspirations flourish abroad, the cause of reform lags in the United States. Americans today are anxious about their country's future, angry and cynical toward government, and uneasy about the deepening problems of poverty, violence, and homelessness that beset their society. And yet unlike antebellum reformers, who engaged in a far-reaching effort to address their society's most profound problems, contemporary Americans seem paralyzed, powerless to enact solutions.

With the advantage of hindsight, it is possible to understand why reform flourished in pre–Civil War America, and the contemporary United States finds it so difficult to act. Many antebellum reformers had an optimism and a faith in progress that few of their cynical, tough-minded, contemporary counterparts feel as strongly. Inspired by a secular and sacred faith in the possibility of fundamental change, antebellum Americans did not perceive their society's problems as intractable. Having grown up in the wake of a revolution that had transformed society, inspired by religious faiths that held out a vision of a more perfect future, they felt great personal confidence in the possibilities of social change. Few Americans today share this optimistic sense. The contemporary United States remains a wealthy and powerful country, but it is also too frightened about its economic future to be very idealistic. Unlike the antebellum reformers, who were inspired by a utopian vision stressing communal responsibility and compassion, Americans now concentrate on private endeavors—family life, sports, consumerism—or turn to paranoid and exclusionary "reforms."

In addition, antebellum society was smaller and more culturally unified. An extraordinarily diverse coalition of reformers found common ground in the struggle to create a new moral order based on the ideals of self-control, self-improvement, humanitarianism, and moral regeneration. It was possible, in a way that it is not now, for reformers to assume that most Americans shared a core of cultural values. The kinds of debates that now rage about the role of men in combating sexual discrimination or the role of whites in challenging racial discrimination did not have the power to obstruct reform. Today, in sharp contrast, American society is deeply riven by what are loosely described as traditional social values, and reform leadership is diluted by racial, ethnic, and gender divisions.

Above all, reform today lacks the grass-roots foundation that provided antebellum reform with much of its power and influence. During the decades before the Civil War, the achievements of reformers depended on their ability to mobilize a vast pan-Protestant network of reform-minded churches and local moral societies. In recent years, however, many of those mediating organizations—such as churches and labor and religious societies have weakened. Lacking a broad base of public support, reform has become a multitude of interest groups, one among many in modern America.

In recent years, there has been a tendency on the part of historians to stress the "ambiguities" of reform: the notion that reforms invariably serve ulterior functions and often help to legitimate new forms of exploitation and social control. And in fact there is a great deal of truth to the view that antebellum reformers were at times morally self-righteous and paternalistic and blind to the implications of their reforms for the poor and the dispossessed. Reformers did, in many cases, acquiesce in the inequities of the wage system and increase

the state's power to discipline and control the poor and the deviant. Nevertheless, it would be a mistake of the highest magnitude to cynically conclude that
antebellum reform was in its essence an instrument of class hegemony or
control.

Antebellum reformers were those Americans who refused to accept the idea
that the existing social order was the best possible, that society must accept its
greatest evils. They created notions of civic and communal responsibility that
have grown increasingly relevant during the past century and a half. They
viewed reform as society's highest endeavor: as an effort to bring social realities in line with the country's aspiration toward perfection. Today, equality
and social justice remain, for many, unfulfilled promises. So long as a disparity
persists between society's highest ideals and its realities, a new age of reform is
sure to arise.

Moralists and Modernizers

Chapter 1

The Specter of Social Breakdown

A nightmare haunted early-nineteenth-century Americans—the specter of social breakdown. In countless sermons, letters, and editorials, thoughtful Americans denounced rising lawlessness, poverty, prostitution, irreligion, and violence, which, if not stopped, threatened to destroy the new nation's democratic experiment. Sidney George Fisher, an upper-class Philadelphian, expressed a fear shared by many when he wrote in his diary in 1844 that the country was "destined to be destroyed by the eruption of the dark masses of ignorance and brutality which lie beneath it, like the fires of a volcano." Nor were turbulence and disorder confined to urban slums or the backwoods. Conflict and instability had even made their way into individual homes, explained William Ellery Channing, one of the nation's leading theologians. "Even in families," he wrote in a discourse in 1835, "we see jarring interests and passions, invasions of rights, resistance of authority, violence, [and] force."

Everywhere one looked—in the growing cities of the North, in the slave South, or on the frontier—lawlessness and violence appeared to be spreading. During the 1820s and 1830s, lynchings, duels, mob uprisings, gang warfare, and convent burnings seemed epidemic. The nation's popular literature was filled with lurid images of frontier violence, urban savagery, and sexual vice, of cheats, cutthroats, tricksters, and con artists.

In New York, the nation's most prosperous city, the popular press gloomily described a carnival of murder. Criminal statistics painted a frightening picture of crime rising far faster than the overall population. Shootings, stabbings, and violent brawls became everyday occurrences. Court reports presented a constant stream of dognappings, muggings, wife beatings, and murder. Between 1814 and 1834, New York City's population doubled, but reports of crime quadrupled to 8,719. The next year, criminal complaints jumped to 10,168. In response to the apparent upsurge in violent crime, fearful citizens armed themselves, carrying guns and nightsticks for defense whenever they went out at night. For added protection, homeowners installed iron grates over their windows.

Particularly distressing were crimes committed by juveniles. Youthful thugs used clubs and cobblestones to rule the streets. Gangs, bearing such names as Plug Uglies, Dead Rabbits, and Bowery B'hoys, prowled the city, stealing from warehouses, junk shops, and private residences.

The most frightening form of lawlessness was mob violence. In a single decade, 1834–44, two hundred incidents of mob violence occurred in New York City. The worst year, 1834, became known as the "year of riots" because of the intensity of the disorders. In April, three days of rioting erupted during municipal elections; the state militia had to be called out to restore order. In July, a mob stormed the home of a prominent abolitionist, carried the furniture into the street, and set it on fire. During the next two days, mobs gutted the city's Episcopal African church and attacked many free blacks' homes. Once again, the state militia had to quell the disturbances.

Adding to a sense of alarm were scenes of heart-wrenching poverty: ragged girls standing barefoot outside hotels, selling matches or begging for pennies; small boys picking through garbage scattered in the streets; fathers stealing boards from the wharves to use as firewood.

Drunkenness and gambling were common sights. Three-card-monte dealers stood on street corners, cheating passersby out of their money. By 1835, there were nearly three thousand licensed drinking places in New York—one for every fifty persons over the age of fifteen. Men and women staggered down sidewalks, begging for money or picking fights with pedestrians. Journalists reported seeing ragged children take whiskey bottles from gutters and guzzle the dregs.

Sexual immorality elicited particular concern. Streetwalkers openly solicited customers outside hotels and in the upper rows of theaters. City authorities published alarming statistics: by 1820, there were at least two hundred brothels, and by 1850, a reported six thousand prostitutes strolled the city streets. Along Broadway at midday, young boys boldly sold pornography—"works of the most indecent and immoral character," the *New York Herald* lamented in 1845.

If the problems facing New York City seemed worse than those elsewhere, the difference was one of degree rather than kind. During the decades before the Civil War, many prominent Americans expressed concern over the vice, immorality, and violence that seemed to be spreading across the country. The *Vicksburg Sentinel* proclaimed that "shooting and cutting of throats appear to be the order of the day." A growing number of Americans feared that the United States was becoming a land of duels, lynchings, and riots, of racial violence and mob uprisings, a land where mobs burned convents, masters sexually abused slave women, and "gentlemen of property and standing" dragged reformers through the streets behind horses, a nation where even a vice president had to carry a gun while presiding over the Senate, lest senators attack each other with canes, knives, or pistols.

Violence was not confined to glittering cities like New York. During the decades following the American Revolution, dozens of observers, foreign and native-born, traveled to the backwoods and hinterlands. Their accounts of their travels created a new awareness among Americans of their country's diversity and contrasts. These observers were particularly struck by the barbaric forms of violence that they encountered: duels, gouging matches, and lynchings.

From the end of the American Revolution until after the Civil War, dueling flourished, particularly in the slave states and the Southwest. In Europe, dueling was confined to the upper classes and the objective was to wound—not to kill—an opponent. A duel was a time-honored way for a gentleman to defend his honor and demonstrate his status and manliness, with a pistol or a rapier, according to the carefully defined code of honor. Typically, a European duel ended with a superficial wound and a ritual reaffirmation of honor. In the South and the West, in contrast, dueling was not confined to the upper class and followed no formal rules. Participants fought each other with shotguns, rifles, and bowie knives. In one duel in 1818, Virginia Senator Armistead T. Mason and his cousin John M. McCarty fought with shotguns at four paces.

In the southern backcountry, other common forms of violence were bloody gouging matches and rough-and-tumble fights, no-holds-barred contests in which men fought all out, kicking each other in the genitals, poking out eyes, and biting off lips and noses. Fighters honed their fingernails and filed their teeth, and used elbows, feet, and fists to injure and disfigure their opponents.

Lynching, too, was widely reported in the South and the West. Lynching was defended as a way of maintaining law and order in areas where there were few established institutions to maintain justice. In one famous incident, the citizens of Vicksburg, Mississippi, in 1835 rid their fair city of gambling and prostitution by raiding gaming houses and brothels and lynching five gamblers.

Some newspapers, such as the nationally known *Niles' Weekly Register,* openly defended lynching as a democratic response to crime. The paper stated, after the execution of an accused murderer in 1834, that "as law, in every country, emanates from the people . . . the unanimous agreement, among the people to put a man to death . . . rendered the act legal to all intents and purposes." In the years before the Civil War, lynching was customarily directed against whites and not blacks—though in one incident in St. Louis in 1835 a mob dragged a free black accused of stabbing a deputy sheriff from a local jail and burned him to death.

In urban areas, mob violence increased in frequency, destructiveness, and class consciousness. Each year brought more reports of rioting. Between 1810 and 1819, there were 7 major riots; in the 1820s, the incidents totaled 21; in the 1830s, there were 115 reported incidents. In 1834, a mob sacked and burned a convent in Charlestown, Massachusetts, near the site of Bunker Hill. Two months later, a proslavery riot swept Philadelphia, destroying forty-five homes in the city's black community. Abraham Lincoln, then a young Springfield, Illinois, attorney, lamented that "outrages committed by mobs . . . [have become] the everyday news of the times."

Perhaps the most graphic symptom of social breakdown, in the eyes of many late-eighteenth- and early-nineteenth-century Americans, was an apparent epidemic of multiple family murders. In 1773, Samuel Brand of Lancaster, Pennsylvania, set fire to his house, where his parents lay sleeping, and shot and killed his own brother; in 1778, Bathsheba Spooner, the daughter of a distinguished Massachusetts judge and general, solicited soldiers to murder her husband; in 1783, William Beadle, a Wethersfield, Connecticut, merchant, slew his wife and four children with an axe. Indeed, of the twelve most widely publicized incidents of family murder between 1600 and 1900, ten took place between 1770 and 1825. These unsettling incidents suggested that savagery and violence were moving even into the recesses of the domestic sphere.

When early-nineteenth-century Americans expressed alarm about lawlessness, violence, immorality, and poverty, they were not simply responding to an increase in the seriousness of these problems (which is difficult to measure, given unreliable records). They were also reacting to a host of other anxieties—about the growth of cities, the spread of industry, changes in gender roles and generational relationships, and, above all, the breakdown of older paternalistic social relationships. Traditional structures of authority—familial, communal, and clerical—were weakening; ties between parents and children, employers and workingmen, seemed to be disintegrating. Ethnic and social diversity were increasing. Each of these developments contributed to the specter of social and moral breakdown.

Rates of urban growth faster than in any previous decade were a major source of alarm. Urban populations grew by 60 percent in the 1820s and again in the 1830s and then exploded in the 1840s, jumping 92 percent. The growth rate was particularly rapid in the nation's largest cities. By 1860, the United States had eight cities with more than 150,000 inhabitants—more large cities than any other country in the world.

During the decades before the Civil War, many Americans uneasily watched the growth of cities. The city, they feared, was a world of strangers, where ties between individuals were attenuated. Popular novelists, such as Ned Buntline (author of *The Mysteries and Miseries of New York*) and George Lippard (author of *New York: Its Upper Ten and Lower Million*), painted lurid descriptions of the realities of urban life that lurked near fashionable shops and glittering storefronts. They described a world of pimps, prostitutes, and pickpockets, of dance halls, vice dens, and houses of assignation, where illicit gambling and sexual activities flourished alongside desperate poverty.

In addition, there was a sudden increase in foreign immigration. At the beginning of the nineteenth century, just 5,000 immigrants arrived in the United States each year. During the 1830s, however, immigration climbed sharply as 600,000 immigrants entered the country. This figure jumped to 1.7 million in the 1840s, when harvests all across Europe failed, and reached 2.6 million in the 1850s. Most of these immigrants came from Germany, Ireland, and Scandinavia, pushed from their homelands by famine, eviction by landlords, and the destruction of traditional handicrafts by factory enterprises. By the 1850s, the Irish composed half the population of Boston and New York, and German immigrants made up a significant proportion of the population in Cincinnati, Milwaukee, and St. Louis. By 1860, in fact, 40 percent of the population of the nation's fifty largest cities was made up of immigrants.

Unprecedented rates of geographic mobility magnified the sense of social breakdown. Each decade, half the residents of northern communities moved to a new town. In Boston, half the population changed residence every one or two years. The rapid movement of people contributed to an image of the city as a land of strangers, a world of anonymity and duplicity, where, the Reverend Rufus W. Clark proclaimed in 1853, one found "nothing open, nothing direct and honest." It was home to cheats and confidence men, "with flattering lips and a double heart. Their language and conduct do not proceed from fixed principle and open-hearted sincerity; but from a spirit of duplicity and management."

The growth of cities was accompanied by far-reaching changes in economic relationships. Between the 1780s and the 1820s, an older, household-centered economy, in which assistants and apprentices lived in or near their employers' home, disintegrated. Young men moved out of rooms in their masters' homes and into hotels and boardinghouses in distinct working-class neighborhoods. The older view that each workman should be attached to a particular master, who would supervise his behavior and assume responsibility for his welfare, declined. In the new conception, labor was a commodity, like cotton, that could be acquired or disposed of according to the laws of supply and demand.

Alongside the transformations in work relations there were profound changes in gender relationships. During the last quarter of the eighteenth century and the first quarter of the nineteenth, young women received unprecedented opportunities to attend school and to work outside a family unit. A growing number of young unmarried women moved to cities and found jobs as servants, fabricators of clothing, factory operatives, and, increasingly, teachers. Women's growing independence heightened sensitivity to sexual morality and sparked intense fears of sexual corruption. Ministers, doctors, and writers of fiction issued impassioned warnings about the dangers of sexual licentiousness, promiscuity, prostitution, seduction, adultery, and rape.

Generational relationships, too, underwent profound changes. By the late eighteenth century, sons and daughters were less and less willing to allow a patriarch to control their labor or their choice of a spouse. Sons left home earlier (in their late teens, rather than their mid-twenties) and also lived farther from their parents' home. At the same time, children gained greater discretion in deciding whom and when to marry. Perhaps the most striking evidence of a breakdown in parental control lies in their declining ability to regulate their children's sexual behavior. By the middle of the eighteenth century, fewer children in New England were willing to postpone sexual relations until after marriage. As many as 40 percent of New England women were already pregnant at the time of marriage. As the economy became increasingly commercial and diversified, children were able to engage in sexual relations prior to marriage and marry early if pregnancy should result.

Nothing contributed more to a sense of social breakdown than the collapse of an older pattern of paternalistic social relationships, which occurred during the late eighteenth and early nineteenth centuries. Earlier systems of apprenticeship declined, and the first labor strikes in American history pitted employees against employers. Further, there were widening extremes of poverty and wealth; the increasing dispersal of families as a result of geographical migration; and a sharp decline in deference to authorities—local elites, lawyers, physicians, and family patriarchs.

Even before the 1820s, a democratic, antielitist impulse began to sweep the country. In all parts of the nation, popular struggles arose against a vast array of social institutions that smacked of special privilege and aristocratic pretension. Established churches, the bench, the legal and medical professions, and even the Bank of the United States all lost their elitist status.

To increase the judiciary's responsiveness to public opinion, most states made local judgeships elected positions. To open up the legal profession, many states allowed any individual to practice law without formal training. Likewise, some states stripped local medical societies of the power to license doctors, allowing unorthodox practitioners, including many women, who prescribed medications based on herbs and roots, to compete with established physicians. Family patriarchs, too, found their legal rights diminished. Courts struck down old laws that required children to receive their father's consent in order to marry.

In cities, traditional paternalistic methods of preserving public order became completely inadequate. Before the 1830s, the nation's cities were "policed" by a handful of unpaid, untrained, ununiformed, and unarmed sheriffs, constables, and nightwatchmen. In New England towns, tithingmen patrolled, armed with long black sticks tipped with brass, searching for drunkards, disorderly children, and wayward servants. These officials made a living by collecting debts, foreclosing on mortgages, and serving court orders. Victims of crime had to offer a reward if they wanted these unpaid law officers to investigate a case.

This system of maintaining public order worked as long as rates of serious crime were extremely low and cities had informal mechanisms for preserving order. Most cities were small and compact and lacked any distinct working-class ghettos. Shopkeepers usually lived at or near their place of business, and apprentices and journeymen lived in or near their masters' house. By the 1820s, this paternalistic pattern of social organization had broken down. The poor and the working class were increasingly segregated by neighborhood. Youth gangs, organized along ethnic and neighborhood lines, proliferated. Older mechanisms of social control weakened.

Drunken brawls, robberies, beatings, and murders all increased in number.

In Philadelphia the number of homicides reached 67 during the period between 1839 and 1845 and then rose to 75 during the next seven years and to 126 in the following seven years. Fear of crime mounted. In 1842, a New York City council report declared that "the property of the citizen is pilfered, almost before his eyes. Dwellings and warehouses are entered with an ease and apparent coolness and carelessness of detection which shows none are safe. . . . Thousands that are arrested go unpunished, and the defenseless and the beautiful are ravished and murdered in the day time, and no trace of the criminals is found."

The collapse of the older paternalistic pattern of social relationships had momentous consequences. First of all, it contributed to a pervasive sense that the traditional social mechanisms controlling individual behavior had lost their grip; that families, local churches, and public authorities were losing their ability to dictate conduct. The result, many feared, was a sharp increase in moral dissolution—debauchery, drunkenness, and various forms of impulsive, vicious, and unrestrained behavior. In the 1820s, the per capita consumption of hard liquor soared to new heights—twice the level today—and duels, lynchings, suicides, and murders appeared to become more common. Second, the weakening of hierarchies and older symbols of authority contributed to a fear that vulnerable individuals were now defenseless against exploitation. With the erosion of traditional and patriarchal forms of social and economic life, who was going to look after the widowed, the orphaned, the impoverished, or the chronically ill? Therefore, one of reform's primary tasks would be to compensate for an apparent decline in morality and communal solidarity.

Changes in the everyday use of language underscored the growing sense of social disintegration. During the late eighteenth century and early nineteenth century, a host of new words entered the English language that were expressive of larger anxieties about impulsive and unrestrained behavior. Words like *incorrigible, intransigent, irredeemable,* and *recalcitrant* suggested a class of people almost beyond society's capacity to control. At the same time, new words described categories of people incapable of self-discipline, such as *addicts* and *alcoholics,* and antisocial types, like *con men, hoodlums, pornographers,* and *psychopaths.*

Alongside these new words, a new vocabulary of exploitation arose. Not only was *exploitation* itself a new word in the late eighteenth century, so too were *manipulate* and *maltreat,* which also suggested the unjust use of another person for one's own profit or advantage. *Destitution* and *poverty-stricken,* however, indicate a new sensitivity to poverty. The realities of poverty and exploitation were, of course, not new; but the growth of cities, the spread of market relationships, and the breakdown of older paternalistic social relationships made these realities visible in a new way.

If long-building social changes intensified social problems, they also spurred debate about how to address them. When thoughtful Americans pondered the problem of social breakdown, they placed much of the blame for disorder upon two basic sources. One was a flawed value system that exalted material gain and individual self-seeking above all else. The other was the apparent weakness of all forms of authority in an increasingly democratic society. Families, churches, and government—all seemed incapable of maintaining moral order.

This diagnosis of the origins of the nation's ills shaped public responses. It led reformers to assert that the country needed a new ethical and moral vision to replace the ethos of selfishness and individualism that dominated American society in the years before the Civil War. Instead of the marketplace mentality that encouraged acquisitiveness and self-seeking, reformers proposed a new ethic of caring and compassion that would recreate a genuine sense of community.

And to address the perceived weakness of familial, church, and governmental authority, antebellum church groups and others began to establish local voluntary societies to oversee public morals, inculcate Christian values, and provide humanitarian care to the unfortunate. To promote public virtue, instill moral values, and shape conduct, reformers spoke of new institutions, ranging from Sunday schools and common schools to new kinds of orphanages, houses of refuge, mental hospitals, and penitentiaries to serve as "crucibles of character." If individuals were to be governed, a growing number of Americans believed, they had to learn how to rule themselves.

As the nation expanded and prospered, Americans could no longer rely on the stabilizing influence of patriarchal families, churches, or constitutions drafted and interpreted by a self-selected "natural aristocracy." In the Old World, said Heman Humphrey, a president of Amherst College, in 1840, "the bayonet of the Czar and the scimitar of the Sultan" could tame citizens "and keep them in subjection." But in a free country, social order would ultimately depend on self-government, on self-restraints embedded in each person's character. Sunday schools, common schools, reformatories, and a host of other institutions would help shape individual character.

The late eighteenth and early nineteenth centuries saw the emergence of a cultural obsession with self-control, a preoccupation with suppressing animal instincts, disciplining the passions, controlling sensual appetites, distancing individuals from their bodily processes, and restraining impulsive behavior. At a time when society threatened to fly out of control, self-discipline and self-mastery became cultural watchwords. Forms of emotional expression and physical behavior that colonial Americans had largely taken for granted were restrained. In the early nineteenth century, respectable middle-class Americans ceased blowing their noses with their fingers and began to use handkerchiefs instead. They began to eat with forks instead of knives and to wipe their hands on napkins instead of their cravats. The old custom of adults and children sharing a bed became distinctly unfashionable.

A flood of etiquette manuals emphasized self-control as the key to respectability, upward mobility, and social harmony. An average of three such books appeared each year in the early nineteenth century, laying out proper standards of manners, deportment, and character building. New, exacting codes began to govern such activities as dining, sneezing, coughing, and spitting. Authorities on etiquette warned readers against slurping their soup, drinking noisily, or ingesting food greedily, since these reduced dining to a mere animal activity. Experts on manners told readers to avoid picking their teeth or nose and never to spit in front of ladies. One popular etiquette manual, James B. Smiley's *Modern Manners and Social Forms,* summed up the essence of proper manners in a single sentence. "A sure mark of good breeding," it declared, "is the suppression of any undue emotion, such as anger, mortification, laughter, or any form of selfishness." Self-control was increasingly regarded as the key to self-improvement and social progress. Only by exercising tight control over every aspect of life—diet, sexuality, manners, and drinking of alcohol—could individuals contain the "bestial" impulses within.

Perhaps the most striking example of the new emphasis on self-restraint was the heightened stress on sexual self-control and a growing concern about the dangers of sexual indulgence. Up until the late eighteenth century, adolescent masturbation appears to have been largely ignored. But beginning at the end of the eighteenth century, intense efforts were made to stamp it out. One American best-seller of the mid-1790s, entitled *Onania,* was a bitter attack against masturbation. An 1834 tract claimed that it was "a monster in our midst," threatening to "sweep in a wide-spread tide of desolation, over our land and the world." Boys were taught to avoid "self-abuse," so that they would acquire the capacity to control all their base impulses.

An intense cultural concern with licentiousness, illicit love, and sexual immorality was apparent not only in books condemning masturbation, but in other best-sellers, such as *Hymen's Recruiting Sergeant* (1799), a denunciation of adultery. Adultery and premarital sex had grown so common, proclaimed an 1834 letter to the *Ohio Star,* that "virgin chastity, and conjugal fidelity, are imaginary virtues."

These concerns can also be seen in the limitation of births in early-nineteenth-century America. In 1800, the American birthrate was higher than that in any European nation. The typical American woman bore an average of seven children. She had her first child when she was about twenty-three and bore children at two-year intervals until her early forties. Had the American birthrate remained at this level, the nation's population would have reached two billion by 1990.

Late in the eighteenth century, however, Americans began to have fewer children. Where the typical American mother in 1800 bore seven children, the average number by 1850 was four or five. By 1900, it had fallen to three and a half. The two basic birth control methods—coitus interruptus (withdrawal) and periodic abstinence (or what is now known as the rhythm method)—both required an ability to regulate sexual impulses. Social mobility and being able to maintain an acceptable standard of living depended on a married couple's discipline and self-control.

During the decades before the Civil War, Americans were intensely concerned with impulse control and shaping character. By *character,* early-nineteenth-century Americans meant the inner behavioral controls (including each person's conscience and will) that determined whether the individual became a criminal or a saint. In a famous phrase, Ralph Waldo Emerson defined character as "moral order through the medium of individual nature." Given the weakness of religious and political institutions, it seemed clear that the very survival of the American experiment in self-government ultimately depended on the character of the American people.

The early-nineteenth-century conception of character differs radically from the concept of personality that has largely replaced it in the twentieth century. The traits associated with a firm character had a strongly moral dimension; they included personal integrity, high ideals, moral courage, a sense of duty, a capacity for hard work, and self-control. In Americans' twentieth-century notion of a well-developed personality, the essence lies in an individual's interpersonal skills and modes of self-presentation: personal charm, poise, self-confidence, tact, and the ability to attract friends and influence other people. For early-nineteenth-century child-rearing experts, the primary goal of socialization was not to nurture a happy, well-adjusted personality, but was to implant a strong will, a capacity for self-discipline, and a sense of duty deep within the individual character.

To early-nineteenth-century Americans, a person's moral character was not innate; it was something that had to be nurtured and shaped. From the English philosopher John Locke and other early modern thinkers, antebellum

Americans derived the notion that human nature was capable of being molded like fresh clay. This belief gave enormous importance to the institutions responsible for nurturing character, such as the family, the church, and the school.

For antebellum Americans, the family was primarily responsible for shaping character. It was within the family, most Americans agreed, that children first learned to respect legitimate authority, to develop a sense of duty and personal responsibility, and to exercise control over their passions. Yet at the same time there was a growing belief that families were becoming less capable of character formation. The very egalitarian and democratic pressures that were transforming American politics also appeared to be eroding parental authority. Heman Humphrey explained that "our children hear so much about liberty and equality," it was "infinitely more difficult to govern children than it used to be."

To help parents cope with the problem of properly raising children, a flood of guidebooks and tracts appeared on "the art and responsibility of family government." The child-rearing literature in the early nineteenth century offered advice that was fundamentally different from that found in earlier works. During the colonial era, such manuals had been addressed to fathers and had argued that the primary task of fatherhood was to make children obedient by breaking their sinful will through physical punishment.

The early-nineteenth-century child-rearing literature also stressed the importance of discipline and obedience, but it recommended very different parental actions. Early-nineteenth-century tracts were addressed to mothers, not fathers, and frowned upon whipping and other forms of corporal punishment, because physical coercion only provoked obstinacy and rebelliousness in children. Instead, the new manuals called on parents to rely upon persuasion and moral influence, including shaming, playing on a child's guilt, and threatening to withdraw love. In this way, parents would produce not merely outward conformity, but a sincere desire within children to obey their parents' injunctions. Bronson Alcott, the father of novelist Louisa May Alcott, applied this new advice in a particularly innovative way. In rearing his daughters, he used a technique he called "vicarious atonement." When his daughters misbehaved, he went without his dinner; and when they were particularly unruly, he had them spank him. By using moral and psychological influence rather than physical punishment, he strove to implant a moral compass within his daughters that could direct their behavior whether he was present or not.

The object of the new child-rearing methods was not merely to secure outward obedience but to shape character and instill a capacity for self-government. In 1841, Catharine Sedgwick, a leading novelist, called self-government "the only effective and lasting government—the one that touches the springs of action, and in all circumstances controls them." Self-discipline could not be instilled by threats, which only produced resentment and "disdain for control" in children; self-government could only be nurtured through moral influence— "methods silent and imperceptible" by which parents inculcated duty and personal responsibility. In a democratic society, where authority more and more depended on consent for its legitimacy, moral and psychological influence proved more effective than physical coercion in shaping character. The ultimate goal of child rearing was to make children develop a sense of duty and obligation without resort to physical coercion.

Yet it was obvious to many antebellum Americans that more families were failing to meet their responsibility to properly shape the character of the nation's young. Failures of family governance offered a persuasive explanation for the sharp increase of violence, robbery, and prostitution. If families had proven inadequate, then it was imperative that other institutions—religious and secular—rise to this huge responsibility.

In 1840, after a visit to the United States, Thomas Brothers, an English observer, offered a bitter retort to those who claimed that the American Revolution had ushered in a new era of freedom and human happiness. "A 'new era' came; and what are the consequences?" he asked in a book entitled *The United States of North America as They Are; Not as They Are Generally Described.* His answer: "Lynching, firing, stabbing, shooting, and rioting are daily taking place." During his visit, Brothers had personally seen a Philadelphia mob deliberately murder free blacks, "destroy their houses, break up their furniture, [and] steal their money." In his book, he quoted newspaper articles describing riots, the burning of convents, and the murders of newspaper editors.

Fourteen years later, another foreign traveler named William Chambers, a Scottish publisher, issued a stern warning that American democracy "contained the seeds of its own dissolution." Racial hatred, class antagonism, a spirit of violence and brutality—all, he wrote in a book entitled *Things as They Are in America* (1857), threatened to destroy America's experiment with self-government and democracy.

During the decades before the Civil War, repeated reports of duels, lynchings, riots, and mob uprisings seemed to confirm the European claim that democracy led inevitably to anarchy and lawlessness. The question that dominated American public life between 1800 and 1860 was how a free society could maintain stability and moral order. Antebellum Americans sought to answer that question through religion, education, and social reform.

Chapter 2

The Promise of the Millennium

Inscribed on the Great Seal of the United States are the Latin words *Novus ordo seclorum*—"a new order for the ages." The notion that the American Revolution inaugurated a new epoch in human history, a new era of virtue, justice, equality, and possibility, was widely shared by late-eighteenth-century and early-nineteenth-century Americans. The Revolution, declared Joseph Priestley, a chemist, an early Unitarian, and an immigrant from England, was nothing less than the harbinger of the millennium—the establishment of God's kingdom on earth. But this fervent optimism and sense of new possibilities was not confined to the religious. Many secular Americans also believed that the United States was the New Israel, destined to lead the world to universal peace and prosperity.

To be sure, millennial hopes were often mixed with fear and foreboding. Many early-nineteenth-century Americans felt a profound sense of peril—from irreligion, godlessness, greed, and anarchy. Nevertheless, the sense that a new age of human history had dawned helped unleash what Ralph Waldo Emerson called the "demon of reform," which flourished with such vigor in pre–Civil War America.

During the last years of the eighteenth century and the first years of the nineteenth, Americans of diverse backgrounds shared a conviction that the

United States would lead the world toward Christ's millennial kingdom, a thousand years of "peace, purity, and felicity," as Timothy Dwight, later president of Yale College, declared in 1776. Inspired by the example of the revolutionaries who won American independence, by the philosophy of the Enlightenment, by the scientific and technological triumphs of the early Industrial Revolution, and, above all, by two critical trends in religious thought—religious liberalism and evangelical revivalism—many Americans believed that their country would take the lead in spreading Christian influence around the globe and combating all forms of tyranny and injustice.

Before the 1770s, millennial thought was often associated with passivity, apathy, and pessimism, as believers patiently awaited the destruction of a corrupt and evil world before the onset of a new era "when time shall be no more." But the success of the American Revolution, the rapid growth in church membership, and the quickening pace of technological and scientific progress stimulated a more hopeful and optimistic view: that the millennium would follow not a violent apocalypse or catastrophic conflagration, but successful efforts to defeat godlessness, irreligion, materialism, and selfishness and to establish a virtuous, just order on earth.

Unlike many present-day millennialists, who are deeply conservative in their economic and social views, profoundly skeptical of reform, and convinced that the millennium will arrive only after a bleak period of wars and natural disasters, their early-nineteenth-century counterparts tended to be much more hopeful. Their millennial vision contributed to a spirit of optimism, a sensitivity to human suffering, and a boundless faith in humanity's capacity to improve social institutions. The moral fervor, the expectancy, and the intense devotion to mission rooted in millennialist ideas inspired early-nineteenth-century efforts at reform and allowed different kinds of reformers to work together.

America's Revolutionary Heritage

One source of inspiration for reformers was the example of the patriots of the American Revolution who had risked their lives and honor to overcome tyranny and injustice. Pre–Civil War reformers pictured their efforts to abolish slavery or to improve the nation's educational system as attempts to realize the republican ideals enshrined in the Declaration of Independence. Proponents of women's rights, world peace, temperance, and abolition all drafted Declarations of Sentiments modeled on the wording of the Declaration of

Independence. Workingmen's parties in New York and Philadelphia in the 1820s, abolitionists in 1830, and proponents of women's rights in 1848 each issued "Declarations of Sentiments" listing "a history of repeated injuries and usurpations" that justified their reforms. Convinced that the sacred principles of the Revolution had been corrupted, reformers sought to revive the Spirit of 1776 by exposing a host of abuses that contradicted the nation's revolutionary principles.

Early-nineteenth-century reformers saw their own crusades as the fulfillment of the political struggles begun during the Revolution. For America's pre–Civil War reformers, the nation's revolutionary heritage remained a standard for measuring present imperfections against a higher ideal.

The theory of natural rights embodied in the Declaration—the idea that "all men are created equal," that they were endowed with certain natural, essential, and inalienable rights—served as a powerful stimulus for reform. The principles of liberty and equality set forth in the Declaration led abolitionist William Lloyd Garrison to challenge the justice of the institution of slavery and encouraged suffragist Elizabeth Cady Stanton to press for equal rights for women.

It is not an accident that many of the nation's leading reformers were members of a specific generation—they were born between 1810 and 1820. Belonging to the new nation's second generation, and lacking any personal experience of the hardships and triumphs of the revolutionary era, these reformers felt an acute "belatedness"—that they had missed the sense of heroic mission and social solidarity experienced by the revolutionary generation. Also, at a time when many respectable careers for the young were becoming overcrowded, reform provided an outlet for intense personal energies and aspirations. For these women and men, reform offered a substitute cause—an opportunity to preserve a virtuous republic in the face of profound challenges: foreign immigration, intemperance, and rapid urban growth. And finally, many reformers were members of a transitional generation that had revolted against Calvinist religious orthodoxy, yet retained a deep sense of moral severity and dedication.

Nor was it accidental that the cause of reform had a particular attraction for residents of New England. Many New Englanders opposed America's second war of independence, the War of 1812, and, after the celebrated American victory in the Battle of New Orleans, found themselves stigmatized as traitors. For those New Englanders who had seen their political power collapse with the demise of the Federalist Party and who were dismayed by the growing separation of church and state, reform seemed a providential means of restoring order and morality to American society. Following the War of

1812, New England adopted a new stance toward the rest of the nation: many embarked on a missionary crusade to make their region's values the nation's.

Philosophy of the Enlightenment

Apart from the nation's revolutionary heritage, the roots of reform could also be found in Enlightenment philosophy. During the eighteenth century, French philosophes, Scottish moral philosophers, and such American thinkers as Benjamin Franklin and Thomas Jefferson developed a set of principles which had enormous importance for reform. One principle was that human beings were not innately sinful, but were basically good. Given a favorable environment, people's moral character would improve. A second principle was that poverty, disease, crime, and ignorance were not inevitable, but could be overcome by reform. By reshaping the environment, reformers could eliminate the causes of human misery. A central message of the Enlightenment was that the human condition was not inevitable; human action could alter it.

Perhaps the Enlightenment's most important contribution to reform was the view that all humanity was born equal in mental and moral capacities, and that environment and circumstance accounted for human differences. As a result, human beings were all entitled to equal respect, regardless of differences in their talents, wealth, and achievements.

The triumphs of eighteenth- and early-nineteenth-century science and technology contributed to a widespread faith in the capacity of human beings to improve society through the use of reason. The steam engine, gas-fueled lamps, potbellied stoves, and interchangeable parts were dramatic examples of humanity's expanding ability to make life better.

Another major intellectual source of the reform impulse was a philosophy imported from Scotland. Common sense realism, based on the psychological writings of philosophers Thomas Reid, Adam Smith, and Dugald Stewart, dominated academic curricula from about 1820 to 1870 and was quickly incorporated into the teachings of the nation's Protestant churches. This philosophy declared that the external world was much as it appeared and that to act properly each person need only follow the moral laws inscribed in one's conscience. Common sense philosophy seemed to offer a providential solution to bitter theological disputes. All theological issues, and even the Bible itself, were accessible to common sense, logic, and reason. Far from being a complicated and mysterious work, which only scholars and theologians could understand, the Bible was a text easily comprehended by almost everyone.

For liberals and conservatives alike, common sense philosophy offered a simple solution to the dislocations and upheavals of the age. Implanted within all people was a conscience—a small, steady voice that stood ready to guide them in the ways of virtue. But the conscience had to be properly nurtured and cultivated, since it constantly had to resist immorality and vice. Families, churches, schools, and moral reform societies would have to play a central role in shaping conscience.

Reform's Religious Roots

Of all the factors that stimulated the growth of reform, the main one was religion. Today, religion—especially the "fundamentalist" kinds of religion that dominated pre–Civil War America—is often conceived of as a conservative force. Social scientists often associate progress with secularization, that is, with the spread of education, technology, and scientific knowledge. And secularization, or the triumph of a scientific worldview, implies a falling away from religious belief. But in nineteenth-century America, as the United States rapidly "modernized," so church membership also increased. Religious commitment was of central importance in inspiring a wide range of reformers.

Almost all the leading reformers were devoutly religious men and women who wanted to deepen the nation's commitment to Christian principles. Proponents of temperance, abolition, and other reforms were convinced that drunkenness or slavery or other social evils were an affront not only to the country's republican values but to Christian morality.

During the eighteenth and early nineteenth centuries, religion was truly the seedbed of social protest and reform. It was no accident that America's first organized efforts to promote social change had religious roots. Among the Quakers in Pennsylvania the American reform impulse was born.

One of several radical religious sects that arose during the English civil wars in the mid-seventeenth century, the Quakers sought to live free from sin and from all enslaving creeds and institutions. They condemned war and refused to bear arms, take oaths, or bow or take off their hats to social superiors. Rejecting an educated, ordained ministry, such sacraments as baptism and the Lord's Supper, as well as a formal theology, the Quakers were "spiritualists" who believed that the Holy Spirit was present in every human heart, and that this "inward Christ" should guide each person's beliefs and actions.

Beginning in the 1670s, many Quakers migrated to the New World, particularly to Pennsylvania, Rhode Island, and the West Indies. Compared to other colonial religious sects, the Quakers were extraordinarily egalitarian. Embracing the idea that the Holy Spirit can speak through both women and men, Quaker women assumed prominent ministerial roles. The Friends rejected the notion that infants are born sinful and with an impaired capacity for reason, and so did not resort to corporal punishment of young children and permitted their offspring to participate in religious meetings from an early age. By the mid-eighteenth century, many Quakers had grown prosperous in trade and manufacturing, but the sect's increasing wealth produced a deep ambivalence. Prosperity and luxury were very much at odds with the traditional emphasis on plainness in speech, dress, and behavior.

During the Seven Years' War (1756–63), Quakers, particularly those living in Pennsylvania, divided over the question of whether or not to support the war effort. Many Quakers who opposed the war were subject to persecution for refusing to fight or to pay taxes. In response, Quaker pacifists sought to purify their sect and raise its moral standards. They reasserted the duty of the individual Quaker to confront social evil and relieve human suffering. As a result, a growing number of Quakers began to take active steps against poverty, the drinking of hard liquor, unjust Indian policies, and, above all, slavery. Between 1755 and 1776, the Society of Friends became the first organization in history to prohibit slaveholding, and Quakers founded the first societies to protest the institution.

In the future, Quakers would join reform movements in far higher numbers than their percentage in the nation's population would suggest. For example, perhaps three-quarters of all the members of antislavery societies formed before 1830 were members of the Society of Friends, and, according to one estimate, 40 percent of all female abolitionists and 19 percent of all pre-1830 feminists were Quaker women. In their desire to combat oppression and human suffering, their emphasis upon personal piety and individual commitment, and their staunch desire to lead the world toward the kingdom of God, the Quakers provided a moral example for later American reformers.

Religious Liberalism

Two significantly different trends in Protestant thought stimulated the rise of reform activity: religious liberalism and evangelical revivalism. Religious liberalism was an emerging humanitarian form of religion that rejected the harsh Calvinist doctrines of original sin and predestination. Its preachers stressed the basic goodness of human nature and each individual's capacity to follow the example of Christ by cultivating proper moral attitudes and behavior. Reason, intellectual freedom, and moral duty were the watchwords of the liberal Christian faith.

Religious liberals tended to reject literal interpretations of the Bible and instead emphasized the importance of reason in interpreting Scripture. They also rejected the orthodox boundaries of the Trinity and, denying the divinity of Jesus Christ, instead viewed him as a moral model whom all humanity should strive to emulate. Regarding God not as an angry and unpredictable Father but as an enlightened parent, liberals emphasized the possibility of salvation for all women and men. Arising partly in reaction against the fervent revivalism of the Great Awakening in the 1730s and 1740s, liberal Christianity sought to substitute reason for revelation. As Charles Chauncy, an early liberal minister put it in an essay entitled "Seasonal Thought on the State of Religion" (1734), "An enlightened Mind, and not raised Affections, ought always to be the guide of those who call themselves Men." But it was not until the early nineteenth century that religious liberalism would adopt clearly defined institutional forms: Unitarianism and Universalism.

William Ellery Channing (1780–1842) was America's leading exponent of religious liberalism. Born in Newport, Rhode Island, and educated at Harvard, Channing served as minister of Federal Street Church in Boston for the last forty years of his life. In 1815, Channing played a major role in a bitter theological conflict that divided New England Congregationalists. During the "Unitarian Conflict," theological conservatives, who emphasized predestination, human depravity, and the infallibility of the Bible, fiercely clashed with liberals whose tenets were free will, the universal brotherhood of humanity, and human reason.

In Baltimore in 1819, Channing delivered a sermon entitled "Unitarian Christianity," which proclaimed the principles of his faith and became the intellectual foundation for American Unitarianism. Emphasizing the importance of human reason in interpreting the Bible, Channing denied that there was a scriptural basis for the orthodox Calvinist beliefs in predestination and original sin. Instead, Channing stressed humanity's basic goodness and its capacity to affect personal salvation and described Christ as a model of moral perfection. In an essay entitled "The Perfect Life" (1831), Channing declared that the sole purpose of Christianity was "the perfection of human nature, the elevation of men into nobler beings." Channing's ideas stimulated many reformers to work toward improving the conditions of the physically handicapped, the criminal, the poor, and the enslaved.

Reluctant to found a new religious denomination, for fear that it would soon impose its own version of orthodoxy, he formed a conference of liberal Congregational ministers in 1820, which was reorganized in 1825 as the American Unitarian Association. Adopting as its slogan "Deeds not creeds," the association stressed individual freedom of belief, a united world under a single God, the mortal nature of Jesus Christ, and the moral and ethical responsibilities of people toward their neighbors. Critics accused the new denomination of downplaying the foundations of religious faith—sin, divine passion, supernatural mystery, and the ecstasy of salvation. And wits mockingly declared that Unitarians, most of whom belonged to the commercial elite in eastern Massachusetts, were dedicated to "the Fatherhood of God, the Brotherhood of Man, and the Neighborhood of Boston." Yet few religious denominations exerted a stronger influence upon American intellectual life (through such figures as William Cullen Bryant, Henry Wadsworth Longfellow, James Russell Lowell, and Francis Parkman) or contributed as many prominent antebellum reformers, including Dorothea Dix, a crusader on behalf of the mentally ill; Samuel Gridley Howe, a staunch advocate for the blind; educational reformer Horace Mann; and Joseph Tuckerman, one of the nation's first advocates for the urban poor.

If Unitarianism drew its support largely from genteel, urban Boston, Universalism was its "lower-class" counterpart, with members in rural, economically marginal areas of New England, though it also gained influence in the Philadelphia area. Like the Unitarians, the Universalists rejected the central tenets of Calvinist orthodoxy, holding instead that God was a benevolent deity who would save all humankind (P. T. Barnum claimed that Universalism was the only religion that "really believes in success"). Sharing the Unitarians' optimistic view of human destiny and the innate goodness of human nature, the Universalists also downplayed theology and stressed conscience and benevolence. Like the Unitarians, the Universalists believed that Christians' fundamental duty was to demonstrate their piety through humanitarian and reformist endeavors.

The Second Great Awakening:
The Revolt against Enlightened Religion

Another source of the reform impulse can be found in the enthusiastic revivals that swept the nation in the early nineteenth century. These revivals sought to awaken Americans to their need for religious rebirth and redemption. Highly emotional meetings were held by preachers in all sections of the country. So widespread were they in the early nineteenth century that they acquired a name, the "Second Great Awakening."

The Second Great Awakening had its symbolic beginning in a small frontier community in central Kentucky. This was one of the most remarkable events in American religious history. Between August 6 through August 12, 1801, thousands of people—perhaps as many as 25,000—gathered at Cane Ridge to fast and pray and take communion. This was the largest attendance at a religious revival in America up until this time, and it was a truly fantastic number. There were only 250,000 people in all of Kentucky, and Lexington, the state's largest city, only had 1,795 residents.

Cane Ridge became an instant legend. Never before had religious piety and fervor been so openly expressed or conversions so numerous. Early in 1801, only about 10 percent of all Kentuckians were formal members of a church; ministers complained about the pervasiveness of deism, rationalism, and religious indifference. Then, in the course of six months, in a series of religious revivals, at least 100,000 frontier Kentuckians, hungry for intense religious experience and eager for a sense of community, joined together in search of religious salvation.

There was not just one minister at Cane Ridge; there were more than a dozen. They came from many denominations: Presbyterian, Baptist, Methodist. There was at least one black minister. The people who attended the camp meeting came from all social classes and social groups; they included Kentucky's governor, prominent landowners, and college-educated ministers; many were young; and perhaps two-thirds were female.

Tales of the "physical exercises" that people experienced at Cane Ridge spread far and wide: weeping, shrieking, groaning, shouting, dancing, trembling, jerking, swooning. A minister named James Campbell left a vivid first-person description of the scene: "Sinners [were] dropping down on every hand, shrieking, groaning, crying for mercy, convoluted; professors praying, agonizing, fainting, falling down in distress."

The outpouring of religious feeling at Cane Ridge soon erupted across the entire country. In 1801 and 1802 revivals broke out in the Carolinas, Georgia, eastern Tennessee, Virginia, western Pennsylvania, and Ohio. Other revivals took place in New England, New Jersey, and New York. Within two years, dozens of ministers, missionaries, and itinerant preachers began organizing camp meetings.

Evangelical Revivalism:
Simple Truth in the Open Air

During the last years of the eighteenth century and the first years of the nineteenth, American religion underwent a transformation as dramatic as any in American history. In a single generation, the tone of religious discourse shifted radically. Enlightenment attacks on institutional religion were overwhelmed by a new conviction that religion was an indispensable vehicle of moral progress.

At the end of the eighteenth century, Enlightenment liberalism and rationalism, and not religious belief, seemed to be what would rule America's future. In 1775, there were probably only 1,800 ministers in a population of 2.5 million. Across the country, church membership was low and falling. According to one estimate, just one American in twenty was a church member. An apparent erosion of religious faith seemed evident in the declining proportion of college graduates entering the ministry. William Ellery Channing commented that "infidelity is very general among the higher classes."

Few of the nation's founders were particularly religious. They were men of the Enlightenment, who valued dispassionate and rational inquiry and rejected religious enthusiasm. Many leaders of the revolutionary generation openly distrusted the clergy, doubted the divine origins of the Bible, and questioned the miracles. George Washington's religious views were not unusual among the founders. He believed that a benevolent divine force governed the universe, but was skeptical of many specific church doctrines. Thomas Jefferson's religious outlook was similar. He considered himself a Christian, and in the *Syllabus,* a work prepared in 1798–99 about his religious opinions, he expressed reverence for the teaching of Jesus Christ as "the most perfect and sublime that has ever been taught by man." At the same time, he apparently did not believe in the divinity of Jesus Christ or in the authenticity of biblical miracles. He repeatedly denounced the clergy for perverting Christianity into "a mere contrivance to filch wealth and power to themselves," as he wrote in an 1810 letter.

During the 1790s, however, alarm over irreligion and secularism mounted. When the new leaders in revolutionary France abolished Christianity and the worship of God, and people founded deist societies in the United States, and, above all, antireligious tracts by Ethan Allen and Thomas Paine (Paine's *Age of Reason* went through eight American editions) were published, Americans feared that skepticism, deism, and rationalism were rapidly spreading. Rationalism, irreligion, and skepticism seemed to be the dominant characteristics of the time. Paine's denunciation of Christianity in the second part of *The Age of Reason* (1795) was particularly bitter: "Of all the systems of religion that ever were invented, there is none more derogatory to the Almighty, more unedifying to man, more repugnant to reason, and more contradictory in itself, than this thing called Christianity." Even at Yale College, soon to become a center of revivalism, students eagerly debated the question, "Are the Scriptures of the Old and New Testaments the Word of God?" In his *Letters from an American Farmer* (1782), a series of extremely popular essays, J. Hector St. John Crèvecoeur, a French immigrant, observed that "religious indifference is imperceptibly disseminated from one end of the continent to the other."

Yet by the 1830s, no Western nation appeared to be more religious than the United States. Reported church membership doubled between 1800 and 1830. In his classic *Democracy in America,* Alexis de Tocqueville, the famous French commentator, observed: "There is no country in the whole world in which the Christian religion retains a greater influence over the souls of men than in America."

The chief vehicle for this unique outpouring of religious faith was the religious revival. Even before the great camp meeting at Cane Ridge, scattered smaller revivals had erupted in eastern Tennessee and North Carolina. The years up to 1865 witnessed almost continual waves of such gatherings. One observer, Methodist Episcopal Bishop Francis Asbury, estimated in 1811 that three to four million Americans attended camp meetings annually.

Evangelical revivalism was the dominant form of religious expression in early-nineteenth-century America. The word *evangelical* refers to a belief that all people must recognize their depravity and worthlessness, repent their sins, and undergo a conversion experience and a rebirth of religious feeling. Two key terms in the revivalists' vocabulary were *ability* and *decision*. In their eyes, all people had the ability to open their heart to the Holy Spirit and to decide whether they would submit to God's will. The great goal of revivalists was to arouse in men and women the recognition of their own sinfulness, so each individual could welcome the Holy Spirit and go through a sudden, dramatic second birth, in which a person could experience the bliss of new life in Christ.

What explains the rapid rise of revivalism? In part, revivals were a response to the growing separation of church and state that followed the Revolution. Just when new state governments deprived established churches of state support (as Virginia did in 1785, Connecticut in 1818, and Massachusetts in 1833), the number of denominations expanded. Revivals increased church membership and ensured that America would remain a God-fearing nation. In the face of disestablishment, Protestants joined forces to combat irreligion.

Yet the popularity of revivals represented something more than a reaction to disestablishment: tens of thousands of ordinary Americans hungered for a more popular, more emotional, less constrained religion. Even in the late eighteenth century, Americans were not as indifferent to religion as church membership statistics might suggest. Many Americans were put off by genteel clergy with aristocratic pretensions, as well as by the older denominations' stress on decorum, unemotional sermons, and formal catechism. They remained ready for forms of religion that addressed their needs and aspirations. Evangelical religious denominations met a popular desire for a religion that the unlearned could understand, a religion that downplayed creeds, articles of faith, and sacramental rituals and instead emphasized conversion.

Revivals also met a growing need for a sense of community and communal purpose. Revivalism was, in part, an attempt to bring order, education, and moral discipline to a disordered and secularized society. At a time of rapid and increasing mobility and mounting commercialism, revivals offered an antidote to secularism and mammonism, to luxury and rampant individualism. The evangelical revivals expressed genuine anxieties: a fear that the nation's expansive energies would erode America's higher values and sense of purpose.

To some extent, revivals transcended class lines, but they had particular appeal to distinct social groups. In the South, the revivals largely attracted the dispossessed, slaves, and free blacks, as well as yeoman whites. In the North, it was the aspiring and upwardly mobile groups, especially in thriving market towns and new cities in western New York and Ohio. Although transient workers tended not to become converts, middle-class women, more permanent, settled workers, and shopkeepers joined the revivals in large numbers, eager to demonstrate that their rise was not at the expense of social organization.

No group was more strongly attracted to revivalistic religion than women, especially younger women. As early as the mid-seventeenth century, women already constituted a majority of members in New England churches. During the Second Great Awakening, female converts in New England outnumbered men by three to two—a fact that contemporaries attributed to women's Christian character. As one early-nineteenth-century minister named Daniel Chaplin stated in 1814, "Women are happily formed for religion" by their "natural endowments," delicacy, piety, sensitivity, and compassion. Indeed, evangelical religion emphasized values that antebellum culture associated with women, including self-sacrifice, service, and commitment to others.

Social circumstances contributed to women's religiosity. Largely cut off from the amoral worlds of business and politics, many women viewed themselves as guardians of morality. At a time when women's lives were undergoing profound transformations—when growing numbers of young women were working outside a home setting and were delaying marriage or not marrying at all—religion provided young women with a sense of identity and purpose. It also provided avenues for self-expression—through church societies, mothers' associations, and charitable and benevolent organizations—and membership in a larger community.

The evangelical revivals left an indelible imprint on antebellum American culture. The rituals of evangelical religion—the camp meeting, the religious revival, group prayer, and mass baptisms along rivers and creeks—were the truly distinctive American experience in the decades before the Civil War. The very vocabulary of politicians was rooted in the language of the nation's revivalists. When Lincoln, in the Gettysburg Address, spoke about a bloody sacrifice, rebirth, and national mission, his words carried haunting echoes of revivalist sermons. The revivals contributed to a conception of the United States as the New Israel, destined to prepare the world for the establishment of God's kingdom on earth. Revivalists stamped a profound sense of mission on America—it was America's special obligation to combat sin in order to lead the world to a golden age of freedom and equality.

A key concept for the revivalists was "sanctification," or what was some-times called "perfectionism." This was the belief that Christians could live truly sinless lives. By making it each individual's duty to combat sin, by tying personal piety and social action together, evangelical revivalism made a profound contribution to the reform impulse. For antebellum evangelicals, sin was not an abstraction, nor was it something metaphysical. It was concrete: dueling, fornication, profanity, drinking hard liquor. To a number of southern Methodists and Baptists and later northern evangelicals, slavery was the sum of all sins. Only when sin was defeated would Christ return to earth. In theological terms, this vision is known as "postmillennialism": Christ's second coming would occur only after the churches had succeeded in converting the unconverted and overcoming moral evil.

Religious revivals had diverse functions in early-nineteenth-century America. They were at once a force for social discipline and for social reform. Many social conservatives viewed evangelical religion as an indispensable tool for taming the frontier and subduing the urban working class by combating violence, profanity, intemperance, and vice. But evangelicalism not only targeted the sins of the poor; it also sought to reform the manners of the rich and high-born, to make them moral as well as genteel. In the words of revivalist Charles Grandison Finney, revivals sought to remove "the starch and flattery of high life": luxury, idleness, fashionable display, and gluttony. Thus evangelical revivalism helped establish a distinctive set of middle-class norms, separate from those of the upper classes and of the lower classes. Revivalists also helped promote the Protestant ethic, since they equated piety and Christian morality with sobriety, thrift, industry, and individual self-discipline. At the same time, however, revivals played a more radical role, calling on the converted to reject corrupt customs and sinful institutions and to build the kingdom of God on earth.

Revivals South and North

The Second Great Awakening spread across antebellum America in a series of great waves. The first began soon after the Revolution and moved from the Cumberland Valley across the South. Beginning with a belief in natural rights and a radical critique of wealth, worldliness, and pretension—and in the case of some late-eighteenth-century Baptist and Methodist churches, militant opposition to slavery—southern evangelists increasingly discarded radical social criticism and accommodated themselves to the established order.

Southern and western revivalists called for total acceptance of the Bible as the literal word of God. Despite many differences, Methodist circuit riders, Baptist and Presbyterian preachers, and a host of itinerant revivalists agreed that all humans were sinners doomed to writhe in Satan's hands for all eternity unless their sins were forgiven. But, they added, forgiveness was possible because Christ had atoned for humanity's sins on the cross. Perhaps the most influential of the early frontier revivalists was a Presbyterian minister named James McGready, a spellbinding orator who was said to make his listeners smell the sulfur in Hell and hear the harps playing in Heaven. At one of the earliest frontier camp meetings, held in the summer of 1800 in Logan County, Kentucky, hundreds of his listeners were "slain in the spirit" and prayed and screamed and cried out for deliverance.

One of the most dramatic consequences of the great southern revivals in the late eighteenth and early nineteenth centuries was the conversion of the enslaved African Americans to Christianity. During the seventeenth century, slaveholders feared that baptized slaves would have to be set free and that the Christian notion of the equality of all human beings would lead slaves to demand their freedom. But by the second quarter of the eighteenth century, a growing number of slave owners concluded that Christianity would make slaves more docile and conscientious, placing them "under strong Obligations to perform [their] duties with the greatest Diligence and Fidelity . . . from a

Sense of Duty to God." The first concerted campaigns to convert slaves to Christianity were led by Quaker, Moravian, and Anglican ministers during the early eighteenth century. Missionaries established schools and taught several thousand slaves to read and recite Scripture. The Great Awakening in the 1730s and 1740s stimulated renewed efforts to promote Christianization, but it was not until the late eighteenth century, when Methodists and Baptists licensed African Americans to exhort and preach, that truly significant numbers of slaves converted to Christianity. Most slaves attended church alongside whites, although a small number of separate black churches (mainly Baptist) began to emerge as early as the 1760s.

Within the Baptist and Methodist churches, slaves began to create a hybrid form of Christianity, blending Christian rituals and beliefs with elements of West African culture. The result was a religion with its own distinctive forms of preaching and worship, characterized by rhythmic sermons, "shouting" and other ecstatic behavior induced by spiritual possession, and forms of singing and dancing influenced by African traditions. Their African heritage gave them a hopeful, optimistic view of life, which contrasted sharply with evangelical Protestantism's belief in human sinfulness. In Protestant Christianity, slaves found an emphasis on love and spiritual equality that strengthened their hopes of eventual deliverance from bondage. Spirituals, such as "Go Down, Moses" with its refrain, "Let my people go," indicate that slaves identified with the Hebrew people, who had overcome oppression and enslavement.

A second great wave of religious ferment, of northern and urban revivals, had a symbolic start at Yale College. For more than six years, Yale's president, Timothy Dwight, struggled to convert his students. Then suddenly in 1801, his efforts met with success. Half of Yale's students underwent conversion. Many flocked to the ministry.

At colleges across the Northeast—among them, Amherst and Williams—conversions became commonplace, with many students entering divinity schools, joining the ministry, and becoming missionaries. Revivals soon spread across New England and particularly western New York with such fury that this region became known as the "burned-over district."

The king of antebellum northern revivalists was Charles Grandison Finney (1792–1875). Born in Connecticut, Finney grew up in western New York, where he studied the law and became an attorney. In 1821, however, he underwent a violent conversion experience, which convinced him that he had "a retainer from the Lord Jesus Christ to plead his case." The story of his conversion became as familiar to many American Protestants as the scriptural account of Paul's conversion on the road to Damascus. His autobiography contains a vivid description. On a Sabbath evening Finney, then a prosperous young lawyer, thumbed through the Bible as part of his research on a court case, uncertain of the meaning of "Mosaic law." He soon began to read the text more closely, overwhelmed by questions he had never before considered. "What are you waiting for?" a voice seemed to be asking. "Are you leading a righteous life?" Gripped by fear, Finney worried that his heart was dead to God. Then it seemed as if he "met the Lord Jesus Christ face to face." The Holy Spirit seemed to be speaking to him, asking him, "Will you doubt?" Finney cried out, "No I will not doubt; I cannot doubt." Suddenly, his sense of guilt and sinfulness was gone. He had been born again.

Despite his rejection of formal theological training, Finney began to convert souls to Christ in the small towns of western New York. He introduced a series of "new measures" to win converts. Finney believed that a revivalist had to be willing to use any measure to lead his listeners to open their hearts to Christ. He used plain, colloquial language in his sermons; he prayed for sinners by name; he held "protracted meetings" in the evenings and they lasted for a week or more; he set up an "anxious bench" at the front of the meeting, where the almost-saved could receive special prayers; and he encouraged women to actively participate in revivals.

With a hypnotic gaze, a clear speaking style honed in courthouses, and illustrations drawn from everyday life, Finney led successful revivals in such fast-growing new cities as Rochester, New York, and Reading, Pennsylvania, and in the nation's largest city, New York. His direct, strong sermons were "like cannonballs through a basket of eggs," declared one observer. His message was simple and direct: Each person is responsible for his or her own sinfulness and has the ability to achieve salvation. Finney told his audience that their efforts could bring the millennium, a thousand years of peace and prosperity that would culminate in Christ's second coming. If only enough people converted to Christ, Finney told his listeners, "the millennium may come in this country in three years."

As a preacher, Finney sought to convert not just the mind but the heart. He wanted his listeners to experience an overwhelming sense of their own depravity and unworthiness; to feel the agonizing despair that he had felt on finding his heart dead to God; to go through remorse and repentance; and to finally experience the ecstatic sense of joy and liberation that was the evidence of a rebirth experience. For Finney, however, conversion was not an end in itself. The true Christian character was revealed in acts of practical benevolence.

Although Finney's main emphasis was on personal moral regeneration, his optimism, his faith in God's benevolence, his dedication to democracy and progress, and his belief in humanity's perfectibility, all contributed to the reform impulse. In his sermons, Finney drew a direct connection between revivals and social reform. "The great business of the church," he proclaimed in an essay entitled "The Pernicious Attitude of the Church on the Reforms of the Age" (1846), "is to reform the world—to put away every kind of sin." It was no accident that many of Finney's converts became active participants in reform—including the abolitionist Theodore Weld and the utopian socialist John Humphrey Noyes. Through their activism, these reformers demonstrated the radical implications of Finney's preaching.

Six decades of religious ferment culminated in a great religious revival that began in Philadelphia in 1856 and in New York City in late 1857. In October 1857, in the midst of an economic panic, noonday prayer meetings began to draw huge crowds to New York City's Fulton Street Dutch Reformed Church. Soon, more than ten thousand men and women a day gathered for prayer meetings held at churches throughout the city. By the spring of 1858, the press carried daily accounts of a nationwide nonsectarian revival, centered not on the frontier or in the new western cities but in the nation's largest metropolises.

Arising partly in response to a wave of bank failures, mortgage foreclosures, and bankruptcies, the great revival of 1857 and 1858 also gave expression to a host of other anxieties, such as the increase in poverty and crime, the growth of cities, and, above all, sectional tensions over slavery. To many Americans, the great revival seemed to offer hope that the divisive issue of slavery would be overcome in a burst of religious fervor. But to many others, North and South, the revival suggested that only their region clung to God's true faith. Antebellum Americans may have "read the same Bible and pray[ed] to the same God," in the words of Lincoln's second inaugural address. But as the era drew to a end, religion had become a source of division rather than a force for unity. In 1837, the Presbyterian church had divided, partly on account of the issue of slavery. In 1844, the Methodist church split for the same reason, as did the Baptist church the next year. Religious feeling, which fueled an unprecedented movement for reform, now propelled sectional antagonism, which brought the nation to the brink of civil war.

Religious Ferment

In 1783, Yale College's president, Ezra Stiles, predicted that three religious denominations—the Congregationalists, the Episcopalians, and the Presbyterians—would dominate the religious life of the new nation. His prediction proved to be entirely wrong. Stiles never imagined that a number of older denominations would quickly expand—notably, the Baptists, Catholics, and Methodists—and that a host of new denominations and movements would soon arise and radically reshape the religious landscape—adventists, perfectionists, primitivists, Christians, Disciples of Christ, Mormons, and separate African American churches.

During the late eighteenth and early nineteenth centuries, the Congregationalist and Episcopal churches grew relatively slowly. The number of Congregationalist churches rose from 750 in 1780 to 2,200 in 1860; the number of Episcopal congregations from 400 to 2,100. At the same time, other denominations—particularly the more pietistic and evangelical sects—expanded at a staggering pace. Baptists grew from approximately 400 congregations in 1780 to 12,150 in 1860; Lutherans from 225 to 2,100; Presbyterians from 500 to 6,400; Methodists from 50 in 1783 to 20,000 in 1860; Roman Catholics from 50 in 1780 to 2,500 in 1860. The African Methodist Episcopal church grew from 5 congregations in 1816 to more than 100 by 1850.

During the decades before the Civil War, America was a veritable "spiritual hothouse," a place of extraordinary religious ferment and enthusiasm. Many new religions and sects arose—among them, the Disciples of Christ, the Mormons, and the Shakers. An influx of foreign immigrants helped create ethnic and linguistic fissures in older churches, such as the Lutheran church and the Roman Catholic church. Older denominations splintered and fragmented, producing diverse forms of Presbyterianism (Old School, New School, Reformed, Associated) and many kinds of Baptist churches (General, Free Will, Regular, Separate). Lay members challenged established authority and demanded changes in ritual. In many churches, women suddenly assumed previously unheard-of roles.

It was a period of truly unprecedented innovation and experimentation in the realm of religion. At a time when religion was losing ground in Europe, America witnessed a remarkable outpouring of religious belief. According to one estimate, three-quarters of the American population in 1860 had a connection with a church. By 1860, the nation's churches reported having 26 million seats for the country's 31 million people.

Behind this explosion of religious enthusiasm and popular evangelicalism lay a broad cultural shift: a weakening of older structures of religious authority and a revolt against Calvinist notions of human depravity and a predestined elect. People sought new forms of religious fellowship, at camp meetings, urban prayer meetings, and Methodist "love feasts." In the increasingly fluid environment of early-nineteenth-century America, sects competed fiercely for members. Charismatic preachers, scorning pessimistic Calvinist views of human nature and recognizing people's ability to speed their own salvation, expressed exuberant confidence in their ability to save souls and promote revivals.

Three currents of popular religious thought exhibited particular vigor and intensity in antebellum America. The first, known as primitivism or restorationism, was a movement to recreate the practices of early New Testament Christianity and strip away ecclesiastical perversions and creeds. The second, millennialism or adventism, was a set of ideas connected with the second coming of Christ and the arrival of an era of earthly peace and the triumph of righteousness mentioned in the New Testament Book of Revelation. The third was the doctrine of holiness—a belief that moral and spiritual perfection and sinlessness were prerequisites for salvation. These intellectual currents contributed to the establishment of a number of new religious sects and denominations and greatly stimulated enthusiasm for personal piety, education, and social reform.

Primitivism

One of the most distinctly American developments in early-nineteenth-century Protestantism was the rapid growth of a religious movement known as the Christians or the Disciples of Christ. This new movement, born in the upper South and the Midwest at the beginning of the century, intended to surmount divisions among Christian denominations by concentrating on what its first leaders considered essential beliefs and tolerating differences on other matters.

The central figures in the movement's founding were Elias Smith, a former New England Baptist minister, who wanted to free republican Americans from subservience "to a catechism, creed, covenant or a superstitious priest"; James O'Kelly, a former Methodist minister in Virginia, discontented with the Methodist church hierarchy; Barton Stone, a former Presbyterian minister in Kentucky, who came to reject such theological notions as the Trinity and predestination on the ground that they conflicted with reason; and Alexander Campbell, a Scottish immigrant, also a staunch advocate of a rational Biblicism. All considered themselves religious reformers, eager to restore Christianity to its original purity. The idea of re-creating the original patterns of New Testament Christianity, of overthrowing outmoded ecclesiastical establishments, and of recognizing the right of common people to interpret the

Bible for themselves, using logic and common sense, fit well with the optimistic, democratic, antiestablishment temper of early-nineteenth-century America. The Disciples of Christ rejected creeds, insisted on liberty of opinion, sought an ecumenical union of all Christians, and emphasized rational interpretation of the Bible. Optimistic in outlook, they upheld the doctrine that a moral sense was implanted in each individual, in sharp contrast to orthodox Calvinism. Although revivalist James McGready, for example, preached that salvation required that each individual undergo a conversion experience, the Disciples' leaders argued that a reasoned belief in the New Testament was enough to bring salvation.

The movement was staunchly reformist. Not only were Christians and Disciples active in temperance, they also had a strong abolitionist tradition— Barton Stone and Alexander Campbell both freed their own slaves. Possessing a deep respect for learning, believing that reason applied to Scripture can lead people to salvation, they established many colleges, including Drake in Iowa, Eureka in Illinois, and Hiram in Ohio, as well as many religious periodicals, including one now known as *The Christian Century*, a leading ecumenical journal.

Millennialism

Visions of the millennium—the return of Christ to earth and the arrival of a thousand years of universal peace and happiness—exerted enormous influence upon pre–Civil War America. Rooted in the books of Daniel and Revelation in the Bible, the millennial impulse took many different forms. Adventists believed that the literal second coming of Christ and the end of the world were at hand. Radical adventists often employed apocalyptic imagery— they expected the imminent destruction of the temporal world, and they predicted that the unrighteous would be purged in a holocaust that would engulf the earth and that the righteous would be resurrected. "Premillennialists" argued that Christ's second coming would precede his thousand-year reign on earth, which would culminate in the ultimate battle between good and evil at Armageddon. More common in antebellum America was an optimistic theological tradition known as "postmillennialism." This was the belief that Christ will return to earth only after the millennium—after clergy, missionaries, and reformers had defeated the forces of irreligion, evil, and vice and set the stage for the triumph of virtue and righteousness.

Antebellum America's millennial consciousness drew upon a variety of sources. In part, one basis was the long-standing view that Americans were, in Herman Melville's words, "the peculiar, chosen people, the Israel of our time," and that the millennium was destined to take place in America. The pace of scientific and technological innovation, the triumphs of the revivalists, and the strength of the nation's republican institutions further contributed to millennial fervor. The invention of the telegraph touched off a dramatic statement of millennialist hopes in *The Ladies' Repository,* a Methodist monthly, in 1850: "This noble invention is to be the means of extending civilization, republicanism, and Christianity over the earth. . . . Then will wrong and injustice be forever banished. Every yoke shall be broken, and the oppressed go free. Wars will cease from the earth. . . . Then shall come to pass the millennium."

Antebellum America spawned many religious sects and communitarian ventures that drew inspiration from their reading of the Book of Revelation. At utopian communities in Oneida, New York, and Zoar, Ohio, and in Shaker communities, men and women sought to live as if the millennium had already arrived. The desire to root out sin and set the stage for the millennium inspired countless missionaries to win the world for Christ. Millennialist visions also stimulated reform movements that attacked drinking, slavery, and other social evils. Millennialist imagery arose with particular intensity during the Civil War, when many Northerners believed that the conflict would cleanse the nation of sin and prepare the way for an age of righteousness. The North, in the words of Julia Ward Howe's "Battle Hymn of the Republic," had glimpsed "the glory of the coming of the Lord" and was fighting to purge the land of sin. Much as "Christ had died to make men holy," Northern soldiers were fighting to set men free.

Perhaps the most dramatic example of radical adventism in antebellum America involved a religious leader named William Miller (1782–1849), a farmer from Low Hampton, New York, who interpreted the Bible to pinpoint the return of Christ "around 1843." A native of Massachusetts, a veteran of the War of 1812, and a dabbler in deism, Miller underwent a dramatic conversion experience, after which he was baptized a Baptist and developed a method for computing the precise time of Christ's return. Joshua V. Himes, a Boston minister and a communications genius, popularized Miller's views in some five million pieces of literature. Tens of thousands of Americans prepared themselves for the imminent arrival of the millennium.

Miller initially predicted that the millennium would commence in March 1843. When his original prediction failed to come true, he first offered March 1844 as the date of Christ's return, and then October 22, 1844. It used to be said that many Millerites abandoned their jobs and property and gathered on hilltops to await the second coming. In fact, Miller's followers gathered at churches and prayed as the end of the world approached.

Although many were disillusioned after the failure of Miller's predictions, a number of the faithful remained convinced that the second coming was imminent. Some disappointed Millerites would follow the teachings of Ellen G. White, herself a Miller convert, which later formed the theological basis for Seventh-Day Adventism. Retaining the belief in the imminence of Christ's second coming, White advocated vegetarianism, forbade alcohol and tobacco, and criticized reliance on drugs and medicine. Other adventists would turn to the teaching of Charles Taze Russell, who believed that the millennium had already commenced but that its final consummation still lay in the future. Russell's successor, Joseph F. Rutherford, would draw upon Russell's teachings when he formed Jehovah's Witnesses in 1931.

Holiness Movements

The quest for holiness exerted a powerful attraction in pre–Civil War America. Many Protestants, mainly Methodist in background, were deeply troubled by the worldliness of established churches and struggled relentlessly to achieve John Wesley's ideal of perfect sanctification—a truly sinless Christian life, a life of purity and piety. Many others, particularly those converted in the revivals held by Charles Finney, sought feverishly to attain Finney's ideal of spiritual and moral perfection. To many individuals active in the pre–Civil War holiness movements, personal piety could be truly expressed only through acts of disinterested benevolence.

The central figure in the antebellum holiness movement was Phoebe Palmer, the daughter of English Methodist immigrants. In camp meetings, holiness revivals, home gatherings, and interdenominational prayer meetings, she converted thousands of Americans and Canadians with the message that salvation could be achieved through total submission to God's will. It was not necessary to wait for an emotional conversion experience; nor was it necessary to "struggle with the powers of darkness," she proclaimed in *The Way of Holiness* (1851). Salvation was immediately open to all who would consecrate themselves to God.

Women played a particularly active role in the holiness movement. Leaders were members of the laity, men and women who had an equal right to preach. It was assumed that both men and women could receive an infusion of the

Holy Spirit and could testify in public to the experience of holiness. Above all, women were especially likely to engage in acts of practical benevolence, which demonstrated their obedience to God's law. Phoebe Palmer herself was a pioneer in urban philanthropy, establishing a mission in Five Points, New York City's most notorious slum, and dispensing assistance to inmates in New York's Tombs prison.

The Mormons

Many of the major strands in antebellum religious thought come together in the history of the Mormon church. These include the "restorationist" impulse to repudiate the legitimacy of existing churches and to restore the true church; the "millennialist" sense that a new age in human history was about to commence; and the "perfectionist" desire to attain personal holiness.

In the history of religion, few stories are more dramatic than that of the Mormons. It has the haunting biblical overtones of divine revelations and visitations, of persecution and martyrdom, of an exodus virtually across a continent, and of ultimate success in establishing a religious society in an uninhabited desert. This story, however, did not take place in a foreign land and in the distant past. It took place in the United States during the nineteenth century.

The Mormon church had its beginnings in western New York, which, during the early nineteenth century, was a hotbed of religious fervor. Methodist, Baptist, Presbyterian, and Universalist preachers all eagerly sought converts. Fourteen-year-old Joseph Smith Jr., the son of migrant farmers who had tried and failed to make a living in Vermont and New Hampshire, listened closely to these preachers, but was uncertain which way to turn. "So great were the confusion and strife among the different denominations," Smith later recalled, "that it was impossible for a person, young as I was . . . to come to any certain conclusion who was right and who was wrong."

In the spring of 1820, Smith went into the woods near Palmyra, New York, to seek divine guidance. Suddenly, he was "seized upon by some power that entirely overcame me." According to his account, a brilliant light revealed to him "two personages," who announced that they were God the Father and Christ the Savior. They told him that all existing churches were false and that the true church of God was about to be reestablished on earth.

Three years later, young Smith underwent another supernatural experience. On the evening of September 21, 1823, "a personage" visited his bedroom and said "that God had work for" him to do. The spectral visitor told him of the existence of a set of buried golden plates that contained a lost section from the Bible describing a tribe of Israelites that had lived in America. The next morning, Smith said, he made his way to nearby Hill Cumorah and proceeded to unearth the golden plates that were deposited in a stone box. He was forbidden to remove them or reveal their existence for four years. Finally, in 1827, Smith received the plates and, with the aid of magic stones, translated them into English. In 1830, the messages on the plates were published as the Book of Mormon.

For Mormons, the visions and revelations received by Joseph Smith Jr., beginning in 1820, marked the dawn of a new age in human history. They signaled the end of "the Great Apostasy," fourteen hundred years during which Catholic and Protestant churches had deluded the world. On April 6, 1830, Smith formally founded the Church of Christ, later renamed the Church of Jesus Christ of Latter-day Saints, and he committed the church to establishing the kingdom of God on earth.

At first, members of the church were mainly relatives and neighbors. In 1830, the church consisted of six elders and just fifty members. But the movement quickly grew. Part of Mormonism's early attraction may be that it spoke directly to the beliefs and yearnings of many antebellum rural New Yorkers. The folk culture of the time paid a great deal of attention to the occult—to diviners who used rods and seer stones to find water or buried treasure, to adepts who performed magic rituals, to clairvoyance and magical talismans and mystical visions, to legends about Indians and mysterious Indian mounds. Joseph Smith had an extraordinary capacity to speak to these people, offering (as poet John Greenleaf Whittier put it) "a language of hope and promise to weak, weary hearts, tossed and troubled, who have wandered from sect to sect, seeking in vain for the primal manifestation of the divine power."

Soon, Smith attracted several thousand followers largely from isolated rural areas of New England, New York, and Pennsylvania and from the frontier Midwest. The converts to Mormonism were usually small farmers, mechanics, and tradesmen who had been displaced by the growing commercial economy and who were repelled by the secularism and rampant individualism of early-nineteenth-century America.

Because Joseph Smith said that he conversed with angels and received direct revelations from the Lord, local authorities threatened to indict him for blasphemy. He and his followers responded by moving to Kirtland, Ohio, near Cleveland, where they built their first temple. It was in Kirtland that the

Mormons first experimented with an economy planned and run by the church. In this community, church trustees controlled the members' property and put members to work building a temple and other structures. Meanwhile, the Mormons set up an unauthorized wildcat bank—a venture that nearly destroyed the church when it failed during the Panic of 1837.

From Kirtland, the Mormons moved to Independence, Missouri, and then to a town called Far West, in northern Missouri. Disputes broke out almost immediately between Mormons and "gentiles," as non-Mormons were called. Beginning in 1832, proslavery mobs attacked the Mormons, accusing them of inciting slave insurrection. They burned several Mormon settlements and seized Mormon farms and houses. Joseph Smith Jr. was arrested for treason and sentenced to be shot, but he managed to escape several months later. Fifteen thousand Mormons fled from Missouri to Illinois after Governor L. W. Boggs proclaimed them enemies who "had to be exterminated, or driven from the state."

In 1839, communities of Mormons, including many converts from Britain and northern Europe, resettled along the east bank of the Mississippi River in the town of Commerce, Illinois. They changed its name to Nauvoo, and it soon became the second-largest city in the state. Trouble arose again, after dissident Mormons published a newspaper denouncing the practice of polygamy and attacking Joseph Smith for trying to become "king or lawgiver to the church."

On Smith's orders, the city marshal and Mormon legionnaires destroyed the dissidents' printing press. Authorities charged Smith with treason, but the Illinois governor gave Smith his pledge of protection. Smith and his brother were then confined to jail in Carthage, Illinois. Late in the afternoon of June 27, 1844, a mob of prominent citizens, aided by jail guards, broke into Smith's cell, shot him and his brother, and threw their bodies out a second-story window.

Why did the Mormons seem so menacing? Why did many western settlers agree with the Reverend Finis Ewing when he said that "the 'Mormons' are the common enemies of mankind and ought to be destroyed"? Today, it is hard to believe that Mormons could ever have been regarded as subversive, since they are known for their abstinence from tobacco and alcohol and their stress on family and community responsibility. Why were they subjected to continuing persecution?

Anti-Mormonism was partly rooted in a struggle for economic and political power. Individualistic frontiersmen feared the Mormons, who voted as their elders told them to and whose trustees controlled their land. Mormonism was also denounced as a threat to fundamental social values. Protestant ministers railed against it, since Mormons rejected the legitimacy of established churches and insisted that the Book of Mormon was Holy Scripture, equal in importance to the Bible. They attacked Mormonism as a preposterous hoax that was played on naive and superstitious minds. The Mormons were also accused of corrupt moral values, especially after 1842 when rumors about polygamy began to spread. Indeed, Mormons did practice polygamy for half a century, which was justified theologically as an effort to reestablish the patriarchal Old Testament family. Polygamy also served an important social function, absorbing single or widowed women into Mormon communities. The novelist Harriet Beecher Stowe denounced polygamy as "a slavery which debases and degrades womanhood, motherhood and family," but contrary to popular belief it was not widely practiced. Altogether, only 10 to 20 percent of Mormon families were polygamous and nearly two-thirds involved a man and two wives.

After Joseph Smith's murder, a new leader, Brigham Young, led the Mormons across a thousand miles of unsettled prairie, plains, and arid desert to a new Zion on the shores of the Great Salt Lake. More than 85,000 Mormon migrants followed. By the time of his death in 1877, there were 125,000 Mormons in Utah.

Today, the Mormon church is one of the fastest-growing religious groups in the United States, and its members are known for their piety, industriousness, sobriety, and thrift. A century ago, anti-Mormons regarded the church as a fundamental threat to American values. Early-nineteenth-century American society attached enormous importance to individualism, monogamous marriage, and private property, and the Mormons were believed to subvert each of these values. If in certain respects the Mormons challenged the values of antebellum America, their aspirations were truly a product of their times. They sought nothing less than the establishment of God's kingdom on earth.

Religious Outsiders

The Mormons were not the only antebellum religious group subject to intense prejudice and discrimination. Catholics, Jews, and northern African American Protestants also faced severe hostility from the dominant culture. Catholics and Jews had to respond to a series of other challenges. These ranged from the weakness of clerical and rabbinical authority, the relative power of the laity, and the increasing ethnic diversity of the American Catholic and Jewish populations. In response to discrimination, antebellum Catholics, Jews, and free black Protestants each formed fraternal lodges, benevolent associations, and mutual benefit societies. These organizations had religious ties but were largely secular in orientation, which allowed them to preserve distinctive group identity while adapting to the problems of education and charity in early-ninetenth-century America.

American Catholicism

No major church grew more rapidly during the pre–Civil War era—or faced more bitter hostility—than Roman Catholicism. Numbering no more than 25,000 in 1776, Catholics grew to 1.75 million by 1850, making them the nation's largest religious group and the country's first truly multicultural church.

Throughout the colonial period, Catholics constituted a tiny persecuted minority, just 1 percent of the population, concentrated in three colonies: Maryland, Pennsylvania, and New York. Few in number, hampered by a shortage of clergy (there were only six priests in the American colonies in 1776 and no bishop), and lacking a regular church hierarchy, the colonial Catholic church was strongly localistic. The Catholic laity not only founded churches but administered them as well through a practice known as "trusteeship."

It was not until after the Revolution that a formal church hierarchy in line with canon law began to be organized—provoking repeated conflicts between bishops and lay trustees over who held title to church property and who had the authority to appoint or dismiss local pastors. During the early nineteenth century, however, American Catholics began the process of institution building, strengthening ecclesiastical authority. By 1829, when bishops from Baltimore, Boston, Charleston, Cincinnati, New York, and Philadelphia met in the First Provincial Council of Baltimore, the Catholic church had established six seminaries, nine colleges, and thirty-three monasteries, convents, and communities of religious women.

Massive immigration from Ireland and Germany between 1820 and 1860 dramatically increased the size of the Catholic church, from 195,000 to 3,103,000, but also generated ethnic tensions within the church. Following the Revolution, the church had been led primarily by English Catholic families from Maryland and by French Catholics. As the composition of the American Catholic population changed, however, Catholics of German and Irish ancestry wanted priests of their own background as well as liturgical practices conforming to their national customs. German Catholics, for example, called for separate parishes, parochial schools, fraternal organizations, and cemeteries, while Irish Catholics, who attached significance to pilgrimages, processions, and wakes, demanded recognition of their customs.

During the antebellum era, American Catholics faced intense hostility and even violence. Anti-Catholicism had deep roots in American culture. The evangelical Protestant revivals in the 1820s and 1830s stimulated a "No Popery" movement. Prominent northern clergymen, mostly Whigs in their politics, accused the Catholic church of conspiring to overthrow democracy and subject the United States to papal despotism. Popular fiction (such as Maria Monk's *Awful Disclosures of the Hotel Dieu Nunnery in Montreal* [1836], which sold three hundred thousand copies before the Civil War) offered graphic descriptions of priests seducing women during confession and nuns cutting infants from the womb and throwing them to dogs. A popular children's game was called "break the Pope's neck." Anti-Catholic sentiment culminated in mobs rioting and the burning of churches and convents. In 1834, following an anti-Catholic sermon, a Protestant mob burned the Ursuline Convent in Charlestown, Massachusetts. A decade later, after Philadelphia's Catholic bishop convinced the city's school board to use both the Catholic and Protestant versions of the Bible in schools, a vicious riot erupted in the nearby suburbs of Kensington and Southwark.

The advent of so many immigrants from Ireland and Germany after 1845 led to a renewed anti-Catholic outburst. Catholics were blamed for a sharp increase in poverty, crime, and drunkenness, as well as subservience to a foreign leader, the pope. Thousands of native-born Protestants responded with outrage when Catholic Archbishop John Hughes of New York declared in 1850 that "everyone should know that we have for our mission to convert the world—including the inhabitants of the United States—the people of the cities and the people of the country, the officers of the navy and the marines, commanders of the army, the legislatures, the Senate, the Cabinet, the President, and all!"

To native-born Protestant workers, Catholic immigrants also posed a tangible economic threat. Rapid inflation followed the discovery of gold in California in 1848. The growth of railroads disrupted local markets and eliminated jobs in river and canal transportation. Economic slumps in 1851 and 1854 resulted in severe unemployment and wage cuts, and native-born workers blamed Irish and German Catholics for their plight and briefly supported the anti-Catholic Know-Nothing political party.

The Catholic church responded to Protestant hostility in a variety of ways. Concerned that many immigrants were only nominally Catholic, the Church established urban missions and launched religious revivals to strengthen immigrants' religious identity. Somewhat similar to the Protestant evangelical revivals, the Catholic revivals featured rousing sermons and sought to encourage religious piety, fervor, and devotion. Catholics also responded to the expansion and intensification of Protestant reform activities in the 1850s by establishing a separate system of benevolent societies, hospitals, orphanages, and sanitoriums to care for the poor, the sick, and the orphaned, as well as trade schools and "houses of protection" for single working women (the first was established in Pittsburgh in 1843). Unlike many Protestant charities and benevolent societies, which sought to reform the character of the poor, Catholic charities were more interested in simply relieving the economic condition of impoverished Catholics. Discrimination in public schools, where many teachers read passages from the Protestant version of the Bible and used texts that portrayed the Catholic church as a threat to republican institutions, led Catholics to establish a separate system of parochial schools. Beginning in New York City in the early 1840s, Catholics embarked on an ambitious program of building a parochial school in every diocese. In these ways, the Church sought to help Catholics, particularly Catholic children, preserve their faith in the face of Protestant proselytizing.

American Judaism

Twenty-three refugees from Portuguese Brazil who arrived in New Amsterdam in the summer of 1654 were the first Jews to settle in the American colonies. Throughout the colonial era, the number of Jews in the present-day United States remained extremely low. At the time of the Revolution, the American Jewish population numbered no more than fifteen hundred. Composed primarily of traders, petty merchants, and artisans, and characterized by a high rate of intermarriage, the colonial Jewish population established few religious institutions. There were no more than five or six Jewish congregations in all the colonies (many established with the financial support of foreign Jews), no Jewish newspapers, and not a single rabbi, reflecting a significant degree of religious indifference and a deep distrust of rabbis and rabbinical authority.

During the first two decades of the nineteenth century, the Jewish population remained small and largely invisible. By 1812, New York City had the new nation's largest Jewish population—just fifty families; Philadelphia had about thirty Jewish families. In 1816, however, the first organized Protestant efforts to convert Jews to Christianity began. These efforts had an ironic consequence, sensitizing Jews to their distinctive identity and encouraging Jewish communities to establish their own schools, hospitals, and synagogues and appoint foreign rabbis as religious leaders.

By 1850, migration from central and western Europe increased the Jewish population from approximately 2,000 to 50,000. Thousands of immigrants from Germany, Poland, Galicia, Lithuania, Hungary, Moravia, and Bohemia in the 1850s tripled the size of the Jewish population to 150,000 (or about half of 1 percent of the nation's total population) in 1860. As the Jewish population grew, synagogues fragmented along lines of nativity, as German, Dutch, Polish, and Portuguese Jews established their own congregations.

A major challenge antebellum American Jews confronted was adapting religious orthodoxy to the realities of American life. Many early-nineteenth-century Jews lived in small towns where it was impossible to obey traditional laws—towns that lacked a synagogue, a mikvah (ritual bath), a ritual circumciser, and a kosher butcher. Moreover, many Jews found it impossible to refrain from working on the Jewish Sabbath, Saturday. Even those who lived in larger Jewish communities were often eager to adjust to the conditions of American life. As early as 1824, a group of Charleston, South Carolina, Jews organized one of the country's first Reformed congregations. Their aim, they wrote in the congregation's constitution, was to modify "such parts of our prevailing system of Worship, as are inconsistent with the present enlightened state of society, and not in accordance with the Five Books of Moses and the Prophets." Contrary to Orthodox practice, they worshiped from an English-language prayer book, with their heads uncovered, while listening to instrumental music. In subsequent years, many other congregations "Americanized" their religious rituals by playing organ music during services, permitting men and women to worship side by side, allowing men to pray without the traditional prayer shawl (tallith) and head covering (yarmulke), and establishing confirmation ceremonies for boys and girls.

If American Jews discarded many traditional injunctions of Jewish law, they also avidly formed a host of community institutions and exhibited strong concern for charity and communal self-help. Even small towns that lacked Jewish congregations often had extrareligious Jewish institutions, such as a B'nai B'rith, a lodge and benevolent society founded in 1843, or a Young Men's Hebrew Association (the first was formed in 1854), as well as separate orphan asylums, burial societies, and charitable organizations to aid Jews unable to support themselves.

Antebellum Jews experienced less discrimination and persecution than Catholics or Mormons, in part because of their small numbers and in part because the Jewish community was scattered and decentralized. They therefore did not provoke among Christians fears of conspiracy. Equally important was an eagerness to assimilate. In antebellum America, most Jews shed distinctive dress and shaved long sideburns and discarded many customs that set European Jews apart. Although they adapted to American life in many ways, Jews vigorously resisted threats to their identity, strongly opposing state laws that limited membership in state legislatures to Christians and that banned commerce on the Christian Sabbath, efforts of Christian missionaries to convert them, and the recitation of Christian prayers in public schools. Antebellum American Jews waged an uneasy balancing act: they struggled to shed the appearance of foreignness and modernize Jewish tradition while sustaining Jewish distinctiveness.

Black Churches

In November 1787, white elders of Philadelphia's St. George's Methodist Church ordered black Methodists to sit in a newly built gallery. Several free blacks refused, including Richard Allen (1760–1831), a former slave, who had supported himself as a brickyard laborer, shoemaker, wagon driver, and woodchopper. Instead, he prayed at the altar. Shaken by his experiences with discrimination, Allen founded the Free African Society of Philadelphia, which is usually considered the first autonomous free black organization in the United States. Seven years later, in 1794, Allen founded a separate black Methodist church, known as Mother Bethel. That same year, Absalom Jones (1746–1818), also a former slave and a former Methodist preacher, formed the African Church of Philadelphia as a racially separate nondenominational church; the church later became St. Thomas's African Episcopal Church.

Discriminatory treatment in white-controlled churches led free black communities across the North to establish separate black congregations in the late eighteenth and early nineteenth centuries. Between 1804 and 1815, separate black Baptist, Methodist, and Presbyterian churches were founded in Boston, New York, Philadelphia, and Wilmington, Delaware. In 1816, Richard Allen formed the first autonomous black denomination, the African Methodist Episcopal church. Five years later, a separate denomination, the African Methodist Episcopal Zion church, was established in New York. By 1820, there may have been as many as seven hundred African American congregations in the country.

During the antebellum period, African American churches developed their own forms of worship that blended African and Christian traditions. Religious services included highly rhythmic singing, dancing, and clapping. African American ministers played an critical role in shaping a distinctive, vernacular American preaching style. During the 1790s, a black evangelist named Harry Hoosier had accompanied the Methodist Episcopal bishop Francis

Asbury in his tours across the southern frontier, where he drew thousands of converts with his dramatic retellings of biblical stories. A black Virginia Baptist preacher named John Jasper became legendary for his ability to string "together picture after picture." Other antebellum black ministers known for their verbal pyrotechnics and "volcanic passion" included Lemuel Haynes and Harry Evans. Their use of repetition, recurrent alteration of sound and expression, humor, striking metaphors, a vivid pictorial style, and stress on the human Jesus transformed American preaching styles.

Although most free blacks were Protestants, some became Catholics. The refusal of the major Catholic religious orders to admit African Americans led to the founding of two orders of black nuns—the Oblate Sisters in 1829 and the Holy Family Sisters in 1842. The first black American priest, James Augustine Healy, was ordained in 1854.

The black churches served as centers of political life, communal self-help, and social reform, and black ministers were community leaders. Absalom Jones, for example, provided schooling in his church; founded one of the first black reform organizations, the Society for the Suppression of Vice and Immorality; distributed one of the earliest petitions against the slave trade; and established January 1, 1808, as a day of thanksgiving in black communities to mark the closing of the African slave trade. Similarly, Richard Allen established church schools and mutual aid societies, and in 1830, the year before his death, he assumed leadership of the First National Negro Convention, a black political organization that met at his church.

Like many white Christians, African American evangelicals were strongly millennarian in their beliefs. Preachers in black Baptist and Methodist churches told their parishioners that African Americans would play a critical role in redeeming white America from the sins of slaveholding and racial prejudice and thereby free the nation to lead the world toward the millennium.

The Post–Civil War Splintering
of the Millennialist Vision

During the first half of the nineteenth century, notions of progress, perfection, and mission nurtured by the Second Great Awakening inspired an impressive array of reform campaigns aimed at social betterment and moral improvement. Convinced that their efforts would usher in the millennium and the second coming of Christ, committed Christians established hundreds of voluntary associations to battle sin, ignorance, crime, and social inequity.

Theological liberals, evangelical Protestants, and rationalists all shared a millennialist faith that America was destined to lead the world to a new epoch of human virtue and improvement.

Even before the Civil War, this hopeful consensus began to fade. During the late 1830s and the 1840s, interdenominational cooperation among churches declined. Having once united to Christianize American society, churches established their own missionary societies, Bible and tract societies, and other benevolent and educational organizations. Denominations themselves broke apart. In 1837, the Presbyterian church divided, one cause being the moral issue of slavery. In 1844, the Methodist church split apart, and the next year, the Baptists divided into the Southern and Northern Conventions.

After the Civil War, divisions among American Protestants widened even further. A relatively cohesive religious culture gave way to a culture riven by class, ethnicity, and conflicting sets of values. A great schism took place in American Protestantism in the late nineteenth century, and the issue was the Bible's status as a divinely inspired text. During the mid-nineteenth century, German scholars subjected the Bible to historical and critical scrutiny. Their findings, imported into the United States after 1850, cast doubt on the factual reliability of the Bible, the traditional dating and authorship, and the authenticity of the miracles described in Scripture.

Meanwhile, Charles Darwin's theory of evolution, laid out in his *Origin of Species* (1859) and *The Descent of Man* (1871), called into question the accuracy of the biblical account of creation. During the early nineteenth century, American Protestants tended to assume that science reinforced divine revelation. But by the late nineteenth century, there was a growing sense that the findings of modern science and religion were at odds. A volume by Andrew Dickson White, former president of Cornell University, entitled *The History of the Warfare of Science with Theology in Christendom* (1896), underscored the growing tension. Protestant modernists discarded many religious beliefs that conflicted with scientific findings; Protestant traditionalists struggled to preserve the tenets of their faith.

Religion would continue to inspire many late-nineteenth-century advocates of reform, especially proponents of the Social Gospel, a movement within liberal Protestantism to apply the teachings of Jesus Christ to social problems. But many conservative evangelicals, adventists, and pentecostals denounced the Social Gospel, in the words of evangelist Billy Sunday, as "godless social service nonsense." Many conservative post–Civil War evangelicals adopted a pessimistic form of biblical interpretation known as "dispensationalist premillennialism." Convinced that the world was incurably corrupt, conservative evangelicals downplayed social action to save souls and patiently awaited a final cataclysm that would purge the world of wickedness and sin.

Nevertheless, the belief that Americans have an obligation to obey a higher law than the Constitution—the absolute moral law of the Bible—would inspire future crusades for social justice. When the Reverend Martin Luther King Jr. issued his stirring pleas for justice and interracial brotherhood, his words carried haunting echoes of evangelical preachers a century before.

Chapter 3

Making the United States
a Christian Republic

THE POLITICS OF VIRTUE

On July 4, 1827, a Presbyterian minister in Philadelphia made a startling proposal. Ezra Stiles Ely challenged the nation's Baptists, Congregationalists, Episcopalians, Methodists, and Presbyterians to join together to form a "Christian party in politics." Declaring that it was "the duty of Christian freemen to elect Christian rulers," he called on the nation's religious majority to drive from political office "heretics, drunkards, and blasphemers" and replace them with truly godly leaders. Ely's dream of a Christian party in politics was never realized. Religious rivalries and sectarian feuding prevented the nation's major religious denominations from uniting around common candidates or a shared political agenda, and opponents bitterly attacked the idea as a breach of the constitutional separation of church and state.

Nevertheless, committed Protestants did join together to form scores of voluntary societies that sought to disseminate Christian values, improve the character of the nation's citizens, and restructure the nation's leisure patterns. During the early decades of the nineteenth century, the evangelical clergy and laity reacted to the growth of cities, the spread of industry, the quickening pace of migration, and widening class divisions by establishing interdenominational reform associations to combat atheism, deism, profanity, Sabbath breaking, lewdness, intemperance, gambling, and other signs of moral disintegration. Societies sprang up to place a Bible in every American home; to enforce the Christian Sabbath; to convert Jews, Indians, and other "heathen" to Christianity; to provide a religious education for the children of the poor; and to curb the heavy use of hard liquor. This vast network of interdenominational voluntary societies, which has come to be known as the Benevolent Empire or the Evangelical United Front, struggled mightily during the 1820s and 1830s to guide an erring nation to righteousness by restoring what the Reverend Lyman Beecher in 1807 called "the moral government of God."

The initial aim of pre–Civil War reform was to uplift the nation's morals and spread Christian values. Inspired by religion, moral reformers sought to suppress prostitution and intemperance and to create a sense of social solidarity between the affluent and the poor. By instilling self-control and self-restraint, moral reformers hoped to counteract the individualizing tendencies of modernization and economic growth.

Of all the manifestations of antebellum reform, none is easier to ridicule than the "missionary" impulse to convert the "pagan" and suppress vice. It is easy to dismiss these efforts to impose middle-class Protestant values upon the poor and the non-Christian as morally arrogant and unduly self-righteous. And yet, as we shall see, evaluating the efforts of the early moral reformers is a difficult task. Initially, these moral reformers were extraordinarily naive; they were largely blind to the intrusive nature their reforms. But over time, they developed a surprising degree of sensitivity to those they hoped to help. Many foreign religious missionaries became defenders of Indians and other non-white peoples, and many urban missionaries became pioneers in the field of social work.

"Practical Christianity"

Behind the moral reformers' efforts to transform the United States into a truly Christian nation lay a foreign example. During the tumultuous years of the French Revolution and the Napoleonic Wars, a group of earnest English Protestants known as the Evangelicals arose within the Church of England. Anxious to overcome religious apathy, revitalize Protestantism, and combat class conflict and the threat of revolution, the Evangelicals offered a model of personal piety and practical Christianity. Extolling moral uplift as the Christian alternative to revolutionary upheaval, the Evangelicals, in cooperation with religious nonconformists (Baptists, Methodists, and Quakers), established a vast array of religious and benevolent societies to teach the poor to read, to suppress sexual vice and ungodly amusements such as cockfighting and bearbaiting, and to abolish the slave trade.

Initially, conservatives denounced the Evangelicals as "the Jacobins of England." Critics characterized their Sunday schools as hotbeds of vice and sedition. But soon such Evangelicals as Hannah More and William Wilberforce gained the cooperation of government leaders in their campaigns to reform public morality. The Evangelicals' dramatic success in persuading the British Parliament to abolish the African slave trade in 1807 offered special inspiration to pious men and women in the northeastern United States.

Deeply dismayed by the collapse of Federalist political power and the disestablishment of churches, these men and women increasingly looked to the example of British Evangelical benevolence as a way to purify public morals and promote virtue. "Liberty without godliness, is but another name for anarchism or despotism," declared Gardiner Spring, a leading evangelical, in 1820. "You have never known a free people without the Bible; with it, they cannot long be slave." But the attraction of reform had a deeply personal dimension as well. For many of the laity, men and women uncertain about finding a meaningful vocation, the missionary activity, Bible and tract societies, Sunday schools, and temperance organizations gave a comforting discipline and direction to their lives.

A sense of religious duty inspired an astonishing range of benevolent societies. Convinced that "the government of God is the only government which will hold society against depravity within and temptation without," as the evangelical magazine *The Way of the Pilgrims* declared in 1831, reformers established societies to suppress vice, punish Sabbath breaking, stamp out intemperance, combat gambling, and curb profanity (the first was founded in Connecticut in 1812). They formed societies to teach the poor to read and write, to distribute religious tracts and Bibles, and to proselytize among the unchurched, Jews, and Roman Catholics. There was even a Society for the Encouragement of Faithful Domestic Servants, established in New York in 1826. These societies marshaled impressive financial resources. Up to 1828, the federal government spent approximately $3.6 million on internal improvements. During the same period, the revenue of the principal benevolent societies totaled $2.8 million.

Perhaps the most striking characteristic of these voluntary societies was their national vision. Inspired by the example of similar associations in Britain, the new societies operated in cooperation, free of clerical domination and of identification with any specific church. As the Philadelphia Sunday and Adult School Union stated in 1818: "Unite and triumph, be then the motto of

Christians." Long before mergers and business consolidation reshaped the American economy, the major religious and benevolent societies joined together and discovered the advantages of national organization. As an anonymous Methodist bluntly stated in the *Christian Advocate and Journal* in 1828: "It is the order of the day to be national. We have our national theaters, national lottery offices, national hotels, national steam boats, and national grog shops. . . . I see no reason why we should not have national societies, since this character gives those societies a popularity and influence they could not otherwise sustain." Religious and benevolent societies were pioneers in the development of nationally integrated forms of organization. In 1830, when the country had just three hundred miles of railroad track, delegates from thirteen states attended the American Sunday-School Union's national convention.

The Benevolent Empire

At the very center of the Benevolent Empire was a small group of Congregationalists and Presbyterians educated at Princeton, Williams, Yale, and Andover Theological Seminary who were informally allied with members of the Baptist, Dutch Reformed, Episcopal, and Methodist churches. A surprising number of the Evangelical United Front's leaders were educated at a single school, the Andover seminary, which Congregationalists founded in 1809 to counteract the influence of Harvard's liberal divinity school. There, each Monday evening, one of the seminary's professors, Ebenezer Porter, held workshops "for devising plans of doing good, and advancing the Redeemer's kingdom at home and abroad, in every practical way," as a reformer named John Adams recalled in 1855. Out of these weekly meetings grew such organizations as the American Board of Commissioners for Foreign Missions, the nation's largest missionary society; the American Tract Society; the American Education Society; the American Temperance Society; and the Association for the Better Observance of the Sabbath.

During the antebellum years, the leaders of the Benevolent Empire struggled to create a wide range of cross-denominational missionary societies, Bible and tract societies, Sunday schools, and temperance societies—all aiming to reshape individual character and instill an ethic of self-control. In an era of convulsive social and economic transformations, of rapid urban growth and western expansion, prayer meetings, Sunday school classes, and benevolent societies not only held out the promise of a nation guided by evangelical principles, such institutions also provided many individual Protestants with a meaningful social identity as participants in a larger spiritual endeavor. At the same time, many members of this empire also embarked on a more activist program to suppress prostitution, enforce the Sabbath, and banish the drinking of alcohol.

In the late 1830s, the dream of all evangelical Protestants together in a common union faded. In 1837, the Presbyterian church split into Old and New Schools, and at the same time Baptists, Methodists, and Episcopalians began to set up their own sectarian missionary societies, Sunday school organizations, and publishing operations. In a series of controversies, critics denounced leaders of the Evangelical United Front for aspiring to become dictators of conscience, who would overcentralize benevolent activities and usurp local intiatives. It was the issue of slavery that ultimately undercut the vision of a Christian union transcending sectarian and regional loyalties.

Bible and Tract Societies and Urban Missions

One of the earliest efforts to strengthen the nation's Christian character and to rescue the nation from unrighteousness was a movement to distribute Bibles and religious tracts. The movement began as a result of a student prank. In 1813, a Princeton undergraduate cut out the pages of the college's chapel Bible and substituted playing cards. Outraged at the sacrilege, many Princeton students formed a Bible society to replace the chapel Bible and to distribute Holy Scripture to the poor and the irreligious. Such societies proliferated rapidly in the United States during the War of 1812. By 1814, there were 69 Bible societies in eighteen states and territories; a year later, the number had grown to 108 Bible societies and 12 tract societies, including many women's Bible societies. As early as 1816, a national organization, the American Bible Society, was founded.

These societies were modeled on the British and Foreign Bible Society, which Evangelicals founded in 1804 to counteract a rising "tide of infidelity and the waves of licentiousness" by spreading Christian doctrine among the English working class. Conservative in its emphasis on social order and deference, the society was nonetheless a pioneer in the application of modern techniques to social problems, conducting social surveys, gathering statistics, circulating questionnaires, and establishing an extensive network of auxiliaries and branches, including separate women's auxiliaries.

The British society's American counterparts proved to be equally innovative, launching the world's first fund-raising drives and purchasing steam presses. The American Bible Society printed three hundred thousand copies of the Bible yearly and the American Tract Society distributed more than three million tracts annually by the mid-1830s. The societies constructed a network of volunteers and agents to canvass neighborhoods and visit families and cajole parents into buying religious tracts. In one remarkable episode, in 1828, the New York Religious Tract Society began an extraordinarily ambitious campaign to distribute tracts to every family in the city each month. In a single month, the society delivered tracts to all but 388 of New York City's 28,383 families.

Convinced that the western frontier was as bereft of religion as "the Valley of the Shadow of Death" (in the words of the Reverend Samuel J. Mills) and that the nation's cities were a "wilderness of sin" (as New York's Female Missionary Society proclaimed in 1818), Bible and tract societies sought to provide "a Bible for every family, a school for every district and a pastor for every thousand souls." What began as an attempt to proselytize among the poor and the unchurched, however, was quickly transformed into something quite different. In city slums and mill towns, urban missionaries began to visit the homes of "the neglected poor." At first, they were content to distribute religious tracts, to exhort and convert slum residents, and to establish mission churches to give "the most deserving and respectable class of the poor, the means of assembling, like their more favored brethren, for the purpose of our common salvation" (as New York's Protestant Episcopal Church Missionary Society stated in 1837).

But as urban missionaries visited slums, jails, and hospitals many came face to face with the stark realities of urban poverty for the first time. According to one report made to the New York Religious Tract Society in 1836: "Almost every-day brings me in contact with cases so appalling and distressing that it requires a nerve of steel to prevent the mind and body from sinking under perpetual excitement." So the missionaries went beyond distributing Bibles and tracts and began offering material assistance, helping the poor with their rent and providing the destitute with food, fuel, and clothing. As awareness of urban suffering, disease, poverty, and other social ills deepened, evangelical missions and tract and Bible societies spawned new organizations to care for the aged, to provide health services for the poor, to reform juvenile delinquents, to care for vagrant children, and to provide poor relief.

In the late eighteenth century, pious upper-class philanthropists had founded the nation's first private institutions to provide financial relief to poor widows, imprisoned debtors, and the chronically ill. Convinced that the afflu-

ent had a duty to ameliorate the conditions of the dependent and the dis-
tressed, these philanthropists nevertheless regarded poverty and suffering as
inevitable. The religious revivals in the early nineteenth century created a new
millennial expectation for urban charity and benevolence, convincing a growing number of middle-class Protestants that a society without sin, misery, and
vice was possible. Initially, these people supported urban religious missions,
but reformers gradually shifted their orientation to the concrete environmental causes of urban problems.

By the 1840s, evangelical societies had built orphanages, free medical dispensaries, and industrial training schools to assist the poor, drawing upon
many middle-class women and men to serve as volunteer teachers, missionaries, friendly visitors, and nurses. Religious philanthropists pioneered a host
of programs now associated with professional welfare services and secular
social work agencies, including vocational classes, job placement services,
fresh-air camps for slum children, public baths, improved housing, and systematic family visits.

The new social agencies continued to bear the marks of their origins:
religious piety was essential to producing self-sufficiency among the poor.
They promoted the spiritual rebirth and moral elevation of the recipients of
their aid. Their goal, said the leader of New York's Association for Improving
the Condition of the Poor in 1844, was "not merely to alleviate wretchedness,
but to reform character." They retained the pious aims of the tract and Bible
societies. As the religious journal the *Independent* noted in 1850: "The physical
and moral are closely allied. The habit of living in squalor and filth engenders
vice, and vice, on the other hand, finds a congenial home in the midst of
physical impurities." Unlike the enlightened secular humanitarians of the late
eighteenth century who had simply sought to ameliorate the conditions of the
poor, the evangelical reformers of the mid-nineteenth century had far broader
goals: to uplift the poor and transform their moral character by combating
idleness, illiteracy, drinking, and gambling and by instilling the values of
industry, sobriety, and thrift.

The most famous pre–Civil War urban missionary was a Boston-born,
Harvard-educated, Unitarian clergyman named Joseph Tuckerman (1778–
1840), whose life dramatically illustrates the shift from moral exhortation to
active benevolence. A college classmate of William Ellery Channing, the nation's leading exponent of religious liberalism, Tuckerman believed that the
essence of the Christian religion lay in action rather than contemplation and
in a recognition of one's personal responsibilities toward one's neighbors. Like
many antebellum reformers, whether liberal or orthodox in theology, Tucker-

man believed that the improvement of society depended upon religion and the cultivation of character. In 1812, he founded the Boston Society for the Religious and Moral Improvement of Seamen—which is often considered to be the country's first urban mission—but it failed because Tuckerman knew nothing about the people he hoped to help. Fourteen years later, in 1826, Tuckerman became a minister-at-large to the unchurched in Boston, and he started visiting the homes of the poor to offer religious counsel.

But Tuckerman was convinced that religion alone offered an insufficient answer to the problems of the poor and the needy. Eager to do something more than merely ameliorate conditions, he sought out the underlying causes of poverty, juvenile delinquency, and alcoholism and would remedy these problems through what he called "scientific charity." He organized savings banks, life insurance, and benefit societies among the poor. In 1834, he set up the country's first agency to coordinate public charities.

Americans today tend to forget religion's central role in the creation of the country's modern social institutions. During the years preceding the Civil War, religion not only gave birth to many colleges, it also inspired the initial efforts to address the needs of the urban poor. In the 1850s, as foreign immigration and urban growth vastly expanded the problems of the poor, the tract and Bible societies devised separate organizations: children's aid societies to assist vagrant slum children; Young Men's Christian Associations to help young rural migrants adjust to urban life without losing their faith; employment bureaus to find jobs for the unemployed; shelters for indigent women and children; inexpensive cafeterias and lodging houses; and programs to place orphans in rural families. These early religiously inspired benevolent institutions were the antecedants of the Salvation Army and settlement houses.

In these cynical times, it is easy to dismiss as patronizing and paternalistic the evangelical reformers' schemes to elevate the working class. Family visitors, for example, were told to visit the poor and point out (in the words of the *Churchman* in 1832) "the true origins of their suffering" and offer "encouragement and counsel along the path to rehabilitation." The evangelical goal of imposing a single morality on a heterogeneous society holds little attraction for a society that stresses cultural pluralism. The moral reformers' efforts to intervene directly in the lives of the poor—through "local voluntary associations of the wise and the good" offering "the moral oversight of the soul" (as Lyman Beecher declared)—seem unduly intrusive to a society that prizes individual liberty.

The very words that the evangelicals used to describe the poor—*immoral, intemperate, defective, wayward*—seem biased and offensive. And especially during the 1850s, when so many immigrants arrived, fear of urban savagery became increasingly pronounced. As the American Sunday-School Union proclaimed in 1856: "The refugee population of Europe . . . congregate in our great cities and send forth . . . wretched progeny . . . to be scavengers, physical and moral, of our streets. Mingled with these are also the offcast children of American debauchery, drunkenness, and vice."

Yet we should be wary of criticizing these moral reformers too intensely. The urban missionaries were not being cynical or hypocritical when they expressed a genuine sense of identity with the urban poor. At a time when earlier bonds of social connectedness were dissolving, when many moral reformers feared that the rich and poor were becoming, in William Ellery Channing's words (1841), "two nations, understanding as little of one another . . . as if they lived in different lands," urban reformers sought to restore social solidarity through charity. Like the professional social workers of a later era, the urban missionaries recognized that poverty, crime, and illiteracy had not merely economic causes, but cultural ones as well.

Sunday Schools

One of the moral reformers' earliest instruments for ensuring that America would be a Christian nation was the Sunday school. In 1791, members of Philadelphia's First Day Society founded one of the nation's first. Deeply disturbed by the tendency "among the Youth of every large city" to spend Sundays "employed in the worst of purposes, to the depravation of morals and manners," the leaders of the First Day Society in 1791 saw the Sunday school as a way to teach poor children to read and write and to forgo "lying, swearing, talking in an indecent manner, or other misbehaviour."

Originating in Britain in the 1780s as a way to train the poor in basic literacy and religious principles—and to keep unsupervised children off the streets on the Sabbath—the Sunday school first appeared in the eastern United States in the 1790s. Sponsored by "enlightened" republican gentlemen of diverse religious backgrounds who regarded education as a way to "promote good order and suppress vice," the first Sunday schools sought (in the words of the First Day Society's founders) to instill "habits of order and industry" and qualify the poor to become "good servants [and] good apprentices." Denied other opportunities to learn how to read and write, many girls, free blacks, and children who toiled in factories turned to Sunday schools in large numbers.

Between 1810 and 1830, as publicly supported free schools and charity schools increasingly assumed the task of teaching working-class children to read and write, a new specifically religious Sunday school emerged, which did not confine its attention to the urban poor. While separate mission schools provided religious instruction to poor children, Sunday schools began to concentrate on preparing the children of church members for conversion. Convinced that during childhood a person's "character usually becomes fixed for life, and for the most part for eternity," the founders assigned Sunday schools the weighty responsibility of ensuring that young people developed the strength of character to resist the "flattering allurements" of a world bent on "seduc[ing] them to ruin," as the *American Sunday-School Magazine* phrased it in 1825.

In 1824, a small group of Philadelphia merchants, largely Episcopalian and Presbyterian, founded the interdenominational American Sunday-School Union to publish inexpensive books, tracts, and magazines for Sunday schools; disseminate instructional materials and guides to Sunday school teachers; centralize fund raising; and sponsor missionaries to organize Sunday schools in rural and frontier areas. An essential element in the Benevolent Empire's drive to make America a Christian nation, the organization had a strong sense of mission—though its paid staff was almost laughably small, two managers and a few clerks and copyists. At a time when the United States lacked a national communications network, the leaders of the American Sunday-School Union sought to construct a chain of evangelical influence reaching across the entire country. The organization announced in its 1829 report that "the responsibility for the character and influence of our WESTERN POPULATION rests to a fearful extent on the American Sunday-School Union."

Proponents of Sunday schools achieved a surprising degree of success. According to an 1832 estimate, 301,358 children in all twenty-four states were enrolled in Sunday school classes—8 percent of all children of Sunday school age. Since the typical child attended only for a year or two, the proportion of children who went to Sunday schools at some point was much higher.

These schools' primary goals were to offer children a basic knowledge of the Bible and the tenets of Protestant morality and to prepare them for conversion. Sunday schools conceived of themselves as "nurseries of piety." In class, children memorized biblical passages, sang hymns, and pondered the theological questions raised in "question books." (The 1829 edition of *Union Questions* asked: "What is it meant to be born again?" and "Who works this great change?") In their teaching, Sunday schools sought to instill in children a sense of the fragility of life and the imminence of death. The books and periodicals in their libraries were filled with tales of childhood piety and deathbed conversions. Despite their reliance on rote memorization, Sunday schools pioneered more liberal methods of pedagogy. In general, Sunday school teachers rejected corporal punishment and substituted an elaborate system of rewards, including certificates for regular attendance, tickets redeemable for Bibles and other books and periodicals, and promotion to the rank of classroom monitor. Sunday schools also frequently staged parades and rallies.

Found on the frontier as well as in urban areas and in the South as well as the North, the Sunday school was not an exclusively middle-class institution. Many industrial laborers, blacks, and Catholics sent their children to these schools, and some actually became teachers. The schools sometimes gave poor children free clothing, books, and magazines and took them on picnics and excursions. Sunday schools played a particularly important role in frontier and rural areas, where they were often the first religious institutions. As one missionary reported to the American Sunday-School Union in 1859, "Most, if not all, the Churches of the West of recent formation, have grown out of Sunday-schools previously existing." These religious schools were the result of local efforts in diverse communities, but their promoters regarded them as part of a larger national effort to inculcate Christian values and national cohesion.

Some of the enthusiasm of Sunday school promoters flagged in the 1850s, when the difficulty of reaching the native-born and immigrant poor increased. As early as 1847, the American Sunday-School Union observed, "Our object has always been to reach the masses, but we cannot get to them." In 1859, a Philadelphia leader reported that poorer children were abandoning Sunday schools, explaining that "they contrast their personal appearance with the well dressed children around them, and through pride will not attend." Following the Civil War, the Sunday school—once conceived in millennialist terms as the chief mechanism for evangelizing the nation's children—fell into the more prosaic role of educational adjunct to individual church congregations.

Conquering the World for Christ

Many leaders of the Benevolent Empire dreamed of extending evangelical principles across the entire earth in preparation for Christ's second coming. In 1832, Calvin Colton, a prominent journalist and a graduate of Yale College and Andover Theological Seminary, conveyed the evangelical sense of mission in graphic terms: "Every one knows . . . that the design of Christianity is to bring back this apostate world to God. . . . It is to reduce the world, and the whole world, by a system of moral means and agencies." The image of nine-tenths of the human race "destitute of instructions of the Scripture" and destined "to eternal death" (as a Boston tract declared in 1830) haunted the evangelical imagination and inspired extraordinary missionary campaigns to convey "a knowledge of Christ to millions of perishing men" in Burma, Ceylon, Liberia, and elsewhere.

In the 1920s and 1930s, the spectacle of thousands of American missionaries promoting religious conversion and civilization around the world caused intense embarrassment among many major Protestant denominations. A growing number of critics questioned the missionaries' right to impose American culture upon others and accused them, sometimes unfairly, of serving as agents of American economic and political interests. As a result, the missionary movement foundered. A century earlier, the missionary crusade to evangelize and civilize "heathen" lands was, in size and resources, one of pre–Civil War America's largest movements, gripping the consciences and enlisting the support of thousands of church members. As the Baptist minister and the future president of Brown University, Francis Wayland, proclaimed in 1823, "The missionary cause combines within itself the elements of all that is sublime in human purpose, nay, combines them in a loftier perfection than any other enterprise."

Inspired by the biblical injunction to "go to the world and preach the gospel" and by the view of America as Christ's messenger with a special obligation to spread Christian civilization across the globe, missionaries served "Indians of the wilderness, the depressed African . . . the remote settler on the frontier, and . . . the poor." Their aim, the American Board of Commissioners for Foreign Missions stated at its second annual meeting in 1811, was to bring "nations betrayed, enslaved, weltering in . . . blood, and shrouded in a starless night of infidelity . . . to the rising glories of the Sun of Righteousness."

Although there were sporadic attempts to convert slaves and Indians to Christianity in the seventeenth and eighteenth centuries, sustained missionary activities date from the early nineteenth century. Looking back at the colonial era, the Reverend Francis Brown in 1814 found it odd "that Protestant Christians of the last two centuries did not make more vigorous and systematic efforts to evangelize the world. . . . Our fathers prayed," he commented, "but they did not act." Though somewhat exaggerated, this comment is basically true. With a few notable exceptions, colonial missionary efforts were limited to establishing congregations among unchurched whites.

During the seventeenth century, perhaps twelve Puritan ministers actively evangelized Native Americans. The best-known was John Eliot, who transcribed sermons and the Bible into the Massachuset language and gathered converts into fourteen distinct Christian communities. In the early eighteenth century, the Anglican Church's Society for the Propagation of the Gospel in Foreign Parts dispatched 309 agents to the colonies, not one of whom lived among the Indians. More active were the Society in Scotland for Promoting Christian Knowledge (whose most famous missionary, David Brainerd, preached to the Delaware Indians of New Jersey and Pennsylvania), Congregationalists (including Eleazar Wheelock, who trained some fifty Algonkian and Iroquois Indians for missionary work), and particularly the United Brethren or Moravians (who founded a number of Christian communities among the Delaware) and the Quakers. A variety of other churches sent missionaries to eighteenth-century America, but they worked largely among the white population: Scottish Presbyterians among Scot-Irish frontiersmen; itinerant Baptist preachers; and Methodist lay preachers.

Then, during the new republic's early years, the first interdenominational American missionary societies arose, eager to convert Indians and the unchurched in the West and in the fast-growing cities on the Atlantic seaboard. The first was the Society for Propagating the Gospel among the Indians and Others in North America, formed in 1787. Emulating contemporary British societies, such as the Baptist Missionary Society (1792), members of the Presbyterian, Baptist, and Dutch Reformed churches founded the New York Missionary Society in 1796.

Many early American missionaries attended Williams College in western Massachusetts, and they decided to dedicate their lives to missionary activity while attending a prayer meeting held on a haystack. They founded the nation's largest missionary organization, the American Board of Commissioners for Foreign Missions, in 1810. By the 1850s, the American Board, which was dominated by Massachusetts Congregationalists, accounted for roughly 40 percent of all foreign missionaries. Two of the Williams undergraduates—Adoniram Judson and Luther Rice—became Baptists and formed the Baptist Board for Foreign Missions in 1814, the second-largest missionary organization.

Various churches established their own missionary societies—the Methodists organized theirs in 1819, the Episcopalians in 1821, and the Old School Presbyterians in 1837. Nevertheless, most missionary activity was interdenominational, carried on through such organizations as the United Foreign Missionary Society, established by the Presbyterian, Dutch Reformed, and Associated Reformed churches in 1817, and the American Home Missionary Society, formed in 1826 by Presbyterians and Congregationalists.

Many early missionaries had a peculiar mixture of motives. On the one hand, many were convinced that humanity "descended from the same common parents," as the American Board stated in "Address to the Christian Public" (1811). They felt a humanitarian obligation to assist non-Christians and bring them to the light of Christ. On the other hand, many agreed with Richard Furman, who addressed a Baptist convention in 1814, that non-Christian religions were largely worthless—"absurd, sanguinary, and obscene"—and believed that they had a special responsibility to subdue "the world 'to the obedience of Christ.'"

Antebellum missionaries targeted the entire world for redemption. In all, about 10 percent of antebellum missionaries served the American Indians. The American Board of Commissioners for Foreign Missions sent about one-fifth of its personnel to Hawaii, one-eighth to East Asia, and one-tenth to Africa. Old School Presbyterians dispatched missionaries to West Africa and India; Reformed Presbyterians to the West Indies and Syria; Methodists to Liberia and Greece; Lutherans to India and Liberia; Disciples of Christ to Turkey, India, China, the West Indies, and Europe; and the United Brethren to West Africa.

One of the missionaries' initial goals was to Christianize and assimilate Native Americans, making them, as Samuel A. Worcester explained in 1816, "English in their language, civilized in their habits, and Christian in their religion." In 1817, the American Board established missions and schools among the Cherokee, Choctaw, Creek, and Chickasaw Indians who lived in what would become the South's cotton belt. In quantitative terms, these efforts were remarkably unsuccessful. By 1829, only fifteen hundred Native Americans had been converted to Christianity.

Nevertheless, the missionaries were able to prove that Indians were capable of adapting to changing conditions. By the late 1820s, the Cherokee, who lived in northern and western Georgia, western North Carolina, and eastern Tennessee, encouraged by the missionary Samuel Worcester and a native minister named Galagina (who later adopted the name Elias Boudinot), developed a written alphabet, opened schools, established churches, built roads, operated printing presses, published a weekly newspaper, and even adopted a constitution. (Traditionalists within the Cherokee Nation, who opposed these modernizing, assimilationist efforts, later murdered Galagina.)

Unfortunately, the discovery of gold on Cherokee land caused thousands of white settlers to encroach on their territory. Missionaries helped mobilize northeastern Congregationalists and Presbyterians to resist Georgia's efforts to seize control of Cherokee land. When Worcester defied a Georgia law designed to dispossess the Cherokee, he was imprisoned.

In two important legal cases, *Cherokee Nation* v. *Georgia* (1831) and *Worcester* v. *Georgia* (1832), the Supreme Court denied Georgia's right to extend state laws over the Cherokee people and held the federal government responsible for keeping white intruders off Indian lands. With the strong support of northeastern church groups, fifteen thousand Cherokee joined in a protest against President Andrew Jackson's Indian removal policy, under which the Cherokee were to exchange their tribal lands for new land in Oklahoma and Arkansas. Despite vigorous resistance from missionaries and church groups, some forty thousand Native Americans were removed from Georgia, Alabama, and Mississippi during Jackson's presidency.

Another major area of missionary activity was the Hawaiian Islands. In 1819, the American Board sent a team of seventeen missionaries and teachers to what were then known as the Sandwich Islands. By the late 1830s, there were approximately ninety American missionaries and several hundred native workers in Hawaii. They converted more than eighteen thousand communicants out of a total population of one hundred thousand.

In terms of resources, missionary enterprises were one of the largest reform movements in pre–Civil War America. In the 1820s, the income of the American Board of Commissioners for Foreign Missions averaged $40,000 a year—three times the budget of the American Temperance Society and ten times larger than that of the Prison Discipline Society or the American Peace Society. In 1828, the American Board stood second in income among the country's thirteen leading benevolent societies. The American Bible Society was first, with an income of $143,000; the American Board second, with $114,000; the American Tract Society third, with $69,000. Over a sixty-year period, the foreign mission movement deployed some two thousand missionaries. By the 1860s, there were sixteen major American missionary societies. Missionary efforts to redeem the world, in turn, fed into other reform movements. The first attempts to promote the entry of women into colleges and medical schools were justified on the grounds that they would serve as missionaries (or as wives of missionaries).

During the twentieth century, missionaries have often been accused of cultural arrogance and of forcing non-Christians to divest themselves of their indigenous cultures. One antebellum missionary actually proposed that in exchange for a twelve-dollar contribution to educate a heathen child for a year, a donor would receive the privilege of naming the baptized child. Criticisms of cultural insularity are not new; indeed, similar remarks were voiced even before the Civil War. Herman Melville lived in the Sandwich Islands for seven months and, in his novel *Typee: A Peep at Polynesian Life* (1846), claimed to support "the cause of missions in the abstract." Nevertheless, he was convinced that the missionaries had undermined the local culture and exploited the native population economically. As he acidly phrased it, "The small remnant of the natives [have] been civilised into draught horses, and evangelized into beasts of burden."

Some antebellum missionaries, to be sure, did view non-Christians as benighted heathen and extolled the superiority of American civilization, but many others displayed a surprising sensitivity to the integrity of indigenous cultures. They learned native languages and sought to free themselves from doctrinal and cultural provincialism. They favored independent, self-governing, self-supporting native churches and openly criticized political and economic interests that threatened indigenous societies. And, as in the case of the Cherokee, many tried to help native converts resist white encroachment and exploitation.

The most outspoken exponent of respect for indigenous cultures was Rufus Anderson, the senior secretary of the American Board of Commissioners for Foreign Missions. Like many early participants in missionary activity, he was educated at Andover Theological Seminary. His philosophy, which he spelled out in an address in 1845, has a surprisingly modern ring. While he believed that "the civilization which the gospel has conferred upon New England is the highest and best . . . that the world has yet seen," he also believed that it was wrong for missionaries to reorganize "the structure of that social system, of which the converts form a part" and called on missionaries to respect indigenous economies and patterns of "family government, [and] social order." As his words suggest, contemporary Americans have no monopoly on sensitivity toward third-world cultures.

From Moral Uplift to
Social Activism

The Evangelical United Front drew support largely from the Northeast, from the rising professional and mercantile classes, from upwardly aspiring tradesmen and artisans, from many middle-class women, and from rural Congregationalist and Presbyterian farmers. The Benevolent Empire, in turn, ignited intense opposition from religious conservatives who distrusted evangelicalism; from the Baptist, Methodist, and Roman Catholic poor who objected to the reformers' paternalism and condescension; from wealthy patricians hostile to middle-class reformers' tone of moral superiority; and from many Democratic politicians who decried elites who sought to use government to promote moral reform.

From the very beginning, the Benevolent Empire caused stiff resistance among those who opposed clerical interference in politics. Many antebellum Americans were repelled by the specter of educated, northeastern churchgoers building a network of institutions to spread puritanical conformity throughout the country. When the American Sunday-School Union tried to obtain a charter from the Pennsylvania legislature in 1828, a Democratic state senator named John Hare Powel denounced the proposal as an aristocratic plan to make Presbyterian clergymen "dictators to the consciences of thousands" through a campaign of mass indoctrination. Other critics condemned the promoters of Sunday schools and missionary societies as "canting fanatics" and "pious pickpockets" who received millions of dollars in tax exemptions.

Yet the most vociferous opposition to the Benevolent Empire was generated by a series of crusades to eradicate sin and make the nation live up to Christian values—campaigns to suppress urban prostitution, to enforce the Christian Sabbath, and to curb the drinking of hard liquor. In launching these campaigns, evangelicals devised the methods and tactics that would later be used in more radical reforms to win women's rights and abolish slavery.

Prostitution

In 1816, the Hill, a notorious slum neighborhood in Boston known locally as "Mount Whoredom," was inhabited by "drunkards, harlots, spendthrifts, and outcasts." Members of the Boston Female Society reported seeing "ardent spirits . . . retailed without restraint" and the "holy Sabbath [spent] in frolicking and gambling, in fighting and blaspheming." There, men and women of the worst character engaged "in scenes of iniquity and debauchery too dreadful to be named."

In August 1823, Boston's mayor Josiah Quincy attempted to clean up this center of sexual vice by closing down taverns and dance halls, where sailors, mechanics, and apprentices met women and took them back to their lodgings. Two years later, residents of Boston's North End wearing blackface and carrying pitchforks, heavily damaged several brothels and houses of assignation in their neighborhood, ripping open featherbeds and tossing them out the windows. The artisans, small tradesmen, and laborers who took part in this action may well have been motivated by an understanding that many prostitutes were recruited from their class and that their entire neighborhood was stigmatized as immoral.

Prostitution first became a major social issue in the United States between

1810 and 1820. At the time, no laws specifically prohibited prostitution (prostitutes might only be charged with lewdness, nightwalking, vagrancy, or disorderly conduct), and brothels advertised openly in newspapers and guidebooks. In Boston, one observer claimed that there were more than two thousand prostitutes in 1817—or one out of every fourteen women between the ages of twenty and forty-five. This estimate may not have been wholly exaggerated; historians today estimate that 5 to 10 percent of young antebellum women in major cities engaged in prostitution, at least part time. Usually these women were young (records indicate that 75 percent were under the age of twenty-five) and participated in prostitution for short periods of time (an 1858 survey in New York found that 60 percent of the women had been prostitutes for no more than three years).

Prostitution was, of course, nothing new. During the colonial era, prostitutes could be found in all the major seaports, where there were large numbers of sailors and soldiers, and many impoverished unmarried women flocked to such towns in wartime. In the early nineteenth century, however, a variety of factors contributed to the sudden explosion of concern about sexual license. Earlier mechanisms that had controlled the leisure activities of young urban males were breaking down, as more and more young men lived in boardinghouses in distinct working-class neighborhoods, outside a family and free of a master's supervision. Meanwhile, increasing numbers of single young women were arriving in cities, where they discovered that prostitution paid twice as much as domestic service or factory work.

Evangelical reformers experienced a "thrill of horror" upon discovering the existence of "palaces of the passions" and "dens of abortion" within their cities, as a reform newspaper, *McDowall's Journal,* stated in 1834. In every major city, centers of prostitution arose within blocks of city wharves and commercial districts: on Boston's Ann Street, in New York's Five Points, and on Philadelphia's St. Mary's Street. Gambling dens, dance halls, and, most notoriously, the third tier in theaters became well known as rendezvous points for prostitutes and their clients. Older methods of sexual control had clearly broken down.

In colonial Connecticut and Massachusetts, as many as half to two-thirds of all criminal prosecutions involved morals offenses, such as fornication, blasphemy, profanity, and adultery. In those colonies, men were as likely as women to be punished for offenses against Christian morality, usually through some form of public shaming (for example, being driven—naked—in a cart through a town's streets). During the late eighteenth and early nineteenth centuries, as the number of assaults and crimes against property increased, criminal prosecution of private moral offenses declined sharply. Public sexual offenses—such as lewdness and nightwalking—continued to be punished, but female prostitutes, and not their male customers, were the ones most likely to receive stiff fines or confinement in a house of correction. Following an 1830 raid on a Boston brothel, the men received four-dollar fines while the women got four to five months in the house of correction.

During the 1820s, protests against prostitution increased. As early as 1822, Boston's City Missionary Society set up its first house of refuge to rehabilitate prostitutes and other "wayward" young women by providing them with religious exhortations and instruction in household tasks—such as weaving, sewing, ironing, and laundering. In succeeding years, many refuges were founded along similar lines, including institutions run by Catholic nuns (Boston's was called "The House of the Good Shepherd").

The nation's foremost crusader for moral purity was John R. McDowall, a Princeton divinity student who was sent to Five Points, New York City's worst slum, in 1830 to distribute religious pamphlets for the American Tract Society. He visited tenements, prisons, and hospitals—and was shocked to discover that many women in these institutions were prostitutes who lacked any other way to support themselves.

To combat this "gangrenous canker," McDowall, with the support of reform-minded philanthropists Lewis Tappan and Arthur Tappan, formed the New York Magdalen Society and opened a house of refuge for "depraved and abandoned females . . . who have deviated from the path of virtue." His first annual report brought unwelcome public notoriety. McDowall claimed that ten thousand women in New York City earned their living as prostitutes and that their customers included men from some of the city's most prominent families.

Like many future reformers, McDowall found himself attacked for simply discussing the problem he had uncovered. *McDowall's Journal,* a weekly newspaper, offered graphic reports on abortion, child murder, and venereal disease, sparking widespread public denunciation. Abortion was so widespread, the newspaper warned in 1833, that "dead infants are frequently found; sometimes in privies, wells, sewers, ponds, docks, streets, [and] open fields." *McDowall's Journal* was denounced by the *New York Commercial Advertiser* in 1836 as a corruptor of public morals, as "a sort of Directory of Iniquity—a brothel companion, . . . the most foul and loathsome journal that ever suffered the cheek of modesty." An 1833 edition of the *Morning Courier and New York Enquirer* claimed that *McDowall's Journal* was calculated to poison the imagination of virtuous women "and make them adepts in all the mysteries of human corruption!" A New York grand jury condemned the paper as "an obscene and demoralizing publication" that was "grossly obscene and dangerous." In the face of public attack, McDowall's society disbanded.

In 1834, however, the drive against prostitution in New York resumed, this time under female leadership. Members of the New York Female Reform Society (directed by Lydia A. Finney, revivalist Charles Grandison Finney's wife), walked into brothels and prayed for the prostitutes and their patrons. Members also visited prostitutes in jail and lobbied for state laws that would make male solicitation of prostitutes a crime. In their monthly journal (which boasted a circulation of nearly seventeen thousand), members publicized the stories of men who went to prostitutes (including the story of one prominent New Yorker who procured a young, innocent woman, only to discover that she was his own daughter). The society threatened to publish the names of men who frequented brothels, announcing in 1835 that if "the licentious . . . are not ashamed of their debasing vice, we will not be ashamed to expose them."

Aware that moral exhortation alone was not enough to end prostitution, the society in 1837 established a new house of refuge for prostitutes seeking to reform, opened an employment agency for "respectable unprotected females, especially the fatherless and the orphan," and distributed charity to the poor. By 1839, the organization claimed to have 445 auxiliaries in the Northeast, largely in New England.

In retrospect, one of the most striking characteristics of the female moral reform societies was their strong gender consciousness. Directed and staffed mostly by women (including wives of artisans and small shopkeepers as well as teachers, boardinghouse keepers, and other less affluent women), the organizations vocally attacked the double standard of sexuality morality, blamed prostitution on male lechery and on women's limited economic opportunities, and denounced the inequity of punishing prostitutes while brothel keepers and male patrons went free. In its first issue in 1838, the New England Moral Reform Society's journal, *The Friend of Virtue*, stated pointedly that the organization had a duty to protect other women from male exploitation: "to guard our daughters, sisters, and female acquaintances from the delusive arts of corrupt and unprincipled men" and "to bring back to the paths of virtue those who have been drawn aside through the wiles of the destroyer."

Moral reform societies played an important transitional role in the rise of modern feminism. In 1838, the New York society's journal carried a very early critique of a husband's authority over his wife, denouncing the "tyranny exercised [in] the HOME department, where lordly man, 'clothed with a little brief authority,' rules his trembling subjects with a rod of iron, conscious of entire impunity, and exalting in his fancied superiority." Born out of an evangelical faith that sexual vice could be eliminated, female moral reform societies provided many middle-class women with their first opportunity to encounter and work closely with the poor—an experience that would give rise to many urban charities for the orphaned, the widowed, and the unemployed. A new sense of sisterhood, transcending social class, began to emerge. In the 1870s and 1880s, female moral reformers would establish a series of new protective institutions to insulate vulnerable young women from the perils of the city, ranging from Young Women's Christian Associations to travelers' aid societies, boardinghouses for single women, and employment agencies for the jobless.

Sabbatarianism

Before it revised its laws in 1792, Massachusetts required all residents to attend public worship each Sunday. Anyone who missed a full month of Sabbath services faced a stiff fine. Massachusetts also imposed fines on anyone who swam on the Sabbath, or walked unnecessarily, or engaged in business on Saturday evening or Sunday. An English traveler who visited New England in 1740 commented: "Their observation of the sabbath . . . is the strictest kept that ever I yet saw anywhere." No one was allowed "to take air on the Common" or to hunt or fish or to play any sport. And "if two or three people, who meet one another in the street by accident, stand talking together,—if they do not disperse immediately upon the first notice, they are liable to fine and imprisonment." Even after the code was revised, Massachusetts forbade Sabbath travel and required residents to attend religious services once every three months.

Voltaire, famous French philosopher of the Enlightenment, once said, "If you wish to destroy the Christian religion you must first destroy the Christian Sunday." Many early-nineteenth-century church leaders shared this belief and feared for the future of religion in America if the Sabbath was not honored. In the late 1820s, they led a vigorous campaign to encourage its observance—a crusade that provided a model for later campaigns against alcohol and slavery.

The major battleground was an 1810 law that required the nation's ten thousand postal officials to conduct business on Sunday. For nearly two decades, the law aroused little opposition. Then the completion of the Erie Canal—the 364-mile-long "big ditch" that connected the Great Lakes and the Atlantic Ocean—ignited outrage at construction, transportation, and commerce on the Sabbath. Rochester, New York, became the center of the struggle. In 1828, as a result of the canal, Rochester was the nation's fastest-growing city (it had not even existed twenty-eight years earlier). Its ministers and respectable townspeople were appalled by the blare directly outside their house of worship, First Presbyterian Church, even on the Sabbath. Together with Lyman Beecher, one of the nation's leading Congregationalist ministers, and Lewis Tappan, a prominent New York City merchant and ardent supporter of moral reform, they formed the General Union for Promoting the Observance of the Christian Sabbath, with auxiliary chapters from Maine to Ohio.

To many men and women who were uneasy about their society's rapid growth and mounting materialism, respect for the Sabbath became an important symbol of whether Americans were prepared to place spiritual values ahead of success. The Sabbath should be "a day of rest, of family life and introspection," later declared G. Stanley Hall, who would become a pioneering social scientist. "It not only gives seriousness and poise to character and brings the saving fore-, after-, and over-thought into the midst of a hurrying objective and material life, . . . but it teaches self-control, self-knowledge, and self-respect."

The Sabbatarians virtually invented the tactics that would be used in future reform movements, collecting signatures on petitions, distributing tracts, staging rallies, and demanding that Congress respond to their outcry. Sabbatarians flooded Congress with more than 440 petitions, demanding an immediate end to Sunday delivery of mail. Those who signed were primarily artisans and shopkeepers. The more militant Sabbatarians, led by Tappan and a Rochester publisher named Everard Peck, took direct economic action. They denounced seven-day stage companies, ferry lines, and shipping firms, organized boycotts of businesses that operated on Sunday, and even formed a Sabbatarian stagecoach line to provide transportation between Albany and Buffalo.

By 1830, the Sabbatarian movement had gone down to defeat. A Senate report in 1829 pronounced that Congress was not the proper tribunal to determine the laws of God. Congress voted to continue Sunday delivery of mail. In 1832, the leading Sabbatarian organization disbanded, demoralized by widespread popular disapproval. Nevertheless, the movement left an indelible mark on pre–Civil War reform. Not only were the Sabbatarians among the very first reformers to attempt to use economic and political protest to achieve their goals, they had decisively demonstrated that serious Christianity required dedicated protest against perceived social evils.

Temperance

Today, the nineteenth- and early-twentieth-century crusade against hard liquor conjures up negative images: futile efforts to prohibit alcoholic beverages and hatchet-wielding moralists seeking to impose their own puritanical beliefs. However impractical the crusade may seem today, in the decades before the Civil War the campaign against liquor was the unifying reform, drawing support from countless middle-class Protestants, from skilled artisans, clerks, shopkeepers, laborers, free blacks, and Mormons, as well as from many conservative clergy and southerners who were otherwise hostile to reform. It was also a remarkably successful movement, inspiring a dramatic reduction in per capita consumption of alcohol. Called the temperance movement, the antebellum crusade against hard liquor in fact advocated "intemperance"— teetotal abstinence.

The movement's roots can be traced to the late eighteenth century, when a number of individual Quakers, Congregationalists, Presbyterians, and Methodists began to denounce alcohol as a threat to the health and morals of the new republic. The most influential early proponent of temperance was Benjamin Rush, a Philadelphia physician and signer of the Declaration of Independence. Rush was also the author of *Inquiry into the Effects of Ardent Spirits upon the Human Mind and Body,* which warned that hard liquor could destroy a person's health and even cause death and concluded that drinking was a major contributor to "vices, diseases . . . suicide, death, the gallows."

In part, the rise of temperance agitation represented a response to an actual upsurge in heavy drinking. At the end of the eighteenth century, alcohol was an integral part of American life. Many people believed that downing a glass of whiskey before breakfast was conducive to good health. Instead of coffee, people took a dram of liquor at eleven and again at four o'clock as well as drinks after meals "to aid digestion" and a nightcap before going to sleep. Campaigning politicians offered voters generous amounts of liquor during campaigns and as rewards for "right voting" on election day. On the frontier, one evangelist noted, "a house could not be raised, a field of wheat cut down, nor could there be a log rolling, a husking, a quilting, a wedding, or a funeral without the aid of alcohol." By 1820, the typical adult American consumed more than 7 gallons of absolute alcohol a year (compared to 2.8 gallons today). Consumption had risen markedly in two decades, since farmers used more and more corn to make cheap whiskey, which could be transported more easily than bulk corn. In the 1820s, a gallon of whiskey cost just a quarter, a great deal less than rum, tea, or coffee.

But the rise of the temperance movement was not simply a response to an increase in drinking. It reflected broader concerns that alcohol led to economic waste, polluted youth, and created crime and poverty. Particularly in its earliest stages, the campaign against drinking—like the early campaign for Sunday schools—drew support from local elites. These included leading merchants and clergy motivated by a sense of moral stewardship and communal responsibility, Federalists anxious about their declining status, and other wealthy individuals (often of rural backgrounds) who associated excessive drinking with poverty, crime, vice, and the breakdown of the hierarchical eighteenth-century social order. Typical of the early temperance organizations was the Massachusetts Society for the Suppression of Intemperance, founded in 1813 by gentlemen upset by the spread of drunkenness, social disorder, and disrespect for society's upper classes. Especially shocking was that Boston had one grog shop for every twenty-one adult men. The goals of these early organizations tended to be quite limited, stressing self-control rather than abstinence and opposing only distilled, and not fermented, alcohol. It is remarkable that the Massachusetts Society served wine at its meetings.

The evangelical revivals in the 1820s and 1830s transformed temperance into a mass movement. For evangelicals, drinking and temperance were visible symbols of sin, repentance, and redemption and of the practical power of the gospel. Lyman Beecher viewed temperance as a test of humanity's capacity to improve itself spiritually and morally: "Immense evils," he wrote in a sermon entitled "The Nature, Occasions, Signs, Evils, and Remedy of Intemperance" (1826), "afflict communities, not because they are incurable, but because they are tolerated, and great good remains often unaccomplished merely because it is not attempted."

Holding a millennialist faith in the possibility of moral progress, evangelical Protestant reformers relied on "moral suasion" to convince drinkers that abstinence was in their spiritual and economic self-interest. Many reformers were particularly critical of moderate drinking, which helped keep saloons and distilleries in business and set a bad example for those susceptible to alcohol's attractions.

The stage was set for the appearance of an organized national movement against liquor. In 1826, the nation's first formal national temperance organization was born: the American Society for the Promotion of Temperance. Led by socially prominent members of the clergy and laity, the new organization called for total abstinence from hard liquor. Within three years, 222 state and local antiliquor groups labored to spread this message. By 1835, membership in temperance organizations had climbed to 1.5 million and an estimated 2 million Americans had taken the pledge to abstain from distilled spirits.

During the 1820s and 1830s, drinking became a potent cultural symbol. Clergymen declared that drinking hard liquor was ungodly. Physicians linked alcohol to a variety of physical ailments. Many middle-class women blamed alcohol for causing the abuse of wives and children and the squandering of family resources. Societies for the prevention of pauperism blamed drink for crime and poverty. Many businesspeople identified drinking with inefficient and unproductive employees. To a rising middle class of professionals, small businesspeople, and manufacturers, temperance became a critical symbol of self-improvement, self-respect, progress, respectability, and upward mobility. It is not surprising to learn that Abraham Lincoln, an upward-aspiring product of the hard-drinking midwestern frontier, resolved early in life to abstain from alcohol.

Temperance reformers did not rid the nation of the demon rum, but they helped reduce annual per capita consumption from seven gallons in 1830 to less than three gallons a decade later. Four thousand distilleries were forced to close their doors. Fewer employers provided workers with eleven o'clock or four o'clock drams, and some businesses began to fire employees who drank on the job.

The 1840s brought two critical shifts in the temperance movement. The first was the emergence in Baltimore in 1840 of the Washington Temperance Societies, which originated among reformed alcoholics. On the night of April 2, 1840, in a Baltimore tavern, a group of confirmed drinkers decided to attend a temperance lecture at a nearby church. After hearing the lecture, the drinkers decided to pledge themselves to total abstinence and attract other recruits.

In the face of a protracted economic depression (known as the Panic of 1837), the new organization drew support from thousands of skilled artisans, clerks, and laborers. Unlike the more staid evangelical reformers who sought their converts largely among church members, the Washingtonians were loud, boisterous, and dramatic. They staged cold-water picnics, parades, and mass meetings at which reformed drinkers offered vivid personal testimony of the social degradation they suffered under the influence of alcohol. The Washingtonians provoked ambivalence from old-guard temperance advocates, who feared that "emotion is supplanting reason." Nevertheless, by 1843, the Washingtonians claimed that half a million drinkers had signed their pledge.

Perhaps the most famous platform orator was John Bartholomew Gough (1817–86), an English immigrant who arrived in America at the age of twelve and claimed to have spent seven years incapacitated by drink. Known as the "poet of the d.t.'s," Gough became notorious for his dramatizations of the horrors of drunkenness (such as choking his own wife or placing his child next to an open fireplace) as well as for the lurid stories that were part of his lectures, including the tale of a drunken man who roasted his two-year-old daughter on a fire. Denounced as a "clown" and a "buffoon," Gough vividly recounted the nightmarish visions that had filled his drunken youth, of oceans of blood and knives thrust into his skin. The emotional intensity of his orations was legendary. In his autobiography, Gough described his performances. "What fills the almshouses and jails?" he recalled asking. "What brings yon trembling wretch upon the gallows? It is drink. . . . Snap your burning chains, ye denizens of the pit, and come up sheeted in the fire, dripping with the flames of hell, and with your trumpet tongues testify against the damnation of the drink!"

During the 1840s and 1850s, temperance songs (with such titles as "Dear Father, Drink No More") and fictional literature proliferated, including "Horrid Case of Intemperance," which described a drunken man burned to death in a blacksmith's fire; *John Elliott,* about a drunken husband who drags his wife by her hair; and *The Glass,* in which a boy, locked in a closet by his drunken mother, chews off his arm to avoid starvation. The most famous temperance tract was Timothy Shay Arthur's melodramatic *Ten Nights in a Bar Room, and What I Saw There* (1854), a graphic description of Joe Morgan's descent into unemployment, poverty, and wife abuse after he begins to drink. The story reaches a tragic climax when Joe's daughter Mary sings, "Father, dear Father, come home with me now," at the saloon door, only to die after being struck by a thrown bar glass. The novel sold more than four hundred thousand copies.

A second major development in the temperance movement in the 1840s was the lessening of moral suasion in favor of laws prohibiting the manufacture or sale of distilled spirits. Temperance reformers became convinced that the temptations of alcohol had to be eliminated. Declared the Reverend Leonard Bacon: "You might almost as well persuade the chained maniac to leave off howling, as to persuade him to leave off drinking."

The sudden arrival of hundreds of thousands of immigrants from Ireland and Germany stimulated the shift from temperance to prohibition. Between 1830 and 1860, nearly 2 million Irish arrived and 893,000 Germans in the United States. In Ireland, land was in such short supply that many young men were unable to support a family by farming. The only solution was to delay marriage and socialize with other young men in "bachelor groups," a ritual that often involved drinking. These immigrants probably drank no more than most native-born Americans prior to the 1830s, but immigrants were denounced for their supposed penchant for liquor.

Partly in response to the influx of immigrants, Maine passed the nation's first statewide prohibition law in 1851 (which led to prohibition laws often being referred to as "Maine laws"). The leader of the drive for prohibition laws was Neal Dow, a Quaker businessman in Portland, Maine, who had been shocked to discover that there were five hundred "common drunkards" and one thousand "addicts to excessive use" in his hometown. "I saw health impaired," he later wrote, "capacity undermined, employment lost. I saw wives and children suffering. . . . I found helpless victims of a controlling appetite that was dragging them down to ruin." Like many early temperance proponents, Dow knew the perils of alcohol firsthand, since one of his uncles was an alcoholic. Evangelicals had viewed a refusal to be tempted by alcohol as a sign of grace, but Dow believed that the state, in the interest of public safety, had to remove temptation.

For a brief time, many states followed Maine's example—by 1855, thirteen of the thirty-one states had Maine laws. Soon, however, immigrants and anti-reform groups, who considered prohibition laws to be an infringement of property rights, succeeded in building antitemperance coalitions. The Republican party feared that prohibition would diminish support for its central issue—opposition to the extension of slavery—and undermine its appeal to Irish and German Catholics and German and Scandinavian Lutherans. So leaders omitted prohibition from the party platform. By 1865, only five states still had prohibition laws.

From Moral Reform to
Secular Humanitarianism

Even before the Civil War, the character of moral reform had visibly shifted. The reform organizations that emerged during the mid-1840s and 1850s tended to be more tough-minded, more realistic, and more professional and bureaucratic than their predecessors. They emphasized the importance of environment in causing social evils and aimed at a more scientific approach to benevolence.

This new orientation was apparent in the National Quarantine and Sanitary Convention of the late 1850s, the precursor of the American Public Health Association, which saw civic cleanliness as a solution to the problems of epidemic disease. By the 1850s, the failure of quarantines to combat the spread of cholera, for example, led the NQSC to try to get rid of urban filth and impure water supplies by cleaning up slaughterhouses, breweries, stables, dairies, and piggeries; improving drainage, privies, and sewage systems; and demolishing overcrowded, poorly ventilated slum tenements and building better housing for the poor.

The shift in emphasis could also be seen in the commitment of New York's Association for Improving the Condition of the Poor (founded in 1843) to "scientific philanthropy." Convinced that the poor frequently abused local charitable organizations by applying for relief at several different agencies, the association introduced professionalism and carefully coordinated procedures. To eliminate fraud and ensure the moral elevation of the poor, the association established strict, standardized principles of eligibility for relief, and employed paid agents and trained volunteer visitors to investigate needy families. By 1853, the association had divided Manhattan into 337 districts, with agents in each to monitor more than sixty-five hundred clients. Viewing relief as a last resort, the association built model tenements, opened medical dispensaries, and lobbied on behalf of health and housing legislation.

The Civil War greatly intensified—and bureaucratized—efforts to promote moral uplift. In the spring of 1861, following the Battle of Bull Run, the North's YMCAs formed the Christian Commission to promote "the spiritual good of the soldiers in the army, and incidentally, their intellectual improvement and social and physical comfort." By 1864, the commission had assigned to each of the Union armies a director who coordinated the efforts of 2,217 "delegates," many of whom were women. Like earlier urban and foreign missionaries, these delegates distributed religious tracts and Bibles; they also offered comfort to wounded or dying soldiers. In 1864 alone, the delegates distributed nearly 570,000 Bibles, 500,000 hymnals, 347,000 magazines, and 13 million pages of tracts. The Christian Commission also held frequent prayer meetings and religious services and provided soldiers with "oranges, lemons, onions, pickles . . . shirts [and] towels," which were "given and distributed in the name of Jesus."

The other major philanthropic organization to emerge during the war was the Sanitary Commission. Its task was to coordinate relief for wounded Union soldiers. Like the Christian Commission, the Sanitary Commission drew its leaders and supporters from local religious societies, but it gave expression to a radically new conception of religious benevolence, emphasizing efficiency and deploring sentimentality. "Its ultimate end," declared a commission report, "is neither humanity nor charity. It is to economize for the National service the life and strength of the National soldier." Run by a group of prominent citizens (including landscape architect Frederick Law Olmsted, Unitarian minister Henry W. Bellows, and humanitarian crusader Samuel Gridley Howe), the commission created a core of professional paid agents to distribute medical supplies, organize hospitals, gather statistics, and devise formal procedures for providing relief. The reliance on paid agents rather than volunteers and on professional canvassers to raise funds sparked criticism—Walt Whitman denounced the agents as "hirelings . . . always incompetent and disagreeable." Scientific benevolence was a Sanitary Commission watchword: a board of experts determined how relief was to be distributed, much to the dismay of nurses who were forbidden to dispense aid until the experts had made their decisions.

In their emphasis on professional organization, rules, efficiency, and scientific analysis of social problems, the Christian Commission and the Sanitary Commission clearly pointed to the future of American benevolence. Moral reform was gradually giving way to secular, bureaucratic humanitarianism.

Chapter 4

The Science of Doing Good

CREATING CRUCIBLES OF
MORAL CHARACTER

In lower Manhattan, just a one-minute walk from Broadway, stood the most notorious slum of the early nineteenth century. Located at the intersection of five city streets, Five Points was the epitome of crime, filth, and violence. Its streets, lined with brothels and saloons and infested with dirt and disease, were inhabited by New York's most destitute and degraded citizens. Five Points was also home to the city's most repellent industries: slaughterhouses, tanneries, and "bone mills," where animal bones were ground into dust. "All that is loathsome, drooping, and decayed is here," wrote English novelist Charles Dickens in *American Notes* (1842), a description of his visit to the United States.

The names of Five Points' tenements—the Gates of Hell and Brickbat Mansion—reflected the area's squalor. The most miserable tenement, the Old Brewery, was said for nearly fifteen years to house a thousand debauched poor and to average a murder a night. One of its inhabitants, a little girl who shared a basement room with twenty-five others, was stabbed to death over a penny she had begged. Her body supposedly lay untouched in a corner for five days.

From 1820 onward, Five Points was a dreadful place, "as miserable a haunt of vice and misery as . . . was ever . . . witnessed in Europe," commented Edward Dicey, an English visitor. It was the nation's capital of sin and iniquity, "the most notorious precinct of moral leprosy" in the country. The Plug Uglies and other gangs roamed Five Points' crime-infested streets. Here, observed George G. Foster, a popular writer, in 1850, one saw haggard women "bare-headed, bare-armed, and bare-breasted," muttering obscenities and "inviting passers-by, indiscriminately, to enter" brothels and saloons. A single square block housed seventeen "temples of love," including Rosina Townsend's notorious Palace of the Passions.

At the very time that evangelical Protestant moral reformers sought to save the nation from anarchy and mobocracy by founding urban and foreign missions and Sunday schools and crusading against prostitution, Sabbath breaking, and intemperance, humanitarian reformers in America, England, and Europe started new social institutions to address the mounting problems of crime, delinquency, poverty, ignorance, and physical disability epitomized by Five Points. These included the workhouse for the poor; the asylum for the insane and the physically handicapped; the urban hospital for the ill and the infirm; the house of refuge and reformatory for homeless or delinquent youth; the penitentiary for the criminal; and the common school for the young.

This institutional approach to social problems represented a radical departure from earlier responses to deviance and dependence. Colonial Americans did not rely on institutionalization or incarceration as the primary way of treating the criminal, the indigent, the mentally ill, the orphaned, or the delinquent. They failed to develop specialized institutions for the sick, the disabled, the criminal, the poor, and the mentally ill. By the mid-nineteenth century, in contrast, caretaker institutions had become society's preferred response to problems of criminality, delinquency, indigence, insanity, and physical disability.

Today, the fortresslike penitentiaries, reformatories, orphan asylums, and mental hospitals of the Jacksonian era stand as relics of a seemingly more repressive and less enlightened past. But all these institutions were inspired, to varying degrees, by a utopian faith that it was possible to solve social problems and reshape human character—to eradicate pauperism, rehabilitate criminals, cure insanity, and remedy all social evils—by removing individuals from corrupting outside influences and instilling self-control through moral education, work, rigorous discipline, and an orderly environment. During the early nineteenth century, European visitors flocked to see these grand theaters "for the trial of new plans in hygiene and education, in physical and moral reform."

Yet these new institutions had a dual aspect. In theory, they were to provide the deviant and the dependent with a familial environment in which to learn to overcome violent or intemperate habits. Prison wardens, almshouse keepers, asylum doctors, and other institutional authorities were supposed to use the very same techniques that child-rearing manuals prescribed to progressive parents to strengthen their children's moral character: they were to substitute psychological forms of discipline for physical restraint and learn to manipulate natural emotions—guilt, shame, and sympathy—in order to instill a capacity for self-control.

For all the talk about reform, moral uplift, and rehabilitation, however, these institutions also served a custodial function, removing the deviant and the dependent from the larger society. Over time, this custodial function became more and more pronounced. Even before the Civil War, overcrowding and a lack of state funds and trained personnel transformed many of these institutions into human warehouses, where a population consisting largely of lower-class immigrants and the chronically mentally ill was subjected to strict surveillance, regimentation, and corporal punishment.

It was not a coincidence that asylums, workhouses, a new prison system, and other institutions for social control emerged in the United States and western Europe during the late eighteenth and early nineteenth centuries. At a time when elites on both sides of the Atlantic were beginning to embrace the doctrine of laissez-faire, minimal government regulation of the economy, problems of destitution and dependence proliferated. Thus it seemed critical to find solutions appropriate in a free-market society. The new prison system, asylums, and workhouses of the early nineteenth century all were supposed to provide a benevolent form of social control, replacing the family government and stable communities of the past. These caretaker institutions were to offer a nonauthoritarian way of deterring pauperism, resocializing criminals, alleviating mental illness, and teaching the deaf and the blind to read and write.

Even though the emergence of these "crucibles of moral character" was a transatlantic phenomenon, there was something distinctively American about institutional reform in the antebellum United States. A religiously fired, millennialist optimism infused the rhetoric of the founders of penitentiaries, houses of refuge, orphan asylums, insane asylums, and common schools. These reformers often spoke in apocalyptic terms, decrying the breakdown of family discipline and the dangers of communal disorder, but they did not regard these new institutions as bulwarks against anarchy and social collapse. Rather, they viewed these asylums as models for society and as instruments of liberation and emancipation. The asylum would free the mentally ill and the disabled from confinement in attics, cellars, and jail cells. The common school would erase class lines and promote social mobility. The prison and the reformatory would remove criminals from the temptations of vice and eradicate the underlying source of crime. It is a pointed historical irony that the period of growing laissez-faire also marked the beginning of a new public paternalism, in which public institutions took on the moral prerogatives, presumed benevolence, and good will previously invested in kinship and local communities.

The Discovery of Poverty

In 1819, financial panic struck the United States: banks failed in record numbers, factories shut down, mortgages were foreclosed, and laborers were left jobless. One foreign observer estimated that half a million Americans were out of work. The panic was frightening in its scope and impact. Agricultural prices fell by half. Land values declined by 50 to 70 percent. The downswing swept like a plague across the country. In Pennsylvania, land values plunged from $150 an acre in 1815 to just $35 in 1820. In Cincinnati, bankruptcy sales occurred almost daily. In Philadelphia, 1,808 individuals were committed to debtors' prison; in Boston, the figure was 3,500.

For the first time in American history, the problem of urban poverty commanded widespread public attention. In New York City in 1819, the Society for the Prevention of Pauperism identified 8,000 paupers out of a population of 120,000. The next year, the society found 13,000. Fifty thousand workers were said to be idle in New York, Philadelphia, and Baltimore. To address the growing problem of destitution, newspapers appealed for old clothes and shoes for the poor, and churches and municipalities distributed soup. Baltimore set up twelve soup kitchens for the poor.

By 1823, the panic was over. But it left a lasting imprint on American attitudes toward the poor. For one thing, the panic led to a growing awareness of poverty as an economic condition caused by low wages, unemployment, illness, and the vicissitudes of the business cycle. For another, it sharpened distinctions in the public mind between paupers and the "respectable poor," who were impoverished but not degraded. And finally, the panic sparked demands that the prevailing system of poor relief be abolished. Like their English contemporaries, many American reformers believed that the traditional system encouraged dependency by extending automatic rights of relief to the idle. They sought to eradicate pauperism by establishing workhouses and poor farms.

At the beginning of the nineteenth century, poor relief was governed by laws dating to the seventeenth century, which made kin liable for supporting poor relatives and defined poor relief as a local responsibility. Each town, county, or parish was responsible only for its own residents. As a result, localities routinely denied aid to the migrant poor, or forcibly removed them to the towns from which they had come. While some of the indigent received "outdoor relief"—maintenance in their own home—others were leased or auctioned off to lowest bidder, who agreed to provide room and board in exchange for labor. Many localities contracted to board the poor with another family. Indigent children were often separated from their parents and placed in apprenticeships. A few colonial seaports, such as Boston, New York, and Philadelphia, established almshouses for the poor. But these were not modern poorhouses, since they did not require inmates to work and did not prohibit the use of alcohol.

In the 1800s, poverty was an increasingly visible problem in American cities. By the early 1820s, the first urban slums had arisen near Boston's Ann Street and New York's Five Points. Many Americans believed then that poverty was caused by "indolence, intemperance, and sensuality," by "idleness, dissipation, and worthlessness." But astute observers in the 1820s, such as Mathew Carey, author of "Essay on the Public Charities of Philadelphia" (1828), recognized that poverty had structural roots: wretched wages, sickness, disability, and a "deficiency of [regular] employment."

Periodic poverty was an inescapable fact of life for the antebellum urban laboring classes. Frequent unemployment was a serious problem. In Massachusetts, more than 40 percent of all workers were out of a job for part of the year, usually for four months or more. Fluctuations in demand, inclement weather, interruptions in transportation, technological displacement, fire, injury, and illness—all could leave workers jobless. Families were especially likely to suffer poverty at two specific stages: when children were too young to contribute, and when a father was no longer able to work, as a result of old age or disability.

The realities of antebellum poverty are vividly illustrated by a legal case in Newburyport, Massachusetts. The police arrested a man named John McFeaing in 1850 for stealing wood from the wharves. The man pleaded "necessity" because he could not find work, and an investigation substantiated his claim. His wife and four children lived "in the extremity of misery. The children were all scantily supplied with clothing and not one had a shoe to his feet. There was not a stick of firewood or scarcely a morsel of food in the house." During the early nineteenth century, the situation of the McFeaing family was far from unique. Many day laborers, coal heavers, dockworkers, and other unskilled workers earned just a dollar a day—far less than what contemporaries considered to be a subsistence income. Such people migrated frequently in search of employment, knowing that illness, injury, or interruption of employment threatened them with destitution.

The Panic of 1819 convinced many Americans that the prevailing system of poor relief was inadequate. During the early years of the nineteenth century, the costs of relief soared. In Massachusetts, for example, spending on poor relief doubled between 1801 and 1820. And abuses were rife. The poor were often shunted from one town to another. Many towns spent more money on litigation—to avoid responsibility for providing relief—than it would have cost to support the poor. The practice of apprenticing poor children and auctioning off paupers was particularly liable to abuse. Investigators uncovered many instances of cruel or neglectful treatment. In 1820, a New Yorker named Abijah Hammond commented acidly: "Most of the poor are *sold* . . . to purchasers nearly as poor as themselves, who treat them . . . more like brutes than human beings." The most compelling complaints lodged against the existing poor laws were that they encouraged idleness and sapped any incentive to industry by providing relief payments indiscriminately and unconditionally. The laws, declared an 1821 report by a Massachusetts committee on the state's pauper laws, failed to differentiate between the "worthy" and the "unworthy" poor, between those "wholly incapable of work, through old age, infancy, sickness or corporeal debility" and the able-bodied poor.

The poorhouse appeared to offer a providential solution to the problem of poverty. It promised to accomplish economic and humanitarian goals simultaneously: to reduce relief expenditures, deter applications for relief, curb abuses in the prevailing poor laws, alleviate distress, and break the cycle of poverty by inculcating steady work habits and transforming the character and the behavior of the poor. By isolating and segregating inmates and deliberately making poor relief degrading, the poorhouse would establish the principle of "less eligibility"—that able-bodied paupers would not be better off than the working poor—therefore discouraging the able-bodied from seeking relief. More positively, adoption of the poorhouse system would end the practice of auctioning off paupers and apprenticing poor children. It would provide a refuge for the migrant poor. Most important of all, the poorhouse would eradicate poverty's root causes by curbing intemperance and instilling the habits of industry that would allow the poor to become truly independent.

By mid-century, it was already apparent that the poorhouse had failed to fulfill its founders' objectives. A report by a New York state senate committee in 1857 said the poorhouses in that state were "badly constructed, ill-arranged, ill-warmed, and ill-ventilated." Inmates lacked proper food, clothing, ventilation, and heat in winter, contributing to shockingly high rates of mortality. In one workhouse in Erie County, New York, one in every six inmates died in a single year. Widows, prostitutes, children, drunks, the mentally ill, tramps, and beggars—"all classes and colors, all ages and habits"—were confined together indiscriminately, according to an 1855 letter to the New York secretary of state. "The ill and the maimed, the filthy and the diseased," an 1857 investigation in New York found, "are crowded in the same rooms . . . wrapped in wretched blankets more like beasts than human beings."

The essential reason for the poorhouse's failure lies in a contradiction between the institution's deterrent and rehabilitative goals. Poorhouse advocates had promised that the new institution would cost less than outdoor relief and would further reduce relief expenses by deterring applications for public assistance. But this insistence on cutting costs was at odds with the institution's reform goal: to resocialize the poor so they could become productive members of society. Staffs had no professional training, and corruption and graft were widespread. Few poorhouses offered inmates useful work or vocational training; one almshouse actually put the poor to work walking on treadmills. And many inmates were too old, too young, or too infirm to engage in much productive work. In practice, workhouses frequently became little more than dumping grounds for the poor, especially the immigrant poor, neglected children, and the disabled. In New York State during the 1850s, children made up fully 25 percent of the poorhouse inmates, and the deaf, the blind, and the mentally ill another 25 percent.

As early as the 1850s, it was clear that poorhouses failed to function as their architects anticipated. The poor found ways to manipulate the poorhouse: many young men took temporary refuge there during the winter or times of unemployment and hardship, and the sick and elderly poor, unable to support themselves and lacking kin to care for them, remained for prolonged periods. Despite reformers' best efforts, however, the poorhouse never entirely replaced outdoor relief, which provided assistance to three or four times as many poor people. Most widows, children, old people, and the sick and the disabled continued to receive relief outside of institutions.

The movement to institutionalize the poor in workhouses was one aspect of a much broader trend toward institutionalization. Penitentiaries, reformatories, mental hospitals, and residential schools for the deaf and the blind were all part of an institution-building impulse.

The Challenge of Crime
in a Free Society

During the decades preceding the Civil War, humanitarian reformers began to see crime as a social problem—a product of a faulty environment and flawed character—rather than as a product of human depravity. Instead of whipping criminals, locking them in stocks, or hanging them, reformers believed that the duty of a humane society was to remove the underlying causes of crime, sympathize and show patience toward criminals, and try to rehabilitate them. By the 1840s, a growing number of Americans believed that expanded education and improved correctional institutions offered the best solution to crime.

Prior to the American Revolution, Americans rarely locked criminals in jail for long periods of time. Punishment generally ranged from hanging (capital crimes) to public whipping, confinement in stocks, or branding (lesser offenses). These public punishments were designed to express the collective disapproval of the community, elicit shame in the offender, and reinforce communal norms. This system was appropriate to a small, tightly knit community, where criminals were not considered to be a separate class of people largely immune to communal pressures.

In colonial America, jails were used as temporary confinement for criminal defendants awaiting trial or punishment, and prisoners were sometimes chained with leg irons, handcuffs, and metal bands around the waist. Conditions in these early jails were abominable. Debtors were confined with criminals, and offenders of both sexes and all ages were confined in large groups in cramped cells. Within these squalid holding pens, prisoners customarily were charged for expenses of food and lodging, and they would starve without the assistance of humane societies. Connecticut actually used an abandoned copper mine as a jail.

By the late eighteenth century, the effectiveness of traditional punishments had clearly waned. Population growth, increasing mobility and migration, and the emergence of a distinct poor population made such sanctions as fines, whippings, and the pillory less effective than in the past. Many states increased the number of crimes punishable by death, but this threat proved ineffective, since grand juries refused to indict for capital offenses and juries refused to convict. In the late eighteenth and early nineteenth centuries, the states seized on a new answer to the problem of crime: penal institutions. There, the "disease" of crime could be quarantined and inmates could be gradually rehabilitated in an environment of discipline and routine. Called "penitentiaries" or "reformatories," these new prisons reflected the belief that hard physical labor and confinement might encourage introspection and instill habits of discipline that would rehabilitate criminals. The new penitentiary represented a real attempt to put religious notions of conversion and repentance to practical use: within penitentiaries, criminals would reflect on their wrongdoings, repent, and reform their character. By 1800, eight of the sixteen states had established prisons.

Two rival prison systems competed for public support. After constructing Auburn Prison, New York State authorities adopted a system in which inmates labored in large workshops during the day and slept in separate cells at night. Convicts had to march in lockstep and refrain from speaking or even glimpsing at each other. In Pennsylvania's Eastern State Penitentiary, constructed in 1829, authorities placed even greater stress on the physical isolation of prisoners. Every prison cell had its own exercise yard, work space, and toilet facilities. Under the Pennsylvania plan, prisoners lived and worked in complete isolation.

A blend of Enlightenment, utilitarian, and practical ideas inspired prison reformers in the North and the South. These included beliefs that incarceration might deter crime and safeguard society by segregating and confining hardened criminals; that penitentiaries might rehabilitate prisoners; and that juries would be more likely to convict if they had an alternative to capital or physical punishment.

Forced labor played a critical role in early prisons. Inmates' labor defrayed prison expenses, occupied them, and, in theory, promoted reformation by instilling diligence and discipline and overcoming habits of idleness, sloth, and vice. Silence, too, was supposed to reform prisoners' character. In the New York institution, total silence was maintained during the day and physical isolation at night. After their look at the prison in 1831, two French visitors, Alexis de Tocqueville and Gustave Auguste de Beaumont, commented: "The silence within these vast walls . . . is that of death. . . . We felt as if we traversed catacombs; there were a thousand living beings, and yet it was a desert solitude."

As prison size grew, however, officials found maintaining order increasingly difficult. Although prison rules forbade conversation, in practice convicts frequently talked to each other, and they cursed and sang obscene songs on the Sabbath. Arson, assaults on guards, and prison escapes were common events. To reassert discipline, wardens imposed harsh punishments, employing straitjackets, solitary confinement, diets of bread and water, "shower baths" in ice water, and whippings.

Female inmates, who made up about 4 percent of the nation's prisoners in 1850, were generally considered irredeemable and consequently suffered harsh treatment and sexual abuse. As New York prison officials reported in 1844: "It seems to have been regarded as a sufficient performance of the object of punishment to . . . leave them to feed upon and destroy each other." In New York's Auburn Prison, female prisoners were crowded together in a one-room attic, its windows sealed to prevent communication with male inmates. To keep the women quiet, the warden employed the stocks—"a chair, with a fastening for the head and all the limbs." Commented a prison chaplain at Auburn: "To be a female convict, for any protracted period, would be worse than death."

Poor diets, overwork, and harsh punishment contributed to an extraordinarily high prison death rate; 5.8 percent of the nation's inmates in 1850 died in prison. Years earlier, observers had already begun to doubt that prison could reform criminals. In 1823, the directors of the Massachusetts State Prison declared: "Convicts are discharged who have no friends, acquaintances or money; or who, by being known as convicts, are avoided as infectious and driven by necessity to commit new crimes. They are willing to labour, but can get no employment; and cannot consent to starve, even at the hazard of new imprisonment."

By 1850, it was clear that the penitentiary would not live up to its founders' promises. Like the poorhouse, the penitentiary aimed to achieve a series of contradictory and ultimately irreconcilable goals: to punish and reform; to deter and rehabilitate; to segregate and resocialize. By mid-century, the institution's custodial role had superseded its rehabilitative aims.

Regional Differences

Prison construction made its greatest strides in the Northeast, but it was not an exclusively northern development. In the South, too, many states experimented with penitentiaries, but in this region a variety of informal, premodern means of dealing with crime existed as well. Unlike the North, which was eager to rationalize and depersonalize the administration of justice, to make punishment less arbitrary and more effective, the South attached greater value to the defense of personal honor through duels, fights, gouging matches, and other highly personalized forms of justice.

In 1796, the Virginia state legislature eliminated the death penalty for all but a single offense—first-degree murder—and built one of the nation's first penitentiaries. Designed by the famous architect Benjamin Henry Latrobe, the structure in Richmond consisted of a series of cells laid out in a semicircle around an observation area, so a small number of guards could keep track of the inmates. Upon arrival, inmates were placed in solitary confinement for one-twelfth to one-half of their sentence—they were to reflect on their crimes and grow penitent. Then inmates began a regimen of forced labor in a large central workshop, making nails, shoes, and leather goods.

Almost immediately, it was clear that the penitentiary was not working as intended. Just six years after its founding, the institution was described as a "truly disagreeable and dangerous" place. The cells lacked heat, and water from a nearby stagnant pond seeped through the walls. Several inmates died; a few went mad.

During the decades before the Civil War, when many northern states, led by Massachusetts, New York, and Pennsylvania, created a modern criminal justice system, complete with penitentiaries and urban police forces, a number of southern states also developed state prisons. Georgia, Kentucky, Maryland, and Virginia all constructed penitentiaries before 1820. In general, however, the slave states relied less on prisons than on informal, extralegal means of resolving disputes, including dueling and organized vigilantism.

There was a marked difference in the nature of crime and punishment in the North and the South, a contrast illustrated most starkly by the distinctions between Massachusetts and South Carolina. In Massachusetts, where urban expansion, high levels of transience, and rapid immigration overwhelmed the ability of traditional mechanisms to control crime and disorder, prosecution of sexual and religious offenses (fornication and blasphemy, for example) declined in the late eighteenth and early nineteenth centuries and prosecution of crimes against property (especially petty theft) and other offenses involving the lower classes, such as drunkenness and vagrancy, sharply increased. Conviction rates were high, reflecting people's intense concern about public order, and offenders were generally punished by confinement in a jail, a house of correction, a state prison, or an almshouse.

In South Carolina, one of two states with a slave majority, offenses committed by slaves were largely handled either through "plantation justice" or by vigilante societies. Among whites, crimes of passion rather than crimes against property were the most common criminal offenses, usually assaults occasioned by verbal insults, disputes over property, or attacks on a person's honor. Incarceration played a relatively small role in punishment; the Palmetto State relied heavily on fines and on corporal punishment, including branding, which continued until 1833, and whipping, which continued until the Civil War.

Sharp regional differences in the treatment of crime would persist throughout the nineteenth century. In an effort to reduce the costs of building and operating prisons, many post-Reconstruction southern states adopted the convict lease system. The state governments established heavy penalties for petty offenses, and leased convicts to corporations or private individuals. Unlike the more modern, impersonal, bureaucratic system of criminal justice that characterized the North, the South continued to rely on a decentralized, informal system of social control.

Juvenile Delinquency

Antebellum reformers were particularly worried about the problems posed by juvenile delinquents. If sent to an almshouse, a poor farm, or jail, they mixed with adult paupers and hardened criminals and were "liable to acquire bad habits and principles, and lay the foundation for a career of worthlessness and improvidence," explained a committee of Philadelphians in 1827. To stop poverty and crime before they began, charity reformers and municipal leaders proposed a new institution: the house of refuge.

Few subjects aroused more concern in the minds of early-nineteenth-century philanthropists than the children of the poor, the "offcast children of American debauchery, drunkenness and vice." Wayward, vagrant, runaway, neglected, indigent youths became common sights in American cities beginning in the 1820s. New York City's Society for the Prevention of Pauperism warned in 1821: "Thousands of children are growing up . . . destitute of . . . superintendence over their minds and morals. . . . A class more dangerous to the community . . . can hardly be imagined."

After 1800, Baltimore, Boston, New York, and Philadelphia opened the nation's first houses of refuge to remove "the vagrant and perilled children of the streets" and to provide moral and vocational training to prevent them from becoming paupers or criminals. Convinced that "youth is particularly susceptible of reform," the founders of the Boston Children's Friend Society spoke for other groups when they declared in 1851 that houses of refuge would ensure that children would not grow up to become "pests to society, and ultimately the tenants of our prisons."

Combining the features of a family, a school, and a prison, the refuges accepted vagrant, abandoned, abused, and orphaned children as well as delinquents. Sometimes, destitute parents temporarily placed children in refuges while they searched for work. Typically, young people spent two to five years in a house of refuge, followed by an apprenticeship to a craftsman or a farmer.

Insisting that their institutions were "an asylum for friendless and unfortunate children, not a prison for young culprits," their founders viewed refuges as preventative and rehabilitative institutions. In 1829, the Society for the Reformation of Juvenile Delinquents in New York expressed the prevailing confidence of reformers that they could prevent crime and poverty "by seeking out the youthful and unprotected who were in the way of temptation, and by religious and moral instructure, by imparting to them useful knowledge, and by giving them industrious and orderly habits, rescuing them from vice and rendering them valuable members of society."

Yet the architecture and internal organization of the houses of refuge bore a striking resemblence to those of prisons. Children slept in large dormitories, labored in group workshops, and ate in silence in a common dining hall. Certainly, many inmates regarded the refuges as prisons, a point they made by frequently setting fires, staging riots, and running away.

Officials imposed a strict routine. In the New York house of refuge, a ringing bell awoke the children at 5 A.M.; after washing and making their bed, the children paraded in the yard, where officials examined their cleanliness and dress. The children then attended morning prayers and school until 7 A.M., when they received breakfast and began to labor in the refuge's workshops, finishing shoes, making nails, or constructing wicker chairs. After an hour for lunch, they worked until 5 P.M. After dinner, their schooling resumed until 8 P.M.

To maintain order, refuge officials used a combination of positive and negative incentives. Well-behaved youngsters were allowed to take unescorted trips outside the institution and to serve as monitors of younger children. Administrators punished unruly behavior severely, inflicting whippings, placing children in solitary confinement, depriving them of meals, and restraining them in leg irons and handcuffs. Children who wet their beds had their names announced in the dining hall. In 1848, a critic named Elijah Devoe declared: "Nothing short of excessive ignorance can entertain for a moment the idea that the inmates of the Refuge are contented . . . On parade, at table, at their work, and in school, they are not allowed to converse . . . Restriction and Constraint are their most intimate companions."

Precisely because the houses of refuge were said to be acting in children's best interest, they possessed powers greater than those of a prison. They could separate indigent and delinquent children from their natural parents. In a landmark case in 1838, the Pennsylvania State Supreme Court turned down a father's request to have his daughter released from the Philadelphia House of Refuge, stating: "The infant has been snatched from a course which must have ended in confirmed depravity; and not only is the restraint of her person lawful, but it would be an act of extreme cruelty to release her from it."

The pre–Civil War houses of refuge established two legal precedents that continue to characterize the juvenile justice system in the United States: jurisdiction over noncriminal behavior (the refuges had the authority to incarcerate juveniles even when the youth were not guilty of a crime) and indeterminate sentencing. A "promiscuous" girl, a "vicious" or "incorrigible" boy, or even an "idle" child or school truant might be placed in a house of refuge until he or she reached adulthood.

By mid-century, the increasing numbers of delinquent and neglected children had outstripped the capacities of the houses of refuge, which were mainly run by private benevolent societies. In response, state governments began to set up a new government-run institution in the late 1840s and 1850s for delinquents—the reform school. Usually located in rural areas, these schools were intended to remove wayward children from the moral contamination of the city and to transform them culturally and even religiously through a regimen of moral instruction, prayer, and physical labor.

In practice, however, the reform schools, like the houses of refuge, failed to live up to their founders' intentions. Harsh discipline and strict regimentation served to "darken, harden, and embitter" many of the young people placed in the institutions. An 1859 fire at the Massachusetts State Reform School for Boys in Westborough (just eleven years after the institution opened) revealed a bleak side to reform-school life. Caused by arson (the work of a disgruntled fifteen-year-old), the fire revealed that three inmates had been in solitary confinement for several months. The three, who had been accused, respectively, of running away, assaulting an institution official, and attempted arson, were manacled to the floor in dark, poorly ventilated cells and fed bread and water.

A variety of factors contributed to the worsening conditions within reformatories—factors that also led to the decline of such antebellum institutions as workhouses, penitentiaries, and mental hospitals. An influx of inmates from the immigrant lower classes undermined enthusiasm for reform. At the same time, the belief that a suitable environment could improve character and inculcate good habits waned.

The Restriction of Corporal and Capital Punishment

Apart from the development of the prison and the reformatory, an important early-nineteenth-century legal development was the drive to outlaw corporal and capital punishment. The first half of the nineteenth century witnessed concerted campaigns in both the United States and Britain to curb the use of physical punishment in schools, prisons, and the navy. The infliction of pain and cruelty came to be viewed as at odds with the religiously rooted ideals of compassion and humanity. In postrevolutionary America, corporal punishment was widespread. During the late eighteenth and early nineteenth centuries, flogging—with a cat-o'-nine-tails (nine twisted cords fastened to a wooden handle), a rod, or a whip—was a common feature of life. In 1799, the U.S. Congress specifically authorized flogging as a punishment for sailors guilty of swearing or drunkenness. Prisons, beset by problems of overcrowding, escapes, and riots, increasingly relied on whippings to control unruly inmates. Teachers frequently used the rod and the whip to correct pupils.

During the first half of the nineteenth century, critics denounced corporal punishment as antiquated, cruel, and ineffective. It was degrading and inhumane, a despotic "relic of feudalism and barbarity" (as Senator John Parker Hale of New Hampshire declared in 1849 in a speech condemning flogging). Corporal punishment, critics charged, was incapable of achieving the true aim of discipline: a capacity for self-government and self-control, which could only be developed through appeals to reason and conscience. Reformers maintained that physical punishment merely nurtured sadistic and cruel impulses in its perpetrators and resentment, anger, and a desire for vengeance in its victims. Practical concerns reinforced moral concerns. For example, physical punishment frustrated the navy's efforts to alleviate its manpower shortage, and corporal punishments in schools provoked hostility from many working-class parents.

Massachusetts was one of the first states to abolish corporal punishment of criminals—the government prohibited whipping, branding, the stock, and the pillory in 1804 and 1805 (1805 was also the year that Massachusetts opened its first state prison). Tattooing of repeat offenders was abolished in 1829. The latter half of the 1840s brought significant restrictions on corporal punishment. In 1846, New York City admonished public school teachers to chastise students only with "great discretion" and in "special cases." Boston and New York also required teachers to record their use of corporal punishment. In the late 1840s, several northeastern states restricted its use in penitentiaries. And in 1850, Congress prohibited flogging in the U.S. Navy.

Another major antebellum reform effort was a movement to outlaw capital punishment. During the colonial era, many crimes—including counterfeiting, rape, and robbery—were capital offenses. In colonial South Carolina, 165 offenses were punishable by death; in colonial Massachusetts, 12. In practice, however, execution rates were lower than such figures might suggest—below 50 percent for those convicted of capital offenses—reflecting the reluctance of prosecutors to press charges that would result in the death penalty and the reluctance of juries to convict.

Prior to the 1830s, most states reduced the number of crimes punishable by death. In Massachusetts, for example, the number fell to six; in South Carolina, to approximately thirty-two. States also began to carry out executions beyond public view, lest the spectacle of hangings stimulate people to acts of violence.

During the 1830s and 1840s, agitation against the death penalty increased. Executive clemency for condemned criminals grew more common—in Massachusetts, for example, two-fifths of those sentenced to death were pardoned. Combining Enlightenment, utilitarian, religious, and practical objections, critics argued that capital punishment brutalized society, failed to deter crime, and was applied capriciously and sometimes in error. In 1847, Michigan became the first modern jurisdiction to outlaw the death penalty, and Rhode Island and Wisconsin soon followed. A number of other states failed to abolish capital punishment but did restrict its use. They removed arson, rape, robbery, and treason from the list of capital offenses and restricted the death penalty solely to cases of first-degree murder.

Abolition of Imprisonment for Debt

Imprisonment for debt also came under attack. During the seventeenth century, colonial legislatures, following English precedent, gave creditors the power to have defaulting debtors imprisoned until their debt was repaid. The incidence of imprisonment for debt grew noticeably during the late eighteenth and early nineteenth centuries. In part, this reflected an actual increase in the amount of lending and borrowing and the number of defaulting debtors. But it also reflected a fundamental shift in business practice. Relations between creditors and debtors became more impersonal, with lenders relying less on a borrower's reputation and more on contracts and the threat of imprisonment. Growing speculation in land companies, turnpikes, canals, banks, and government securities in the wake of the Revolution also contributed to an increase in the incidence of imprisonment for debt. Many promoters and speculators found themselves forced into debtors' prison—among them, revolutionary leader Robert Morris, who spent three years in a Philadelphia jail.

Beginning in the late eighteenth century, imprisonment for debt was increasingly denounced as shocking and irrational. Critics of the practice—many workingmen and prominent businessmen—bombarded the public with startling examples of nursing mothers and aged veterans of the Revolution imprisoned for months over trivial debts. A Boston woman was taken from her three children as a result of a $3 debt; a Vermont man was imprisoned for a debt of 54¢. As late as 1816, an average of six hundred residents of New York City were in prison at any one time for failure to pay debts. Most imprisoned debtors were poor. Roughly 60 percent owed no more than $10, and only a tenth were ever able to repay their debts in full.

Reformers regarded debtors' prisons not only as cruel and inhumane—places of "Death and Torments to Many Unfortunate People"—but as inefficient and counterproductive as well, since jailed debtors were unable to work or care for their dependents and since creditors had to pay jail fees. Imprisonment also came to be viewed as obsolete, given new credit arrangements. After 1800, creditors increasingly extended "secured" loans and then attached the borrower's property or wages when the loan became overdue.

Imprisonment for debt gradually ended as a result of piecemeal reforms. Many state legislatures allowed the indigent to leave jail after taking an oath of poverty. Many states broadened the definition of imprisonment; in 1841, for example, South Carolina declared that an entire judicial district would serve as a "prison." Other states abolished imprisonment for certain groups of debtors. In 1809, New York forbade the jailing of women who owed less than $50; in 1828, it eliminated imprisonment for debt for all women; in 1830, it exempted revolutionary veterans; and the next year, the state abolished imprisonment for debt.

Asylums for the Afflicted

During the decades before the Civil War, many reformers devoted their attention to the problems of the mentally ill, the deaf, and the blind. Unlike colonial Americans, who regarded mental illness, deafness, and blindness as incurable afflictions with supernatural sources, antebellum reformers treated these disabilities as medical problems susceptible to human intervention. They established special institutions—asylums—to provide shelter and a therapeutic environment for people long abused and ignored.

In 1841, Dorothea Dix (1802–87), a thirty-nine-year-old former school-teacher, volunteered to give religious instruction to women incarcerated in the East Cambridge, Massachusetts, House of Correction. Inside the jail, she was horrified to find mentally ill inmates dressed in rags and confined to a single dreary room without any source of heat. Shocked by what she saw, she embarked on a lifelong crusade to reform the treatment of the mentally ill.

After a two-year secret investigation of every jail and almshouse in Massachusetts, Dix issued a report to the Massachusetts state legislature. The mentally ill, she found, were mixed indiscriminately with paupers and hardened criminals. Many were confined "in cages, closets, cellars, stalls, pens! Chained, naked, beaten with rods and lashed into obedience." When officials at the institutions questioned the report's credibility, accusing Dix of "sensational and slanderous lies," Dix enlisted the support of such influential figures as Horace Mann, who encouraged the state to construct a large addition for the insane to the state hospital.

Following her success in Massachusetts, Dix carried her campaign for state-supported asylums nationwide, traveling thirty thousand miles in ten years and persuading more than a dozen state legislatures to improve institutional care for the insane. Congress approved her proposal for a federal system of hospitals for the mentally ill, but President Franklin Pierce vetoed it on the grounds that the federal government would be unwise to assume responsibility for the nation's poor.

The proliferation of mental institutions during the early nineteenth century represented a revolutionary shift in the treatment of mental illness. In colonial America, most "lunatics" or "distracted people" were cared for in much the same manner as any other dependent persons—by their own families—and the indigent were boarded in private residences or bound out to work. Especially violent or disruptive individuals were physically restrained or isolated in a cellar or attic. Only a small number were confined in hospitals, almshouses, or houses of correction.

Seventeenth- and eighteenth-century Americans considered "distracted" and bizarre behavior "a familiar and pitiful sight." Indeed, the historical record suggests that colonial Americans were more accustomed to seeing aberrant behavior than their contemporary counterparts. For example, Joseph Moody, an eighteenth-century Harvard-educated minister, wore a handkerchief over his face for many years; Joseph Belcher, an Easton, Massachusetts, minister, repeatedly went "to church with his pockets full of sermons which he kept reading until dark," long after his congregation had gone home; and in 1770, James Otis Jr., a leading political figure, broke every window in Boston's town hall and fired a gun "madly" out his window.

For the most part, colonial Americans did not regard mental illness as a pressing social problem. The relatively slow pace of life in an essentially agricultural society, the small size of colonial towns and rural villages, the existence of informal mechanisms to monitor behavior, and the strength of kinship ties all contributed to a surprisingly casual attitude toward mental derangement. But even before the American Revolution, as urban populations grew, public concern over "lunatics" began to increase and so did the number confined in hospitals, almshouses, and jails. A petition submitted to the Pennsylvania General Assembly in 1751, calling for the establishment of a hospital for the mentally ill, underscores that concern: "That . . . the Numbers of Lunatics . . . deprived of their rational Faculties, hath greatly increased in this Province. That some of them . . . are a Terror to their Neighbours, who are daily apprehensive of the Violences they may commit; and others are continually awasting their Substance, to the great Injury of themselves and Families."

By the early nineteenth century, many physicians were convinced that modern life itself stimulated nervous irritability, debilitating moods, delusions, and other mental disorders. As an authority named Edward Jarvis claimed in 1852, economic instability, religious enthusiasm, and the pace of social change all produced "more opportunities and rewards for great and excessive mental action, more uncertain and hazardous employments and consequently more disappointments, [and] more means and provocations for sensual indulgence."

Conditions in the early institutions were truly abominable. The first American hospitals to admit the insane (established in Philadelphia, New York, and Williamsburg, Virginia, during the second half of the eighteenth century) relied heavily on physical restraints, bleeding and blistering, cold baths, and potent purgatives. Pennsylvania Hospital confined violent lunatics in a basement room, bound in manacles, leg irons, leather cuffs, and straitjackets. In 1827—fourteen years before Dorothea Dix launched her investigations—the Reverend Louis Dwight, a founder of the Boston Prison Discipline Society, issued a graphic description of the treatment of the mentally ill in Massachusetts jails: "One was found in an apartment in which he had been nine years. He had a wreath of rags around his body, and another around his neck. This was all his clothing. He had no bed, chair or bench. Two or three rough planks were strewed about the room, a heap of filthy straw, like the nest of swine, was in the corner."

Yet the late eighteenth and early nineteenth centuries also witnessed the birth of the notion that insanity could be cured by prompt and proper treatment. Beginning in 1811, Boston, Hartford, and Philadelphia established new institutions and reorganized older institutions, reflecting revolutionary new concepts of mental disease and treatment.

One pioneer in humanitarian care for the mentally ill was Thomas Story Kirkbride, who was just thirty-one years old when he became superintendent of the Philadelphia Hospital for the Insane in 1840. A Quaker, Kirkbride was eager to emancipate the mentally ill from the chains that bound and repressed them. His institution quickly become the foremost private mental hospital in the United States, and the methods of therapy that he developed shaped the treatment of mental illness in America until the 1870s.

In his institution, Kirkbride emphasized "moral treatment" of the mentally ill. First devised in France by Philippe Pinel and in England by William Tuke, moral treatment assumed that mental illness was curable and stressed kindness and patience, rather than fear and punishment. The physician was supposed to act like an enlightened parent exercising a moral influence over the children. The goal was to stimulate a patient's latent reason and capacity for self-control through a highly structured regimen of individualized treatment, handicrafts, manual labor, physical exercise, lectures, parties, and reading.

Kirkbride believed that every aspect of the hospital environment—from the building's architectural design to the nature of the hospital's daily routine—influenced the patients' prospects for recovery. His book, *On the Construction, Organization, and General Arrangement of Hospitals for the Insane* (1854), became the bible of mid-nineteenth-century mental hospital superintendents. It laid out the blueprint for a model asylum. To ensure that the superintendent could keep careful watch over his patients, the hospital—like a prison—had a central building, where the superintendent resided, and several wings. Within the institution, inmates were classified according to their mental condition and degree of illness. To ensure patient privacy and to prevent escapes, the hospital was set off from the surrounding community by a wall—a design feature that reinforced the hospital's jaillike appearance. To help patients gain control over their emotions and powers of reasoning, the hospital emphasized regularity and order—a routine that also made it easier to operate an increasingly large bureaucratic institution.

Much of the impetus for the early growth of asylums came from families who felt incapable of caring for troublesome or mentally ill relatives within their homes. At first, wealthier families might send them to a spa or a health resort. Generally, a family only turned to an asylum in desperation. Many admissions were prompted by suicide attempts, threats of violence, alcohol or drug addiction, or embarrassing public displays of bizarre behavior. Clearly, compared to those in the eighteenth century, mid-nineteenth-century families felt less comfortable about and capable of caring for the mentally deranged at home.

As early as the 1820s, private hospitals were having difficulty adequately addressing the problems of the mentally ill. The largest ones had fewer than one hundred patients in residence at any given time, and they also faced a severe shortage of funds, which led them to admit fewer and fewer charity patients. To provide care for those unable to afford private treatment, the first public mental hospitals were founded during the 1830s. By 1860, virtually every state had at least one public mental hospital.

Worcester State Hospital, which opened in Massachusetts in 1833, was one of the first such hospitals established in line with the latest psychiatric and medical theory. The history of the Worcester hospital is the story of the gradual breakdown of reformers' utopian hopes. Samuel B. Woodward, Worcester's superintendent from 1833 to 1846, believed that insanity could be cured by creating a sympathetic, clean, and orderly environment for the mentally ill and avoiding all repressive forms of physical restraint. Although Woodward prescribed a variety of drugs, including narcotics and stimulants, to treat physical derangements of the brain and the nervous system, primary emphasis was placed on moral therapy—an individualized program of productive labor, religious observance, and attendance at lectures. Woodward claimed to cure more than 80 percent of the patients admitted to his institution.

Yet even before Woodward retired in 1846, an increase in the hospital's patient population made it more difficult to offer individualized treatment. In 1832, the Massachusetts state legislature required Worcester to accept all dangerous lunatics confined in Massachusetts jails, almshouses, and houses of correction, as well as all people referred by the courts. As a result, more patients were unsuited for therapy, on account of senility, syphilitic infection of the brain, alcoholism, or violent insanity. But there was no proportional increase in state funding.

The 1840s and 1850s not only brought a heavy influx of indigent patients suffering chronic problems, but many of these were impoverished Irish Catholic immigrants, which aggravated class and ethnic tensions within the institution. Patients from wealthier families withdrew and entered the private hospitals that continued to offer individualized moral therapy. In 1856, in an effort to retain paying patients, Worcester separated patients' quarters along class lines, but to no avail.

Woodward's successor as superintendent, George Chandler, tried to maintain a program of moral therapy. But heavy patient loads, understaffing, and inadequate state funding transformed Worcester from a caring, therapeutic institution into a bureaucratic, custodial institution. Instead of serving as a physician caring for patients, Chandler became a full-time administrator, preoccupied with day-to-day operations. To cut costs, he was forced to rely on poorly paid nurses and attendants, who treated the indigent Irish Catholic immigrant patients with hostility and disdain. To manage the increasingly large institution in an efficient, systematic, and orderly manner, the new superintendent emphasized standards and routines, placed physical restraints on disruptive and violent patients, and administered morphine and opium to keep them calm.

The gradual shift toward custodial care took place in many mental hospitals in the 1840s and 1850s. Some institutions, such as New York's Lunatic Asylum on Blackwell's Island and the Boston Lunatic Asylum, were aptly described as "man-kennels" or "legalized cesspools," welfare institutions that made few pretenses of providing therapy. Instead, they offered cheap custodial care to the indigent and to immigrants—the New York asylum used convicts as attendants.

New psychiatric theories that stressed the physical basis of insanity and its incurability further contributed to the transformation of hospitals from therapeutic into custodial institutions. A new generation of physicians rejected moral therapy as unscientific, emphasized the hereditary and physical bases of insanity, and expressed a growing pessimism about whether mental disease was curable. After the Civil War, experts on insanity attributed mental illness to untreatable physical causes—such as lesions of the brain, concussions, and syphilis—to heredity, and to moral causes (intemperance, vice, immorality, and the stresses of nineteenth-century society, such as excessive ambition and overwork).

Resentment of immigrants reinforced the custodial orientation of mental hospitals. An influential 1854 study by Massachusetts physician Edward Jarvis, which supposedly proved that immigrants took a disproportionate advantage of public hospitals, discouraged state support for mental asylums.

In general, the superintendents of antebellum mental hospitals were benevolent and well-intentioned men who genuinely believed that insanity, like any physical illness, was treatable. Although they placed more emphasis on physical restraints than would today be acceptable, and removed the mentally ill from local communities and, thus, visits by relatives and friends, these asylum doctors set high standards of patient care. Certain social and economic realities nevertheless ensured that mental hospitals would fall far short of their architects' hopes. By the 1850s, state legislators had begun to treat public mental hospitals as dumping grounds for the indigent (especially indigent immigrants), the chronically ill, and the violently uncontrollable. Public mental hospitals grew larger and more prisonlike, more bureaucratic and impersonal, contributing to the insane asylum's image as a repressive, therapeutically ineffective "snake pit."

Deafness and Blindness

English novelist Charles Dickens and other contemporaries considered her story "one of the wonders of the educational world." At the age of two, Laura Bridgman, the daughter of a Hanover, New Hampshire, farmer, was stricken with scarlet fever, which left her blind and deaf. A year later she lost her power of speech as well as most of her sense of taste and smell.

In 1837, when she was seven, her family placed the girl under the care of Dr. Samuel Gridley Howe. To teach her to recognize the letters of the alphabet, Howe gave her kitchen utensils and other common household items on which he had pasted labels with raised letters. The young girl handled the objects and began to associate them with the letters' shapes. Then, to allow her to communicate with him, Howe gave her a set of metal type, on which each letter of the alphabet was embossed. By the end of the first year, she had learned to spell out words using the metal type. She could do so with her hands and fingers as well. Soon she learned how to write. Educator Horace Mann was so struck by her success that he wrote: "I should rather have built up the Blind Asylum than have written *Hamlet*."

During the late eighteenth and early nineteenth centuries, the founders of residential schools for the deaf and the blind joined with enlightened reformers in Europe to break with a long tradition of regarding deafness and blindness as untreatable disabilities. For centuries, Europeans regarded the deaf and the blind as defective—as lacking the full attributes of humanity. It was a commonplace of Christian thought that deaf people were incapable of achieving religious salvation, since they were unable to hear the word of God (a view rooted in a passage in Paul's Epistle to the Romans, "So then faith cometh by hearing, and hearing by the word of God"). Not only were the deaf unable to speak, they were also—for reasons not fully understood even today—unable in many cases to read. In the late eighteenth century, Samuel Johnson, the English essayist, poet, and lexicographer, described deafness as "the most desperate of human calamities," since it meant living in total isolation, unable to acquire an education or to communicate with other people. Under European and colonial American law, the blind and the deaf and dumb were classified as idiots.

During the late eighteenth century, new ideas about deafness and blindness began to be expounded. A pioneer in the education of the deaf was an eighteenth-century French cleric, Abbé Charles Michel de l'Epée. Eager to provide the deaf with a religious education, the abbé made a point of closely observing deaf people in Paris. And he made a momentous discovery: deaf people interacted with each other and communicated through hand signals. The abbé studied this language, and in 1755 he opened a school that used hand signs to teach the deaf to read and write French. At the time of his death in 1789, he had founded twenty-one schools for deaf people in Europe.

Like the movement to teach the deaf to read and write, humanitarian efforts to educate the blind began in late-eighteenth-century France. In 1771, a twenty-six-year-old Frenchman, Valentin Haüy, the Father of the Blind, entered a Paris café, where ten blind musicians sat on a platform before a jeering crowd. The men wore dunce caps, asses' ears, and grotesque robes. Their eyes were covered with lensless spectacles. Shocked, Haüy vowed that he would do away with such an "outrage to humanity": "I will make the blind read!" he declared. It took thirteen years for Haüy to fulfill his pledge. In 1784, he opened the first residential school for the blind. During the late eighteenth and early nineteenth centuries, schools for blind children appeared in many European countries. By the time of Haüy's death in 1822, there were five schools for the blind in Britain, two in Ireland, and twelve in as many countries in Europe. The United States, however, had not yet established a single school for the blind.

The first American school for deaf children was a short-lived venture organized in 1815 on a Virginia plantation. Organized by John Braidwood, grandson of the founder of Braidwood Academy, a leading school for the deaf in Edinburgh, Scotland, Cobbs School taught orally (emphasizing lip-reading) rather than through signing. Quite different was the first permanent school for deaf persons, founded in 1817 in Hartford, Connecticut. Unlike Cobbs School, the Connecticut Asylum for the Education and Instruction of Deaf and Dumb Persons was a nonprofit, state-supported residential school, which relied primarily upon deaf teachers who instructed their pupils using a mixture of sign language (a manual and visual mode of communication with its own grammar and structure), signed English, and finger spelling. The new school was animated by a deep religious optimism. In its first annual report, the school proclaimed that education was essential if deaf people were to be "rescued from intellectual darkness" and "brought to a knowledge of the truth as it is found in Jesus."

Leading the effort to establish the school was Mason Fitch Cogswell, a Yale-educated physician, whose daughter Alice had lost her hearing as a result of meningitis. After urging Connecticut ministers to determine the number of deaf children in the state (a survey conducted between 1812 and 1815 found eighty-four), Cogswell persuaded Thomas Hopkins Gallaudet (1787–1851), a Congregational minister educated at Yale and Andover Theological Seminary, to travel to Europe to learn about the education of deaf children.

While studying at the Royal Institution for the Deaf in Paris, Gallaudet met Laurent Clerc, a thirty-year-old deaf graduate of Abbé de l'Epée's school, who agreed to introduce French teaching techniques to the United States. At the Hartford academy, Clerc used French sign language to teach deaf students to communicate with their hands. Over time, French sign language incorporated the hand signals brought to the school by local students to form what is now known as American Sign Language.

Soon other states established residential schools patterned after the Connecticut Asylum, beginning with New York in 1818 and followed by Pennsylvania in 1820, Kentucky in 1823, Ohio in 1827, Virginia in 1838, and Indiana in 1843. By 1857, the United States had nineteen residential schools for deaf persons (including schools in Iowa, Louisiana, Missouri, and Texas). These institutions offered vocational training, typically in bookbinding, carpentry, printing, and shoemaking.

These schools also created communities of deaf persons able to communicate through sign language. The growing sense of community among deaf people was evident in the 1850s and 1860s. Some indications were the founding of their first formal organization, the New England Gallaudet Association of Deaf-Mutes; the appearance in 1860 of their first monthly periodical, the *Gallaudet Guide and Deaf-Mute's Companion;* and the founding, four years later, of Gallaudet College, the first college for deaf people.

The late nineteenth century brought a sharp reaction against sign language and residential schools. In 1880, the International Congress of Educators of the Deaf, convinced that sign language was an imprecise and defective form of communication that impeded the integration of deaf people into the cultural mainstream, forbade the use of sign language and finger spelling in schools for the deaf, and instead emphasized speech and lip reading. The emphasis on oral instruction produced a shift from deaf to hearing teachers, and by 1920, approximately 80 percent of deaf students were instructed using purely oral methods (compared to just 7.5 percent in 1882). The late nineteenth century also witnessed widespread efforts to replace residential schools with less costly day schools.

The first American schools for blind children in Boston, New York, and Philadelphia opened in 1832 and 1833. The inspiration behind the founding of these schools was complex, mixing religious, economic, and humanitarian motives. Partly, the impetus came from parents who wished to ensure that their blind children received an education; partly, there was a concern about the mounting number of indigent blind beggars on the streets. Privately financed, these institutions were patterned after European schools. By 1860, another eighteen residential schools had opened. Many of them were originally designed to care for and educate a wide range of "defective children"— including the deaf and the "feeble-minded," as well as the blind—and all but one (an asylum in Maryland) were state operated.

Samuel Gridley Howe, whom the poet John Greenleaf Whittier called the Cadmus of the Blind, was the central figure in American efforts to educate the blind. After graduating from Brown University and Harvard Medical School, Howe enlisted with the Greeks in their war for independence from the Ottoman Empire, and then, for forty-four years, headed Perkins Institution. He was an active proponent of many humanitarian causes—abolition of slavery, humane treatment of the mentally ill, and universal free education. From the very start, Howe committed his school to educating all blind children, regardless of race. "I should no more think of refusing to help one of my fellow mortals on account of the color of his skin," he wrote in 1832, "than the color of his hair."

Before opening his school, Howe followed the example of Thomas Hopkins Gallaudet and went to Europe to study the methods of teaching the blind. But he found most European schools to be "beacons to warn rather than lights to guide." Rather than offering a serious education, most of them were mere workshops where the blind spun thread, knitted, and mended clothing. He felt that the schools were overly regimented and showed little concern for their students' individuality. Above all, he thought the schools smothered their students with pity and condescension, doing little to teach the blind self-reliance. In sharp contrast, the primary goal of his school was to teach blind children "to rely with confidence upon their own resources, to believe themselves possessed of the means of filling useful and active spheres in society." His institution's motto became "Obstacles are a thing to be overcome."

Howe's experiences in opening his school quickly became the stuff of legend. He found his first two students, Abby and Sophia Carter, by accident, when he stopped at a tollhouse near Andover, Massachusetts. He later wrote—with an astonishing lack of humility—that they were "brought providentially to meet messengers sent of God to deliver them out of darkness." To better understand what it was like to be blind, the hero of the Greek revolution frequently blindfolded himself. After less than six months, his school was out of funds; in 1833, he staged a public exhibition of his students before the Massachusetts state legislature, which responded by granting the school a $6,000 annual appropriation.

Finding that employers refused to hire the blind and that many families provided inadequate care for blind adults, he established in 1840 the nation's first "sheltered workshop" for the blind. "In this department the blind feel perfectly independent," he wrote in the workshop's 1841 report, "being assured of the bread they eat; and if any surplus remains to them, it is far more prized than would be ten times the amount of alms."

The single greatest problem facing Howe and other educators was how to teach the blind to read and write. Determined "to preserve the strictest analogy between the means of educating the blind and the sighted," Haüy used paper printed with raised letters. Other educators experimented with systems of knotted strings and letters carved on wood or metal blocks. Howe initially taught students the alphabet by pasting string in the shape of letters on pieces of cardboard. Later, he devised a system known as Boston Line Type, consisting of simplified angular versions of roman letters.

Educators would later find all these methods to be mistaken. Linear type proved to be unsatisfactory for the blind, since the human fingertip could not easily make out the letters. A truly effective language of the fingers was devised by Louis Braille, a student at the National Institution for the Blind in Paris, in 1834, but this system was not widely adopted before the second half of the nineteenth century. Instead of using the ordinary alphabet, Braille's new alphabet consisted of raised dots arranged in a six-dot "cell" (three dots high and two dots across).

In 1866, at a ceremony marking the laying of the cornerstone of the New York State Institution for the Blind at Batavia, Howe reflected upon his experience and expressed deep misgivings about asylums for the blind. Looking back, he wondered whether residential institutions had done blind people a disservice by separating the sightless from the seeing: "All great establishments in the nature of boarding schools, where the sexes must be separated; where there must be boarding in common, and sleeping in congregate dormitories; where there must be routine, and formality, and restraint, and repression of individuality; where the charms and refining influences of the true family relation cannot be had—all such institutions are unnatural, undesirable, and very liable to abuse. We should have as few of them as is possible, and those few should be kept as small as possible."

It is a great irony that Samuel Gridley Howe, the individual most responsible for establishing residential schools for the blind, very much wanted to discourage the development of separate communities for them. By the end of his life, he was convinced that when the disabled lived together, isolated in their own asylums, their infirmities were reinforced and they became less able to function in ordinary society. He lamented in an undated draft of an essay from the 1850s, "The more they become like each other and the more unlike ordinary persons—hence the less fitted for ordinary society." Accordingly, he rejected any applicants who could be taught in public schools, educated males and females in separate cottages, and refused to hold reunions of Perkins graduates, fearing that they might marry each other.

The Struggle for Public Schools

The early nineteenth century, as we have seen, was a key era of institution building, when many of modern society's caretaker institutions—poorhouses, penitentiaries, reformatories, mental hospitals, and residential schools for the blind and the deaf—were created. Despite many differences, these institutions shared certain characteristics. They were designed to care for the afflicted, shelter the indigent, and rehabilitate the criminal, by placing them in a benevolent and therapeutic environment where all would learn "order, regularity, industry, and temperance." Antebellum reformers, convinced that the nation faced grave perils from the spread of social disorder, the breakdown of family discipline, and the huge number of foreign immigrants, yet confident in the shaping power of environment, looked to these institutions, in the words of French observers Alexis de Tocqueville and Gustave Auguste de Beaumont, as "the remedy for all the evils of society."

The most important of the new specialized antebellum asylums was the common school, the public elementary school that served all children who lived in the surrounding area. By the second half of the nineteenth century, no other nation spent more on public education than the United States. And no other nation invested public education with higher responsibilities: to promote individual opportunity; to prevent a hardening of class lines; to shape character and compensate for neglectful parents; to create a unified civic culture transcending class, ethnic, regional, or sectarian identification; and to instill the values and skills necessary in a rapidly changing society: basic literacy, punctuality, obedience, and self-discipline. Educational reformer Horace Mann summed up the millennial expectations many antebellum Americans assigned to public schools. In the introduction to the *Common School Journal* in 1841, he said: "The common school is the greatest discovery ever made by man. . . . Other social organizations are curative and remedial; this is a preventive and an antidote. . . . Let the Common School be expanded to its capabilities . . . and nine tenths of the crimes in the penal code would become obsolete; the long catalogue of human ills would be abridged."

Of all the ideas advanced by antebellum reformers, none was more radical than the principle that all American children, of whatever social rank, should be educated to their fullest capacity and at public expense. From the early days of settlement, Americans have attached special importance to education. During the seventeenth century, the New England Puritans required every town to establish a grammar school to ensure that all young men would be able to read the Bible (a requirement later repealed). In the late eighteenth century, Thomas Jefferson popularized the ideas that a democratic republic required an enlightened and educated citizenry and that government had a duty to promote education in order to foster a meritocracy based on talent and ability. The revolutionary generation proposed elaborate schemes for federal aid to education and for a national university; little came of these plans. It was up to early-nineteenth-century educational reformers to extend these ideas and struggle to make universal public education a reality.

The campaign for public schools has been the subject of intense historical controversy. An earlier generation of educational historians treated the creation of public school systems as one of the greatest achievements of American history. In the face of bitter opposition, the United States became the first nation in the world (with the qualified exceptions of Prussia and the Netherlands) to establish systems of universal, free, compulsory, tax-supported, nonsectarian public education.

More recently, revisionist scholars have charged that much of the impetus for public schooling stemmed from fear of the lower classes, especially immigrants, and they claim that a primary goal of educational reformers was to melt down ethnic identification and condition children to accept their place in the social order. Far from being vehicles of social equality and economic opportunity, public schools served the needs of an emerging capitalist economy, enhancing workers' productive skills but also defusing discontent and becoming instruments of indoctrination and social control. Instead of promoting equality of opportunity, schools produced a sense of inadequacy and self-contempt in many poorer children. Schools, according to this revisionist point of view, had a "hidden curriculum," rewarding docility, passivity, obedience, and punctuality and penalizing creativity and individuality. Revisionists, denying that public schools were a potent force for social or economic equality, also charge that the educational system was from its inception highly unequal and failed to meet the needs of Catholics, immigrants, blacks, and women.

Not surprisingly, there is truth in both points of view. From their beginnings in the early 1830s, public schools were intended to serve a variety of ideological functions: a mechanism for shaping character, an antidote to social dissolution, a means of overcoming class lines, and a vehicle for integrating "uncouth and dangerous" elements into the fabric of American life. But contrary to what some revisionists have suggested, the major ideological goals of public schools were to produce an enlightened citizenry and to spread basic literacy and a knowledge of science and technology. Moreover, public schools were not the product of a monolithic conspiracy among reformers, businessmen, and clergy. In fact, the movement for public schools was highly diffuse and was the result of many local efforts.

The campaign for public schools began in earnest in the 1820s, when religiously motivated reformers in the Northeast advocated public education as an answer to poverty, crime, and deepening social divisions. Convinced that human character was capable of being shaped for good or evil, reformers believed that in a republic it was essential that one institution mold character in the proper direction. Schools would preserve social harmony and guarantee freedom by disciplining and controlling the young.

In a famous essay entitled "A Plea for the West" (1835), Lyman Beecher, the prominent Congregationalist minister whose daughter, Harriet Beecher Stowe, wrote *Uncle Tom's Cabin,* made the case for public schooling in particularly vivid terms: "We must educate, we must educate, or we must perish by our own prosperity. If we do not, short from the cradle to the grave will be our race. If in our haste to be rich and mighty, we outrun our literary and religious institutions, they will never overtake us." Afraid that growth and expansion, if unchecked and so not balanced by virtue, would result in anarchy, Beecher saw public schooling as the only antidote to social disorganization. It is no accident that Massachusetts, the last state to disestablish churches, was the first to construct an educational establishment. Public schools from the start were designed to assume the ordering and stabilizing role of churches. Indeed, many European societies—including Prussia and the

Netherlands—adopted public schools shortly after disestablishing churches. In each of these countries, the school was supposed to mold common loyalties and values in the interest of national unity.

Proponents of public schools tended to exaggerate the weakness of American education before their reforms. At the beginning of the nineteenth century, the United States had the highest literacy rate in the world: approximately three-quarters of all adult men and women could write their own name. In part, this reflected a variety of informal ways of educating children. Prior to the 1840s, apprenticeship was a major form of education. Many youngsters learned to read and write in dame schools, in which a woman would take a number of girls and boys into her own home. But even before the advent of the common school, formal schooling was already widespread. Supplementing the apprenticeship were charity schools for the poor, church schools, and private academies for the more affluent. It now appears that the proportion of young people being schooled at the beginning of the nineteenth century, prior to the creation of public schools, was roughly comparable to the proportion in school at mid-century.

This does not mean that school reform was unnecessary. In many ways, the early informal system of education was grossly inadequate. Many dame schools were essentially day-care centers, which took in very young children (often only two or three years of age) so mothers could work. Many private academies admitted pupils regardless of age, mixing young children with people in their twenties. A single classroom might contain as many as eighty pupils. These early classrooms were extremely ill equipped; students brought whatever textbooks their parents had at home, and most learning amounted to rote memorization and monotonous repetition of facts. School buildings were often unpainted, overcrowded, and lacked blackboards, maps, desks, windows, playgrounds, or even outhouses. In addition, the opportunity to attend school was circumscribed. Even "free" schools often required payment of tuition. And many schools required entering students to be literate, barring students whose parents had not taught them to read.

Over time, the situation was getting worse, a result of urban growth, an influx of immigrants, the spread of poverty, and the increasing segregation of neighborhoods by class. The astounding growth of cities in the Northeast made middle-class citizens suddenly aware of gangs of juvenile delinquents, vagrant children, and illiteracy and degradation among the urban poor. At first, many evangelical reformers championed Sunday schools as a way "to reclaim the vicious, to instruct the ignorant, to secure the observance of the Sabbath . . . and to raise the standard of morals among the lower classes of society." By the mid-1820s, however, increasing immigration and mounting social disorder heightened the pressures for public schooling. In 1837, Michigan's first superintendent of public instruction, John D. Pierce, asked rhetorically, "How is this political fabric to be preserved?" His answer: "Only by the general diffusion of knowledge. Children of every name and age must be taught the qualifications and duties of American citizens, and learn in early life the art of self-control—they must be educated."

Yet support for public education was not confined to social conservatives. During the late 1820s, workingmen's parties, especially in New York and Philadelphia, demanded free, tax-supported public schools to counteract a trend toward hardening class lines. Public schools were necessary to ensure equality of opportunity and guarantee that the children of artisans and mechanics shared the same advantages as the children of the rich. "The original element of despotism is a monopoly of talent," declared the Philadelphia Working Men's Party in 1830, "which consigns the multitude to comparative ignorance, and secures the balance of knowledge on the side of the rich and the rulers."

In part, the sudden eruption of working-class agitation for public schools was a response to unemployment and changes in patterns of work. Skilled crafts, previously performed by artisans, were subcontracted out to less expensive unskilled laborers, often to low-paid unskilled children or adolescents. Working-class leaders viewed public schools as a way to promote upward mobility and to remove a source of economic competition.

But public schools also faced staunch resistance. Many local communities opposed the creation of state-directed bureaucracies that would impose common standards and a common curriculum. The devoutly religious were against nondenominational schools. Questions of school finance also stirred controversy. Many believed that the costs of education should be borne exclusively by the parents of children attending school. And many lower-income families could not afford to let their children go to school. Many working-class families received 20 percent or more of their income from children under the age of fifteen; those earnings were essential to the family's survival.

Reliance on female teachers allowed towns to expand schooling without a proportionate increase in spending, because women received half or one-third the wages of male schoolteachers. At first many local school boards feared that female teachers would be unable to discipline rowdy schoolchildren (in Massachusetts in 1844, during a single term, ninety schools were closed following disruptions by rebellious pupils; more than three hundred schools were "broken up" by students during the preceding five years). But local communities came increasingly to believe that women were actually more effective in disciplining schoolchildren. As a woman who taught during the 1840s noted, a male student "who would be constantly plotting mischief against a schoolmaster . . . becomes mild and gentle, considerate and well behaved towards a little woman, simply because she is a little woman, whose gentle voice and lady-like manners have fascinated him." By the Civil War, teaching school had become a predominantly female profession and an increasingly common experience for young, native-born women. An estimated one-quarter of all white Massachusetts-born women served as teachers for two or three years.

In operation, antebellum public common schools tended to follow highly regimented schedules. Individual classrooms contained as many as fifty or sixty students, and despite calls for improved teaching methods that would tap students' imagination and draw out their potentialities, teachers continued to rely on rote memorization, recitation, and strict discipline. Innovations in pedagogy were largely left to private schools.

The nation's leading exponent of public schools was Horace Mann (1796–1859). Like many other Whiggish New England reformers of his generation, he had wrestled as a youth with intense fears of sin and damnation and then had decisively rejected Calvinist orthodoxy and converted to Unitarianism. He nevertheless retained an intense personal piety and an evangelical sense of moral responsibility. Throughout his life he opposed liquor, profanity, and even ballet dancing as sinful. Educated at Brown University and trained as an attorney, he found no satisfaction in the law and sought a higher calling: the education of children. He explained his motivation in a letter to a friend in 1837: "Having found the present generation composed of materials almost unmalleable, I am about transferring my efforts to the next. Men are cast-iron, but children are wax." As a member of the Massachusetts state senate, Mann took the lead in establishing a state board of education and then, following his wife's death, resigned his seat to become board secretary in 1837.

During his twelve years as secretary of the Massachusetts Board of Education, Mann considered himself a "circuit rider to the next generation," waging successful campaigns to double state expenditures on education, establish a state-supported teachers' college, improve the curriculum and lengthen the school year, and assign students to grades according to their age and ability. He was also partially successful in curtailing the use of the rod to discipline students. His goals were to expand educational opportunity, to make school curricula more uniform and teaching more professional, and to place control of educational policy more firmly in the hands of a centralized state board of education.

Today, it is difficult to appreciate the radicalism of many of Mann's ideas. He was attacked as an atheist for opposing formal religious instruction in schools (although he did allow teachers to read from the Bible without additional comment). His proposals for school taxes also were bitterly denounced. But his argument—that property holders have an obligation to succeeding generations—ultimately prevailed. In 1852, three years after Mann left office to take a seat in the U.S. House of Representatives, Massachusetts adopted the first statewide compulsory school attendance law.

Before the Civil War, educational reform made its greatest headway in the Northeast and the Midwest. In the South, education remained largely confined to private academies and informal "old-field" schools. Following the war, Horace Mann's vision—a centralized public school system with a prescribed curriculum, graded classes, licensed teachers, more humane methods of instruction, and a hierarchical administration—became the model for American public education across the country. Today, Americans are far less sanguine than Mann about the effectiveness of public schooling, and few share his confidence that if "the money and talent employed" on armies were "expended on education . . . [it] would bring on the millennium at once" (as he wrote in a letter in 1847). Nevertheless, Americans still assign public schools the task of solving their most pressing and deep-seated social problems: persistent poverty, racial and ethnic separation, and parental neglect.

Obstacles to Education

Prior to the Civil War, educational opportunities for women and nonwhites were severely restricted. Most cities specifically excluded blacks from the public schools; New York and Boston, for example, consigned black children to inferior segregated schools. In 1849, municipalities in New York requested just $396 from the state government to educate eleven thousand African American children. The opponents of black education were quite open about their reasoning. In 1828, the Connecticut Colonization Society denounced equal educational opportunities for African Americans on the ground that that would raise expectations for social equality: "Educate him and you have added little or nothing to his happiness—you have unfitted him for the society and sympathies of his degraded kindred, and yet you have not procured for him . . . admission into the society and sympathy of white men."

In 1832, Prudence Crandall, a Quaker schoolteacher in Canterbury, Connecticut, sparked a major controversy by admitting Sarah Harris, the daughter of a free black farmer, into her school. After white parents withdrew their children from the school, Crandall tried to turn it into an institution for the education of free blacks. Hostile neighbors broke the school's windows, contaminated its well with manure, and denied students seats on stagecoaches and pews in church. In 1833, after the state adopted a law making it a crime to teach black students who were not residents of Connecticut, state authorities arrested Crandall. She was tried twice, convicted, and jailed. After her release, a local mob attacked Crandall's school building with crowbars and attempted to burn the structure. It never opened again.

Despite persistent discrimination, no group exhibited a stronger faith in the power of education to break down social barriers and promote social advancement than African Americans. A "petition of Sundry Colored Persons" (1847) in Boston denounced separate schools in terms that would be used to condemn the segregated schools of the post–Civil War South: "All experienced teachers know that where a small and despised class are . . . confined to separate schools, few or none interest themselves about the schools—neglect ensues, abuses creep in, the standard of scholarship degenerates, and the teachers and the scholars are soon considered . . . an inferior class." Not until 1855 did Massachusetts become the first state to admit students to public schools irrespective of "race, color, or religious opinions."

Women also experienced discrimination in opportunities for education. In colonial New England, grammar schools were restricted to boys only. Many girls learned to read and write at home, in dame schools, or in summer schools. Still, female literacy rates remained relatively low. In 1795, when 90 percent of New England men were able to sign wills, only about 45 percent of women were able to do so. But female educational opportunities and literacy rates increased rapidly after the American Revolution, reflecting the notion that mothers would play a critical role in shaping the new republic's "manners and character." After 1800, girls began to be admitted to the winter terms of rural district schools and urban grammar schools.

Prior to 1810, women were largely confined to learning handicrafts and basic reading and writing. New opportunities arose with the establishment of separate female academies and seminaries for the affluent. Emma Hart Willard opened one of the first academies offering an advanced education to women in Middlebury, Vermont, in 1814. Later, in the Troy Female Seminary, which opened in New York in 1821, Willard offered instruction in mathematics, history, geography, and physics to women preparing to become teachers. Beginning in the 1820s and accelerating in the 1840s, a growing number of cities opened separate public high schools for girls to prepare as teachers in elementary schools. During the 1850s, the high costs of operating sex-segregated high schools led many cities to set up the first coeducational high schools.

Catholics, too, suffered discrimination in the public schools. Many schools took their daily Bible readings from the King James version and used textbooks that described Protestant nations as "more advanced in knowledge" and Catholic countries as tending "toward degeneracy and ruin." In 1828, the Catholic bishop of Boston, Benedict Fenwick, expressed Catholic opposition to the Protestant character of public school textbooks in pointed terms: "All the children educated in the common schools of the country are obliged to use books . . . by which their minds are poisoned . . . from their infancy." Some of the bitterest battles over Catholic requests for state funding of Catholic schools erupted in New York State. After these demands were turned down, Catholics decided to establish separate parochial schools in New York City so children could receive a religious education as well as training in the arts and sciences.

Like many Catholics, the German Lutherans and Dutch Calvinists sought to maintain their own schools as a way of preserving their culture and traditions from contamination. In Ohio, German speakers actually succeeded in persuading the state legislature to require English- and German-language schools whenever seventy-five taxpayers demanded it.

Changes in Higher Education

At the beginning of the nineteenth century, Harvard, the nation's most famous college, graduated just thirty-nine men a year, no more than it had graduated in 1720. The entire undergraduate faculty consisted of the college president, a professor of theology, a professor of mathematics, a professor of Hebrew, and four tutors. And Harvard was not at all atypical. Yale's students studied Greek based on the works of Homer, Hesiod, Sophocles, and Euripides; Latin out of the works of Cicero and Horace; and arithmetic, algebra, and geometry based on the works of Euclid. Noah Webster, author of the nation's first dictionary, admitted grudgingly: "Our learning is superficial in shameful degree . . . our colleges are disgracefully destitute of books and philosophical apparatus."

At the end of the American Revolution, the nation had thirteen colleges. Most offered narrow training in the classics designed to prepare students for the ministry. In many ways, these colleges were little more than glorified high schools. Students enrolled at very young ages, often as early as the age of twelve. During the 1820s and 1830s, colleges raised the age of admission and broadened entrance requirements. In an effort to adjust to the "spirits and wants of the age," Yale College recommended in its "Reports on the Course of Instruction" (1830) that colleges broaden their curricula to include the study of history, literature, geography, modern languages, and the sciences; raise the entrance age; and increase the requirements on students.

During the first half of the nineteenth century, the number of institutions of higher learning rapidly expanded. In 1850, the country had 119 colleges, 44 theological seminaries, 36 medical schools, and 16 law schools. Most new colleges were founded by various religious denominations. While most new colleges, particularly in the South and the West, were church-affiliated, several states, including Georgia, Tennessee, Virginia, and Michigan, established state universities. Prior to the Civil War, sixteen states provided some financial support to higher education, and in New York City by the 1850s, an education, from elementary school to college, was available tuition free.

A few institutions of higher education opened their doors to blacks and women. In 1833, Oberlin College became the nation's first coeducational college, and four years later, Mary Lyon established the first women's college, Mount Holyoke, to train teachers and missionaries. A number of western state universities also admitted women. In addition, three colleges for blacks were founded before the Civil War, and Oberlin, Harvard, Bowdoin, and Dartmouth, among others, admitted small numbers of black students.

A Movement Away from Institutionalization

In 1853, Charles Loring Brace (1826–90), founder of the New York Children's Aid Society, began a far-reaching program to address the problem of juvenile delinquency. Convinced that the causes were parental neglect and a morally contaminated environment, he established lodging houses and reading rooms for homeless and vagrant youths and set up industrial missions, where children (mainly young girls) received free meals and learned how to make clothes. Most remarkably, the Yale-educated charity worker (drawing upon the example of a private charity in Boston) launched an ambitious program to place thousands of slum children on western farms. In the view of the Children's Aid Society, "The best of all Asylums for the outcast child is the farmer's home." Between 1853 and 1929, the society sent nearly one hundred thousand neglected, impoverished, homeless, and delinquent children on orphan trains to rural foster and adoptive families.

Brace viewed the placement of slum children on family farms as an economical and healthy alternative to institutional confinement. In retrospect, however, the orphan-train idea seems at least as open to criticism as the institutions that it partially replaced. Brace was convinced that the thousands of children he sent westward were neglected; in fact, however, most were neither orphaned nor abandoned. Roughly half had at least one parent alive, and were sometimes taken from their families without the knowledge or consent of their parents. Many were the children of Roman Catholic immigrants who, Brace thought, could be saved only by removal from parental influence. However repugnant the orphan train idea may seem to us today, many reformers shared Brace's view that it offered a positive substitute for institutional placement.

By the 1850s, a growing number of humanitarian reformers had begun to question the reformative and curative powers of asylums. Doubting the desirability of special institutions for criminals and disabled persons, Charles Loring Brace and others considered the family the best "reformatory institution." Samuel Gridley Howe, expressing his doubts about the efficacy of asylums for the blind, began to advocate community and family-based care. Enoch C. Wines and Theodore Dwight, two leading prison reformers, condemned expenditures on penitentiaries as wasteful and counterproductive, and they favored the commutation of prison sentences on grounds of good behavior, the establishment of a new system of conditional release, probation, and supervised parole, and the creation of systems providing counseling and employment to facilitate the reentry of prisoners into the community.

Increasingly aware of their institutions' deficiencies and the limited and damaging effects of incarceration, humanitarian reformers experimented with new methods and novel systems of organization. Many of the new reform schools of the 1850s and 1860s were organized into small "families" of forty or fewer children, occupying separate cottages. Many state mental hospitals also adopted the "family" or "cottage" system at mid-century. And yet, despite these efforts at reform, large, bureaucratically organized asylums, orphanages, reform schools, and prisons endured. More than a century and a half later, many of these institutions still survive. As Samuel Gridley Howe bluntly observed in the annual report of the Massachusetts Board of State Charities in 1865: "Institutions . . . so strongly built, so richly endowed . . . cannot be got rid of . . . easily."

Chapter 5

Breaking the Bonds of Corrupt Custom

Following the end of the Napoleonic Wars in Europe and the War of 1812, members of the Massachusetts Peace Society launched an investigation of the number of combatants killed in these conflicts. In 1817, they issued a report that concluded that 5,060,000 had died in the fighting. Then the group estimated the total number of people killed in warfare since the world's creation. It reported that "3,346,000,000 of human beings had been sacrificed to the idol of war."

The year 1815 brought to an end more than a quarter century of war and revolution in the Western world and ushered in a new era of economic growth and pressure for reform. In the United States, that year marked the emergence of the first secular societies in history committed to world peace. Condemning war as a violation of Christian ethics and a barbarous anachronism, peace reformers called for the abolition of war and the arbitration of international disputes. By 1821, reformers founded more than fifty peace societies, and in 1828, local and state organizations joined together to form the American Peace Society.

In its early years, the peace movement embraced a wide range of attitudes toward war, ranging from absolute pacifism to an acceptance of the right to self-defense. In general, the outlook then was gradualist and meliorist, an attitude typified by a report issued by the New York Peace Society in 1818. It stated that the society indulged in "no extravagant and fanciful expectations of a sudden and perfect attainment of" of world peace, since "rooted prejudices and violent passions" could only slowly "be supplanted and subdued." Committed to moral suasion, peace societies distributed petitions, sponsored essay contests, and lobbied for abolition of compulsory militia drills.

During the 1830s, however, a more radical current of pacifism, known as "nonresistance," surfaced, especially among radical opponents of slavery. Nonresistants not only condemned all war as contrary to the gospel of Christ, they renounced capital punishment, prisons, and lawsuits on the grounds that true Christians must "forgive every injury and insult, without attempting . . . physical force or penal enactments," as William Lloyd Garrison maintained in 1835. In 1838, nonresistants broke away from the American Peace Society to form the New England Non-Resistance Society.

Peace advocates staged international congresses in London, Brussels, and Frankfort in the 1840s and early 1850s, but during the 1850s the movement waned. Many abandoned the New Testament ethic of love and turned to acceptance of violence as the only way to abolish slavery. The movement's critics, such as the Reverend A. H. Quinn of Massachusetts in 1866, denounced its commitment to nonviolence as "humbug" and "a living lie." The London Peace Society went even further in 1861, charging nonresistants with "hounding on their countrymen to mutual slaughter." With the coming of the Civil War, the peace movement drifted from public view. But in the 1870s and 1880s, a revitalized peace movement sponsored international congresses, formulated a code of international law, and devised plans for an international court, an international arbitrary system, and a league of nations. Although critics dismissed the movement as visionary, in fact many of its proposals were adopted after World War I.

The antebellum peace movement illustrates in vivid terms the idealism and radical ferment of the pre–Civil War era—when reformers gave new life to the nation's moral ideals by pressing for the abolition of slavery, an end to sexual discrimination, and creation of a more just social order. Striving to live up to Christ's teachings in the Sermon on the Mount, radical reformers laid bare the compromises and contradictions in American society.

Although the reform impulse seemed to fade from public view during the Civil War, reformers never abandoned their causes and would remain a powerful force in American life, agitating for racial equality, woman suffrage, penal reform, and other reforms. Indeed, the very success of their efforts would provoke a conservative reaction in the late nineteenth century—counterreformers would seek to reverse many of their accomplishments by restoring capital punishment in many states, weakening married women's property rights, restricting divorce, and criminalizing abortion.

During the 1830s, a new phase of reform emerged—radical reform—which sought to regenerate society by outlawing war, eradicating slavery, eliminating racial and sexual discrimination, and creating utopian communities to serve as models for a better world. These reformers were radical perfectionists who denied the validity of all laws and institutions that conflicted with the higher law of Christian conscience. Even as more conservative evangelicals sought to rescue American society from godlessness, anarchy, and mobocracy through revivals and organized benevolence, radical reformers sought to liberate individuals from the coercive bonds of slavery, inequality, and corrupt custom.

The Growth of Antislavery Sentiment

The growth of antislavery sentiment stands out as one of the most dramatic changes in moral values in history. As late as the 1750s, no church had discouraged its members from owning or trading in slaves. The governments of Britain, France, Denmark, Holland, Portugal, and Spain openly participated in the slave trade. Slaves could be found in each of the thirteen American colonies, and prior to the American Revolution, only Georgia had sought to prohibit slavery.

Within half a century, however, protests against the institution of slavery had become widespread. By 1804, nine states north of Maryland and Delaware had either emancipated their slaves or adopted gradual-emancipation schemes. Both the United States and Britain in 1807 outlawed the African slave trade. In 1833, Britain emancipated 780,000 slaves in the British West Indies, and in 1848, France and Denmark freed the slaves in their New World colonies.

In the early nineteenth century, the emancipation of slaves in the northern states and the prohibition of the African slave trade generated optimism that slavery was on the road to extinction. Congress in 1787 barred slavery from the Old Northwest, the region north of the Ohio River. Even in the South, slavery appeared to be a dying institution. In Maryland and Virginia, many planters were replacing tobacco, a crop grown by means of slave labor, with wheat and corn, which were not. Leading southerners, including Thomas Jefferson, denounced slavery as a source of debt, economic stagnation, and moral dissipation. A French traveler reported that people throughout the South "are constantly talking of abolishing slavery, of contriving some other means of cultivating their estates." The number of slaves freed by their masters rose dramatically in the upper South during the 1780s and 1790s, and more antislavery societies were formed in the South than in the North. At the present rate of progress, predicted Jonathan Edwards Jr. in 1791, within fifty years it will "be as shameful for a man to hold a Negro slave, as to be guilty of common robbery or theft."

By the early 1830s, however, the development of the Cotton Kingdom and increasingly harsh discrimination in the North proved that slavery was not on the road to extinction. Despite the end of the legal slave trade, the slave population had continued to grow, climbing from 1.5 million in 1820 to more than 2 million a decade later.

The Colonization Movement

A major impediment to emancipation was the widespread belief that blacks and whites could not coexist equally in the United States and that any plan for emancipation required separation of the races. The ideology of the American Revolution underscored the contradiction between slavery and liberty. But many leading members of the revolutionary generation held deeply ambivalent attitudes toward slavery and race. Thomas Jefferson, for example, abhorred slavery and believed that "all men are created equal" in their common possession of a moral sense. Simultaneously, however, he expressed grave doubts about the intellectual equality of the races and felt paralyzed by his fears of racial conflict, stating that we have "the wolf by the ears, we can neither hold on nor let go." Such ambivalence contributed to a spate of proposals for gradual emancipation and for deportation of black Americans.

The first proposal to send African Americans to Africa was advanced as early as 1714. Following the American Revolution, such proposals multiplied. A number of blacks supported overseas colonization in the belief that it provided the only alternative to continued degradation and discrimination. During the 1780s, African Americans in Boston (including Prince Hall, founder of the African Masonic Lodge), in Providence, and in Philadelphia—in alliance with white reformers such as British abolitionist Granville Sharp and American abolitionist Samuel Hopkins of Newport, Rhode Island—developed plans for emigration and African colonization as a way of combating racial prejudice and extending freedom and Christianity to Africa.

Between 1810 and 1820, Paul Cuffe (1759–1817), the son of a former slave and an Indian woman, led America's first experiment in colonization. In 1815,

Cuffe, a Massachusetts Quaker sea captain and shipowner, transported thirty-eight free blacks (eighteen adults and twenty children) to Sierra Leone, a state established by the British on the western coast of Africa. Cuffe hoped to carry Christ's word to Africa and establish ongoing trade between the United States and Africa. He devoted thousands of his own dollars to the cause of colonization.

In 1816, a group of prominent ministers and politicians formed the American Colonization Society to resettle free blacks in West Africa, encourage planters to voluntarily emancipate their slaves, and create a group of black missionaries to spread Christianity in Africa. The colonization society quickly attracted the support of the nation's major political figures, including Thomas Jefferson, James Madison, James Monroe, and John Marshall.

To encourage emigration, the colonization society helped establish Liberia in 1820, a colony and later a country, south of Sierra Leone. During the 1820s, Congress and a dozen state legislatures endorsed the society's activities, and the federal government funded the transportation of free blacks to Liberia. By 1830, the society had brought 1,420 free blacks to Liberia, including Daniel Coker, a cofounder of Philadelphia's African Methodist Episcopal church, and John Brown Russwurm, editor of *Freedom's Journal,* the first black newspaper in the United States.

Many black leaders, such as James Forten and Richard Allen of Philadelphia, who had sympathized with Cuffe's efforts abandoned their support for African colonization, which they now regarded as a program for ridding the country of its growing free black population. A number of African American leaders, including Allen, Forten, and Samuel E. Cornish, began to support emigration to Haiti, the only independent black republic in the Western Hemisphere. In 1824 and 1825, approximately six thousand African Americans migrated to Haiti, but quickly departed. Within a dozen years, no black Americans remained there. Other African Americans favored emigration to Canada.

Most African Americans rejected the very notion of colonization. Proud of being Americans, twenty-five hundred black Philadelphians banded together during the War of 1812 to defend their city from a threatened British invasion. In 1817, a convention held in Philadelphia adopted resolutions bitterly denouncing colonization as a policy "little more merciful than death": "Whereas our ancestors (not of choice) were the first successful cultivators of the wilds of America, we their descendants feel ourselves entitled to participate in the blessings of her luxuriant soil. . . . We never will separate ourselves voluntarily from the slave population in this country."

By the late 1820s, it was apparent that overseas colonization was a wholly impractical solution to slavery. Each year, the nation's slave population grew by roughly fifty thousand. But in 1830, the colonization society persuaded just 259 free blacks to migrate to Liberia.

Early Antislavery Efforts

In the face of the widespread consensus in favor of colonization, many early opponents of slavery confined their efforts to lobbying for state emancipation acts and measures to prevent the kidnapping and sale of free blacks. In late-eighteenth-century New York, leading citizens, including John Jay and Alexander Hamilton, formed the New York Manumission Society. Even though many of its members were paternalistic slaveholding Federalists, the society actively sought to prevent the exportation of slaves from New York to the South and provided legal protection for New York's African Americans.

Perhaps the most surprising antislavery agitation took place in the South. During the late eighteenth century, the American South was unique among slave societies in its openness to antislavery ideas. In Maryland and North Carolina, Quakers freed more than fifteen hundred slaves and sent them out of state. Scattered Presbyterian, Baptist, and Methodist ministers and advisory committees condemned slavery as a sin "contrary to the word of God." Quakers and Moravians in Kentucky and Tennessee played a particularly active role in the southern antislavery movement. One southern abolitionist estimated that there were 106 antislavery societies in the South in 1827, with 5,150 members, compared to just 24 societies in the North, with 1,475 members.

By 1830, however, southern agitation against slavery had largely ceased. Presbyterian, Baptist, and Methodist sects that had expressed opposition to slavery modified their antislavery beliefs. Quakers and Unitarians who were strongly antagonistic to slavery emigrated. By the second decade of the century, southern antislavery sentiment was confined to Kentucky, the Piedmont counties of North Carolina, and the mountains in eastern Tennessee.

The region's leading antislavery advocate was Benjamin Lundy, the Quaker editor of the antislavery newspaper, *Genius of Universal Emancipation,* who, as early as 1821, called for the eradication of slavery and an end to racial prejudice. But even before the decade had ended, Lundy himself had retreated to Baltimore.

Southern authorities stifled public debate. Southern state legislatures adopted a series of laws suppressing criticism of the institution. In 1830, Louisiana made it a crime to state anything that might produce discontent or subordination among free blacks. Six years later, Virginia made it a felony for any citizen to deny the legality of slavery.

The silent pressure of public opinion limited open discussion of the slavery question. College presidents or professors suspected of opposing slavery lost their jobs. Mobs attacked editors who dared to print articles critical of slavery. One Richmond, Virginia, editor fought eight duels in two years. In Parkville, Missouri, and Lexington, Kentucky, crowds dismantled the printing presses of antislavery newspapers. The South erected an "iron curtain" against the invasion of antislavery propaganda.

Only once, in the wake of Nat Turner's famous slave insurrection in 1831, did a southern state openly debate the possibility of ending slavery. This occurred in the Virginia legislature in January and February 1832, but the session ended with the defeat of proposals to abolish slavery, compensate slave owners, and expel all African Americans from the state.

James G. Birney was one of many southerners to discover the futility of working for slave emancipation in the South. Birney was born into a wealthy Kentucky slaveholding family and, like many members of the South's slave-owning elite, was educated at Princeton. After graduation, he moved to Huntsville, Alabama, where he practiced law and operated a cotton plantation. In Huntsville, he developed qualms about slavery and came to work as an agent for the American Colonization Society. Soon his doubts had grown into an active hatred of slavery. He returned to Kentucky, emancipated his slaves, and in 1835 organized the Kentucky Anti-Slavery Society.

In Kentucky, Birney quickly discovered that public opinion vehemently opposed antislavery. A committee of leading citizens in Danville informed him that they would not permit him to establish an antislavery newspaper in the city. When Birney announced that he would go through with his plans anyway, the committee bought out the paper's printer and the town's post-master announced that he would refuse to deliver the newspaper. In a final bid to publish his paper, Birney moved across the Ohio River to Cincinnati, but a mob destroyed his press while the city's mayor watched.

The Emergence of Immediatism

By 1830, it was clear that the nation had reached a dead end on the issues of slavery and race. Colonization was a failure: the removal of a few hundred free blacks to Liberia each year did nothing to put slavery on the path to extinction. In fact, slavery was rapidly expanding. During the 1820s, the number of slaves increased by half a million. A cotton boom had extended slavery into the Old Southwest: western Georgia, Alabama, Mississippi, Louisiana, and Texas.

No single fact better underlined the nation's racial problems than the deteriorating status of free blacks. During the late eighteenth century and the early decades of the nineteenth, free blacks were the most rapidly growing segment of the nation's population, increasing by 82 percent between 1790 and 1800, by 72 percent between 1800 and 1810—the total was 319,000 in 1830. After the Revolution, thousands of slaves were freed, and countless others emancipated themselves by running away. In Louisiana, a large free black Creole population had emerged under Spanish and French rule, and in South Carolina a Creole population had arrived from Barbados. The number of free blacks in the Deep South increased rapidly with the arrival of thousands of light-colored refugees from the revolt in Haiti.

Although free blacks composed no more than 3.8 percent of the population of any northern state, they faced growing legal, economic, and social discrimination. During the antebellum era, free blacks were prohibited from serving in state militias, barred from delivering the mail, denied access to hotels and restaurants, and relegated to segregated schools, separate jails and cemeteries, and "nigger pews" in white churches. On trains, they were confined in pens, like livestock. Most states forbade interracial marriage, prohibited blacks from testifying against whites in court, and all but five states—New Hampshire, Maine, Massachusetts, New York, and Vermont—denied them the right to vote.

Free blacks were the poorest, most downtrodden free laborers in the North. Typically, they lived in tenements, sheds, and stables. An English visitor named George G. Foster described the typical black dwelling in Philadelphia in 1847 as "a desolate pen," six feet by six feet square, without windows, beds, or furniture, possessing a leaky roof and a floor so low in the ground "that more or less water comes in on them from the yard in rainy weather." According to the *New York Express,* the principal residence of free blacks in that city was a house with eight or ten rooms, "and in these are crowded not infrequently two or three hundred souls."

By the 1830s, free blacks in both the North and the South had begun to experience heightened discrimination and competition from white immigrants in the skilled trades and even in such traditional occupations as domestic service. Violence directed against free blacks escalated. During the 1830s, white mobs repeatedly attacked urban ghettos and burned them to the ground. Between 1830 and 1860, many "free" states in the Midwest and the Far West excluded free blacks. The great question facing the nation was whether the future would bring continuing violence or serious efforts to address America's racial problems.

Racial warfare seemed to pose a serious threat. In 1829, David Walker (1785–1830), a North Carolina–born free black who ran a secondhand clothing store in Boston, issued *Appeal to the Colored Citizens of the World*, a militant pamphlet calling for insurrection if whites failed to abolish slavery and treat blacks equally. In ringing terms, he warned whites that "your DESTRUCTION is at hand, and will be speedily consummated unless you REPENT." Two years later, Nat Turner led his rebellion in southern Virginia, during which sixty to eighty slaves killed more than fifty whites. Also in 1831, one of the bloodiest slave revolts in history erupted in Jamaica.

If racial warfare seemed to be one possibility, emancipation also seemed increasingly to be another. In 1833, the British Parliament adopted a gradual-emancipation plan in the West Indies. After prolonged debate, Parliament provided generous compensation to slave owners and established an apprenticeship plan to prepare nearly eight hundred thousand slaves for freedom in Jamaica, Trinidad, St. Vincent, and other possessions.

The success of Britain's abolitionists offered two important lessons to American opponents of slavery. First, emancipation required a massive mobilization of public opinion. The experience of British abolitionists seemed to demonstrate that an aroused public could force politicians to abolish the institution. Second, it was a waste of time to advance specific emancipation plans, since this only produced protracted, futile debate.

The American abolition movement that emerged by the 1830s drew upon the same religious and evangelical ideals that had given rise to earlier movements to distribute Bibles and tracts, to establish urban and foreign missions, and to promote temperance. Rejecting colonization and gradualist remedies for slavery, abolitionists called for slavery's immediate demise.

Many American opponents of slavery had served apprenticeships in movements to encourage public education, Sabbath observance, temperance, and moral purity, and they regarded antislavery as an extension of earlier moral and humanitarian reforms. Many proponents of abolition thought of themselves as moral conservatives; indeed, many were moralistic evangelicals deeply disturbed by the growth of class tensions and the breakdown of the preindustrial social order. But they quickly discovered that if they were to awaken Americans to the evil of slavery, they had to become social agitators.

The nation's most famous abolitionist was William Lloyd Garrison (1805–79). Born in Newburyport, Massachusetts, Garrison grew up with a firsthand knowledge of poverty. His father, a sailing master, abandoned his family when Garrison was just three years old. Having little formal schooling, Garrison educated himself while he worked as a printer's apprentice, a part-time journalist, and the editor of a weekly reform newspaper. In 1829, the twenty-five-year-old Garrison added his voice to the outcry against colonization, denouncing it as a cruel hoax designed to promote the racial purity of the northern population while doing nothing to end slavery in the South. Colonization, Garrison insisted in an address entitled "The 'Infidelity' of Abolition" (1860), was "a libel upon republicanism—a libel upon the Declaration of Independence—a libel upon Christianity." He called for "immediate emancipation," that is, the immediate and unconditional release of slaves from bondage without compensation to slave owners.

On January 1, 1831, he began publishing *The Liberator,* a militant abolitionist newspaper that was the country's first publication to demand an immediate end to slavery. On the front page of the first issue, he defiantly declared: "I will not equivocate—I will not excuse—I will not retreat a single inch— AND I WILL BE HEARD." Convinced that the public would speedily abolish slavery if "all the horrors of the abomination" were "depicted in their true colors," Garrison published authenticated accounts of slaves burned alive or beaten to death by sadistic masters. Before the year 1831 was over, the state of Georgia offered a $5,000 reward to anyone who brought Garrison there for trial.

It is true that Garrison was often self-righteous, dogmatic, and humorless. He tended to conceive of himself as a martyr in a corrupt society and refused to treat slavery as a practical political problem. Yet none of this suggests that he was psychologically abnormal. A devout Baptist—his mother had broken away from her parents' Episcopalianism (and had been turned out of her house as a result)—Garrison epitomized the religious piety and millennial spirit of the Second Great Awakening, and he revealed the radical implications of evangelical religion as well. Convinced that slavery rested on violence against blacks, he eventually extended this logic, seeing violence as the basis of the patriarchal family and of governmental authority. He therefore embraced feminism, pacifism, and other radical reforms. If Garrison's extremism offended many of his contemporaries, it is also true that his uncompromising stance freed antislavery from its subservience to colonization and made racial equality abolition's ultimate goal.

In December 1833, Garrison and some sixty other delegates, male and female, black and white, gathered in Philadelphia to form the American Anti-Slavery Society. The meeting, which included Arthur Tappan and Lewis Tappan, two wealthy New York philanthropists who had supported earlier evangelical causes, denounced slavery as a sin and demanded immediate emancipation without compensation. Most radical was the delegates' call for legal equality of the races, and they launched an unprecedented campaign to mobilize public opinion against slavery.

Within a year, two hundred antislavery societies had appeared in the North, drawing support from Quakers, evangelicals, and Congregationalists; from many upwardly mobile manufacturers, merchants, and artisans; and, most of all, from many women (who contributed well over half the names on antislavery petitions). By 1836, the number of antislavery societies had reached 527; and by 1838, there were 1,300 containing 109,000 members. These local groups mounted a massive propaganda campaign to proclaim the sinfulness of slavery. These societies distributed one million pieces of abolitionist literature, sent twenty thousand tracts directly to the South, and gathered some two million names in an 1838–39 petition campaign.

The most careful studies of abolitionist support have found that the movement's rank and file tended to cluster around Boston, New York, Providence, Philadelphia, western Massachusetts, New York State's Mohawk Valley, and the Pennsylvania-Ohio border. Factory towns were particularly fertile breeding grounds for abolition—hundreds of artisans and factory operatives, along with many aspiring entrepreneurs and shopkeepers, signed antislavery petitions. Relatively young, with very modest property holdings, antislavery proponents were mostly from New England or were transplanted New Englanders of evangelical religious beliefs. It is no accident that the new industrial towns were such an important source of antislavery support. Faced with the breakdown of the traditional craft relationships, anxious to dignify manual labor and dissociate it from the stigma of subservience, residents of those towns were especially eager to distinguish "free labor" from "chattel slavery" and the master-slave relationship.

The initial weapon of the abolitionists was moral suasion. However, that did not imply mere passivity. William Lloyd Garrison declared in a letter in 1858 that the weapons of persuasion included "speech, intellectual enlightenment, protest, contumacy, non-conformity, untiring persistency, indomitable purpose, unconquerable will, moral rebellion, abiding faith in the right, [and] the divine spirit of martyrdom." Many abolitionists had labored in earlier movements for moral reform. Stephen S. Foster, Samuel J. May, Joshua Leavitt, and Theodore Dwight Weld had attended theological seminaries and served in movements to distribute Christian tracts; to enforce observance of the Sabbath; to suppress vice, intemperance, and lotteries; and to educate the poor. They believed that direct appeals to conscience would convince slaveholders that slavery was a moral evil. Abolitionists, Garrison proclaimed in his address "The 'Infidelity' of Abolition," sought "the destruction of error by the potency of truth—the overthrow of prejudice by the power of love—and the abolition of slavery by the spirit of repentance." To spread their ideas, they organized antislavery societies, distributed newspapers and tracts, and circulated petitions.

Abolitionist Arguments

Abolitionists attacked slavery for its illegality, immorality, and economic backwardness. Slavery was illegal because it violated the principles of natural rights to life and liberty embodied in the Declaration of Independence. Justice, Garrison stated in 1860, required that the nation "secure to the colored population . . . all the rights and privileges that belong to them as men and as Americans."

Slavery was sinful, Garrison observed in a letter in 1858, because it violated "all the injunctions of the Gospel, . . . subjecting its victims to every species of torture, degrading them to a level with beasts." In addition, it encouraged sexual immorality and undermined marriage and the family, compelling slaves "to live in a state of uncleanness and pollution surpassed by nothing in Sodom or Gomorrah." Not only did slave masters sexually abuse and exploit slave women, abolitionists charged, but in the older southern states, such as Virginia and Maryland, they bred slaves to sell in the more recently settled parts of the Deep South.

Slavery was economically regressive because slaves, motivated only by fear, did not willingly exert themselves. By depriving their labor force of any incentive for performing careful and diligent work, by barring slaves from acquiring and developing productive skills, planters hindered improvements in crop and soil management.

Abolitionists also charged—correctly—that slavery impeded the development of towns, canals, railroads, and schools. As Ralph Waldo Emerson put it, "Slavery is no scholar, no improver; it does not love the newspaper, the mailbag, a college, a book or a preacher who has the absurd whim of saying what he thinks; it does not increase the white population; it does not improve the soil; everything goes to decay." Emerson's observation is largely accurate. The South did not produce urban centers for commerce, finance, and industry on a scale with those found in the North. The South's transportation system and its industry were primitive by national standards. And compared to the

North, the South established few schools, orphanges, hospitals, or asylums for the mentally ill.

Abolitionist Illusions

Although the abolitionists developed a devastating moral critique of slavery, they held many misconceptions about the institution. In the first place, the abolitionists generally viewed slavery as somehow extraneous to the American experience. They did not understand that slavery was in fact vital: it was the key to the nation's system of racial control. Its existence guaranteed that few African Americans would migrate to the North.

Furthermore, the abolitionists tended to ignore the North's complicity in the slave system. Exports of slave-grown cotton paid for the commodities and technology America needed to begin its Industrial Revolution. Slave agriculture also stimulated the growth of northern businesses. A huge textile industry arose in New England to process the South's cotton. And since the South, like other slave societies, did not develop its own financial and commercial facilities, northern banks, insurance companies, and cotton brokerages became substantial businesses.

The abolitionists labored under other illusions as well. They perceived the slave South as economically backward, but in actuality slavery was not unprofitable. In 1860, the South was richer than any country in Europe except England, an economic level unmatched by Italy and Spain until the eve of World War II. Instead of stagnating, per capita income in the South grew 30 percent more rapidly than in the North between 1840 and 1860, and exceeded the income of the western states by 14 percent.

The abolitionists also tended to believe that slavery was maintained by an extremely small planter oligarchy. We now know that slave ownership was not confined to a small elite. In the first half of the nineteenth century, more than one-third of southern white families either had owned slaves or currently owned them. The average slaveholding varied from four to six slaves; and most slave owners possessed no more than five slaves.

But the abolitionists' greatest misconception was their belief that the public—North and South—would easily embrace antislavery arguments. Having labored in earlier movements aimed at moral regeneration, the abolitionists assumed that they could swiftly persuade ministers and other community leaders that slavery was a moral evil. Instead, they encountered a harsh public reaction in both the North and the South.

Mobs led by "gentlemen of property and standing"—including many locally prominent bankers, judges, lawyers, merchants, and physicians—attacked the homes and businesses of abolitionist merchants, destroyed abolitionist printing presses, disrupted antislavery meetings, and attacked black neighborhoods. The reason: abolitionists represented a direct challenge to the authority of local elites, appealing beyond them to the young, women, and free blacks. Enraged by reports that abolitionists advocated "amalgamation" and "levelling" of the races, convinced that they were dupes of English agents sent "to foment discord among our people," crowds pelted abolitionist reformers with eggs and even stones.

During anti-abolitionist rioting in Philadelphia in October 1834, a white mob destroyed forty-five homes in the city's black community. A crowd stormed a meeting hall where antislavery women were holding a convention and burned it to the ground. A year later, a Boston mob dragged Garrison through the streets and almost lynched him before authorities removed him to a city jail for his own safety. That same year, the citizens of East Feliciana, Louisiana, offered a $50,000 reward for the capture, dead or alive, of Arthur Tappan, president of the American Anti-Slavery Society.

States in both the North and the South debated "gag" laws to suppress antislavery agitation, and the U.S. postmaster general refused to deliver antislavery tracts to the South. In each session of Congress between 1836 and 1844, the House of Representatives adopted gag rules so it could automatically table resolutions or petitions concerning the abolition of slavery.

On November 7, 1837, the abolitionist movement acquired its first martyr. The Reverend Elijah P. Lovejoy was the editor of a militant antislavery newspaper in Alton, Illinois, a town located across the Mississippi River from slaveholding St. Louis, Missouri. Three times mobs had destroyed Lovejoy's printing presses and attacked his house. When a fourth printing press arrived, Lovejoy armed himself and guarded the new press at the warehouse. The anti-abolitionist mob set the warehouse on fire and shot Lovejoy as he fled the building. The following day, opponents of the abolitionists lined the streets and cheered as the mutilated corpse was dragged through the town.

Although anti-abolitionist mobs became somewhat less common after 1840, anti-Negro and anti-abolitionist riots continued to take place during the 1840s and 1850s. The suppression of abolitionists' civil liberties convinced thousands of northern moderates to fear for their own freedom.

Abolitionists never expected such a violent reaction. "When we first unfurled the banner of *The Liberator*," Garrison wrote in 1860, "we did not anticipate that . . . the free states would voluntarily trample under foot all order, law and government, or brand the advocates of universal liberty as incendiaries." This violent response produced fragmentation within the anti-slavery movement.

Division in the Antislavery Movement

By the late 1830s, questions of strategy and tactics increasingly divided the abolitionist movement. Some abolitionists turned to the courts and to the U.S. Constitution as weapons in the struggle against slavery. This tactic came dramatically to public notice as the result of a mutiny on a slave ship that occurred in 1839 (which provided the basis for Herman Melville's 1856 short story "Benito Cereno"). Led by Joseph Cinque, thirty-nine African males and four African children on board the schooner *Amistad* rebelled against their Cuban captors and ordered the two surviving whites to sail to Africa. Instead, the crew sailed northeast at night, hoping to encounter a friendly ship. After six weeks, the USS *Washington* seized the *Amistad* off the coast of Long Island; the Africans were jailed.

Abolitionists sued for their freedom on the grounds that the Africans had been illegally enslaved and shipped into Cuba in violation of an Anglo-Spanish treaty and that their revolt represented lawful self-defense under international law. Other arguments advanced by the abolitionists were that the Africans had been free at the time the *Amistad* had been seized, and should not therefore be confined to jail; and further that under American law, illegally imported slaves were to be returned to Africa.

Former president John Quincy Adams, now seventy-four years old, argued the case before the Supreme Court. He defended the slaves' revolt as a clear expression of America's revolutionary principles: the Africans had "vindicated their own right of liberty" by "executing the justice of Heaven" upon a "pirate, murderer, their tyrant and oppressor." The abolitionists' arguments prevailed; both a federal district court and the U.S. Supreme Court ruled on the rebels' behalf, holding that since the international slave trade was illegal, the rebels should be freed. In the end, the Africans returned to Sierra Leone.

Despite this victory, William Lloyd Garrison and his supporters grew increasingly alienated from the broader society. Outraged by the violence directed against abolitionists, convinced that violence lay at the very heart of American society, the Garrisonians believed that slave emancipation would require a revolutionary transformation of American values. In Boston in 1838, they held a "Peace Convention" at which the delegates condemned war and repudiated "all human politics . . . and stations of authority." The Garrisonians rejected capital punishment, lawsuits, prisons, and every other institution that relied on the threat of physical coercion for its authority. Even before the Civil War, American pacifists and nonresistants began to call for the creation of international institutions to arbitrate disputes among nations.

Many younger abolitionists, frustrated by the slow pace of change, wanted more forceful protests against slavery and racial prejudice. A dispute at Lane Theological Seminary in Cincinnati symbolized a growing division between activists and moderates. Lane had been founded as a center of western evangelicalism. In 1834, Theodore Weld, a thirty-one-year-old student at the school, led eighteen days of intense discussions of slavery and convinced his fellow students to set up schools in Cincinnati's black ghetto. Lane's president, the Reverend Lyman Beecher, and the board of trustees expelled the antislavery students, many of whom subsequently became agents for the American Anti-Slavery Society.

At the 1840 annual meeting of the American Anti-Slavery Society in New York, abolitionists split over such questions as women's right to participate in the administration of the organization and the advisability of nominating abolitionists as independent political candidates. Garrison won control of the organization, and his opponents—who tended to be religious evangelicals— promptly walked out. From this point on, no single organization could speak for abolitionism.

One group of abolitionists looked to politics as the way to end slavery, and they founded political parties, such as the Liberty Party. The party, formed in 1840 under the leadership of Arthur Tappan and Lewis Tappan, Gerrit Smith, a wealthy upstate New York landowner, and James G. Birney of Alabama, a former slaveholder, called on Congress to abolish slavery in the District of Columbia, end the interstate slave trade, and cease admitting new slave states to the Union. The party also sought the repeal of local and state "black laws," which discriminated against free blacks.

In its first campaign in 1840, the Liberty Party nominated Birney for president, and he received less than seventy-one hundred votes—mainly from the burned-over district in western New York. Although William Lloyd Garrison called the results "ludicrous and melancholy," Liberty Party supporters persisted. In 1844, the party nominated Birney again, and he polled sixty-two thousand votes, capturing enough votes in Michigan and New York to deprive Whig candidate Henry Clay of the presidency.

The period from 1844 to 1848 witnessed a series of bitter defeats for the antislavery forces. In 1844, Congress narrowly approved the annexation of

Texas, adding a new slave state to the Union. Then, in 1846, the Mexican War erupted. As a result of this conflict, the United States acquired one-third of all Mexican territory—creating the possibility of new slave states in the Southwest. "Bigger pens to cram with slaves" was the way poet James Russell Lowell put it.

Yet these defeats also created new opportunities for political abolitionists. In Massachusetts, the Whig Party splintered, and Conscience Whigs (in contrast to Cotton Whigs) threatened to defect. Likewise in New York, antislavery Democrats, known as Barnburners because of their willingness to burn down the Democratic "barn" to rid the party of its proslavery elements, threatened to leave their party. In 1848, these factions merged with the Liberty Party to form the Free-Soil Party and nominated Martin Van Buren for the presidency.

The political abolitionists' critics accused them of capitulating to political expediency. Unlike the Liberty Party, which was dedicated to the abolition of slavery and to equal rights for African Americans, the Free-Soil Party narrowed its demands to the abolition of slavery in the District of Columbia and the exclusion of slavery from federal territories. The Free-Soilers sought to appeal to moderate and conservative Whigs by adopting a broad economic platform. It called for a homestead law to provide free land for western settlers, high tariffs to protect American industry, and federally sponsored internal improvements. Campaigning under the slogan "Free soil, free labor, free men," the new party polled nearly three hundred thousand votes in the presidential election of 1848 (roughly 10 percent of all votes cast) and gained enough votes in New York and Ohio to determine the election's outcome, helping to elect the Whig Zachary Taylor to the presidency and a dozen Free-Soil candidates to Congress.

The Free-Soilers' radical critics frequently denounced the party as racist. Unlike the Liberty Party, the Free-Soil Party refused to disavow racial discrimination in its national platform. Some Free-Soilers, especially many Barnburners from New York, held openly racist views and favored new laws to keep blacks out of the western territories. Yet for many Free-Soilers, downplaying the issues of abolition and Negro rights was simply a tactical decision to garner political support. As the famous black abolitionist Frederick Douglass commented: "What is morally right is not at all times politically possible."

In many northern states, Free-Soilers actively campaigned for civil rights for African Americans. In Wisconsin, for example, Free-Soilers led an unsuccessful campaign to extend voting rights to free blacks, and in Connecticut they attempted to restore voting rights that had been stripped away in 1814. In

Ohio in 1849, Free-Soilers were successful in repealing laws that prohibited free blacks from entering the state, attending public school, and testifying in court cases involving whites. In Massachusetts, Free-Soilers campaigned against segregated railroad cars and public schools and struggled to open the state militia to blacks.

Radical Abolitionism

Other abolitionists, led by Garrison, took a more radical direction, advocating civil disobedience and linking abolitionism to such other reforms as women's rights, the abolition of war, and the elimination of capital punishment. The radicals questioned whether the Bible represented the word of God, withdrew from membership in established churches that condoned slavery, and called for the voluntary dissolution of the Union.

Refusing to place political expediency over moral purity, the Garrisonians embraced radical perfectionist doctrines. Taking the position that "it is the duty of the followers of Christ to suffer themselves to be defrauded . . . and barbarously treated, without resort to either their own physical energies, or the force of human law," Garrison and his supporters established the New England Non-Resistance Society in 1838. Members refused to vote, to hold public office, or to bring suits in court. In 1854, Garrison attracted notoriety by publicly burning a copy of the Constitution, which he called "a covenant with death and an agreement with Hell" that "should be immediately annulled."

Like some members of the New Left during the 1960s, the most radical abolitionists challenged established conventions and sought to create new noncoercive, nonhierarchical relationships and institutions. When abolitionists Angelina Grimké and Theodore Weld married in 1838, they did so in a ceremony without a minister and without a vow of wifely obedience. Stephen S. Foster, one of the most notorious of the radical abolitionists, repeatedly disrupted church services by standing up and denouncing slavery. At Hopedale Community in Milford, Massachusetts, in 1842, abolitionist Adin Ballou attempted to create a community of Christian nonresistants which would operate without force or coercion. This community attracted roughly three hundred residents at its peak in the mid-1850s. In each of these ways, radical abolitionists sought to eradicate the myriad forms of slavery in American society.

In the long run, the split within antislavery ranks between reformists and radicals worked to the advantage of the cause. Henceforth, northerners could support whichever form of antislavery best reflected their views. Moderates could vote for political candidates with abolitionist sentiments and not be accused of holding radical Garrisonian views or of advocating violence for redress of grievances.

Black Abolitionists

Blacks played a vital role in the abolitionist movement, leading campaigns against colonization, supporting antislavery newspapers (free blacks made up three-quarters of *The Liberator*'s subscribers), and staging protests against segregated churches, schools, and public transportation. Though denied positions as officers and decision makers, African Americans helped found many of the leading antislavery societies and made substantial monetary contributions to the activities of white abolitionists.

Free blacks also initiated independent attacks on slavery and racial discrimination. Starting in 1830, when black delegates from eight states met in Philadelphia, African American leaders held annual conventions to coordinate efforts to abolish slavery and repeal discriminatory black codes. Many of the nation's most prominent black leaders were Baptist and Methodist ministers, including Samuel D. Cornish, Henry Highland Garnet, Samuel Ringgold Ward, and Theodore S. Wright. These religious leaders organized boycotts against segregated schools, demanded the repeal of black laws that restricted the rights of free blacks, and established industrial training schools.

In New York and Pennsylvania, free blacks launched petition drives for equal voting rights. Northern blacks also had a pivotal role in the Underground Railroad, which provided escape routes for southern slaves through the northern states and into Canada. Black churches offered sanctuary to runaways, and black "vigilance" groups in New York and Detroit offered physical resistance to slave catchers.

Fugitive slaves, such as William Wells Brown, Henry Bibb, and Harriet Tubman, advanced abolitionism by publicizing the horrors of slavery. Their firsthand tales of whippings and separation from spouses and children combated the notion that slaves were content and undermined beliefs in racial inferiority. Tubman (c. 1815–1913), who was born a slave on Maryland's Eastern Shore and escaped slavery in 1849, risked her life by making at least nineteen trips into slave territory in order to free as many as three hundred slaves. Slaveholders posted a reward of $40,000 for the capture of the Black Moses.

Frederick Douglass was the most famous fugitive slave and black abolitionist. His early life illustrated many of the cruelties of slavery. He was born in 1818, the son of a Maryland slave woman and an unknown white father. At the age of six, he was sold away from his mother to work on a plantation owned by one of the largest slaveholders on the Eastern Shore. At the age of fifteen, he was sold again. Then he was rented out to a local farmer known as a "Negro breaker." After repeated beatings and whippings by this cruel farmer, Douglass fought back and defeated him in a fist fight. After this, he was no longer punished. In 1838, at the age of twenty, he escaped from slavery by borrowing the papers of a free black sailor.

In the North, Douglass became the first runaway slave to speak out on behalf of the antislavery cause. When many northerners refused to believe that this eloquent orator could possibly have been a slave, he responded by writing an autobiography that identified his previous owners by name. Although he initially allied himself with William Lloyd Garrison, Douglass later started his own newspaper, *North Star,* and supported political action against slavery. During the 1850s, Douglass backed the Republican Party, even though the party called for an end to the expansion of slavery, not its immediate abolition. An assimilationist who envisioned an America where all racial and ethnic differences would dissolve into "a composite American nationality," Douglass was the nation's most eloquent critic of racial inequality. He spoke out bitterly against the hypocrisy of a nation that was dedicated to the principles of liberty and equality of opportunity and that perpetuated slavery. For slaves, he declared in a speech in 1852, the Fourth of July was "mere bombast and fraud, deception, impiety, and hypocrisy—a thin veil to cover up crimes which would disgrace a nation of savages." During the Civil War, he encouraged the Lincoln administration's gradual steps toward making emancipation a war aim, and after the war he favored black suffrage, full legal equality, and the enactment of civil rights laws to provide physical protection for freedmen and guarantee their right to participate in a free market.

During the 1850s, many African Americans grew increasingly pessimistic about the possibility of overthrowing slavery. Colonizationist sentiment appeared again among free blacks. In the fifteen months following passage of the federal Fugitive Slave Law in 1850, some thirteen thousand free blacks fled the North for Canada. In 1854, Martin Delany (1812–85), a Pittsburgh doctor who had studied medicine at Harvard, organized the National Emigration Convention to investigate possible sites for black colonization in Haiti, Central America, and West Africa. The grandson of a Mandingan prince, Delany, who thanked God "for making him a black man," temporarily moved his family to Canada. But when the Civil War broke out, he actively recruited black troops in New England and became a major, the first black officer in the Union army. After the war, he worked for the Freedmen's Bureau in South Carolina, but a growing disenchantment with Reconstruction prompted him to support emigration to Liberia in the late 1870s.

While some African American leaders supported colonization, other blacks argued in favor of violence. Black abolitionists in Ohio adopted resolutions encouraging slaves to escape and called on their fellow citizens to violate any law that "conflicts with reason, liberty and justice, North or South." A meeting of fugitive slaves in Cazenovia, New York, declared that "the State motto of Virginia, 'Death to Tyrants,' is as well the black man's as the white man's motto." By the late 1850s, a growing number of free blacks had concluded that it was just as legitimate to use violence to secure the freedom of the slaves as it had been in establishing the independence of the American colonies.

Abolitionism and the
Sectional Crisis

During the 1850s, as the American political system became incapable of containing the sectional disputes that had smoldered for more than half a century, abolitionists had heightened opportunities to influence the nation's politics. The adoption of the Fugitive Slave Law in 1850, which stripped accused runaways of the right to trial by jury and the right to testify in their own defense, provoked outrage in the North. Attempts to enforce the new law aroused wholesale opposition. Eight northern states attempted to invalidate the law by enacting "personal liberty" laws, which forbade state officials to assist in the return of runaways and extended the right of jury trial to fugitives.

The free black communities of the North responded defiantly to the 1850 law, providing sanctuary to perhaps fifteen hundred fugitive slaves along the Underground Railroad. Others established vigilance committees to protect free blacks from kidnappers who were searching the North for runaways.

Riots against the Fugitive Slave Law erupted in many cities. In Christiana, Pennsylvania, in 1851, a gun battle broke out between abolitionists and slave catchers, and in Wisconsin, an abolitionist editor named Sherman M. Booth freed Joshua Glover, a fugitive slave, from a local jail. In Boston, federal marshals and twenty-two companies of state troops were needed to prevent a crowd from storming a courthouse to free a fugitive named Anthony Burns.

Following the passage of the Kansas-Nebraska Act of 1854, which opened those territories to white settlement and declared "inoperative and void" the

Missouri Compromise prohibition on slavery in the northern half of the Louisiana Purchase, abolitionists found new opportunities to mobilize public opposition to slavery. Political abolitionists played a leading role in organizing the Republican Party, which committed itself in its platform to combating the twin barbarities, slavery and polygamy. Even before the Kansas-Nebraska law had been passed, Eli Thayer, a businessman and educator from Worcester, Massachusetts, had organized the New England Emigrant Aid Company to promote the emigration of antislavery New Englanders to Kansas to "vote to make it free."

In Kansas in 1856, John Brown, a fifty-six-year-old Connecticut native and an ardent abolitionist, played a critical role in leading opposition to slavery. After hearing that proslavery forces had burned buildings in Lawrence, Kansas, and that Senator Charles Sumner of Massachusetts had been assaulted on the Senate floor by a proslavery southern congressman, Brown declared that "something must be done to show these barbarians that we, too, have rights."

A devout, Bible-quoting Congregationalist who believed that he had a personal responsibility to overthrow slavery, Brown announced that the time had come "to fight fire with fire" and "strike terror in the hearts of proslavery men." On May 24, 1856, Brown and six companions dragged five proslavery men and boys from their beds at Pottawatomie Creek, split open their skulls with an axe and cut off their hands. A war of revenge broke out in southeastern Kansas. A proslavery newspaper declared: "If murder and assassination is the program of the day, we are in favor of filling the bill." Some two hundred people were killed in the guerrilla conflict.

Up until the Kansas-Nebraska Act, most abolitionists had been averse to the use of violence. They had hoped to use moral suasion and other peaceful means to eliminate slavery. By the late 1850s, however, the abolitionists' aversion to violence had faded. In 1858, in an address before the New England Peace Convention, William Lloyd Garrison complained that his followers were growing more and more warlike. They spoke of "cleaving tyrants down from the crown to the groin." On the night of October 16, 1859, violence came, and once again John Brown was its instrument.

As early as 1857, Brown had begun to raise money and recruit men for an invasion of the South. He gained financial support from six prominent abolitionists—Dr. Samuel Gridley Howe, the Reverend Thomas Wentworth Higginson, the Reverend Theodore Parker, Franklin B. Sanborn, Gerrit Smith, and George L. Stearns. He told his backers that only through insurrection could this "slave-cursed Republic be restored to the principles of the Declaration of Independence."

On May 19, 1859, Brown met with Frederick Douglass, the celebrated black abolitionist and former slave, in an abandoned stone quarry near Chambersburg, Pennsylvania. For three days, they discussed whether violence could be legitimately used to free the nation's slaves. The Kansas guerrilla leader asked Douglass if he would join a band of raiders who would seize a federal arsenal and spark a mass uprising of slaves. "When I strike," Brown said, "the bees will begin to swarm, and I shall need you to help hive them." Douglass answered no. He regarded Brown's plan as suicidal. Earlier, Brown had proposed a somewhat more realistic scheme, to launch guerrilla activity in the Virginia mountains, providing a haven for slaves and an escape route into the North. Douglass considered Brown's new scheme hopeless.

John Brown's assault against slavery lasted less than two days. At eight o'clock Sunday evening, October 16, Brown led a raiding party of some eighteen men to Harpers Ferry, Virginia, seized the federal arsenal and armory, and sent out detachments to round up hostages and liberate slaves. Within hours, militia companies from villages surrounding Harpers Ferry trapped Brown's men in the armory. Early Tuesday morning, U.S. marines, commanded by Colonel Robert E. Lee and Lieutenant J. E. B. Stuart, broke through the brick walls of Brown's stronghold and took the abolitionist prisoner. A week later, Brown was put on trial in a Virginia court (even though his attack had occurred on federal property). The proceedings lasted six days. Brown refused to plead insanity as a defense, and he was found guilty of treason, conspiracy, and murder and was sentenced to die on the gallows.

The trial's high point came at the very end, when Brown was allowed to make a five-minute speech, which helped convince thousands of northerners that this grizzled man of fifty-nine was a martyr to the cause of freedom. Brown declared that he had come to Virginia to liberate the slaves. "If it is deemed necessary," he told the Virginia court, "that I should forfeit my life for the furtherance of the ends of justice and mingle my blood with the blood of millions in this slave country whose rights are disregarded by wicked, cruel, and unjust enactments, I say let it be done."

December 2 was Brown's execution date. Before he went to the gallows, Brown wrote out one last message: "I . . . am now quite certain that the crime of this guilty land will never be purged away but with blood." Across the North, church bells tolled, flags flew at half-mast, and buildings were draped in black bunting. Ralph Waldo Emerson compared Brown to Jesus Christ and declared that his death had made "the gallows as glorious as the cross." William Lloyd Garrison, previously the strongest exponent of nonviolent opposition to slavery, announced that Brown's death had convinced him of "the need for violence" to destroy slavery. He told a Boston meeting that "every slaveholder had forfeited his right to live," if he opposed immediate emancipation.

The Abolitionist Legacy

To their opponents, the abolitionists were fanatical agitators who knew little about slavery, failed to develop realistic plans to abolish the institution, and deserted the freedmen after the Civil War. This line of argument is almost completely incorrect. Far from being misguided fanatics or deluded extremists who generated a needless war, the abolitionists in fact expressed the moral passion necessary to awaken Americans to the moral evil of slavery and begin the process of eroding racial prejudice. Lacking established institutions to work within, the abolitionists had to experiment with new ways to mobilize public opinion: antislavery societies, petition and pamphlet campaigns, and the founding of third parties.

The abolitionists played a pivotal role in mobilizing northern public opinion against southern slavery. In the end, it was not the abolitionists' moral arguments that turned many northerners against slavery, but the contention that an aggressive southern slave power had seized control of the federal government and threatened to subvert the republican ideals of liberty and equality. Beginning as early as the 1830s, abolitionists formulated the notion that an arrogant and ruthless slave power threatened the civil liberties and the economic prosperity of white northerners. Many northerners who were otherwise apathetic about the moral issue of slavery came to accept the abolitionist charge that the slave power had entrenched slavery in the Constitution, caused financial panics to sabotage the northern economy, dispossessed Indians of their native lands, and incited revolution in Texas and provoked war with Mexico in order to expand the South's slave empire.

Some northerners came to accept the more extreme charges that the slave power was seeking through court decisions and congressional compromises to legalize slavery in the North as well as the South and that the southern slavocracy had secretly assassinated two presidents—William Henry Harrison and Zachary Taylor—and had unsuccessfully conspired to murder three others—Andrew Jackson, Franklin Pierce, and James Buchanan.

Some white abolitionists, it is true, were tainted by racial prejudice, adopted a paternalistic and condescending attitude toward black abolitionists, and refused to socialize with African Americans. In a letter in 1855, James McCune

Smith, a black abolitionist, observed: "It is a strange omission in the Constitution of the American Anti-Slavery Society that no mention is made of Social Equality either of Slaves or Free Blacks, as the aim of that Society." Bound by their own class and culture, many white abolitionists judged individuals not by the color of their skin, but by the degree to which they conformed to middle-class Protestant ideals of industry, self-discipline, and personal piety. But a surprising number were racial egalitarians who favored equal civil rights for African Americans and who demonstrated courage and persistence in fighting racial bias. In state after state, abolitionists took the lead in fighting for Negro suffrage and for repeal of the black codes designed to preserve white supremacy. If they failed to eradicate racism, they did succeed in dramatizing the issue of civil rights.

It is certainly the case that many abolitionists were blind to some of northern society's inequities and injustices. Despite their heated rhetoric and their radical challenge to the institution of slavery, most abolitionists accepted uncritically the wage-labor system of the North. Many of them believed strongly in the ideals of self-discipline, self-help, and free labor, and they opposed the struggles of urban workers for labor unions and the eight-hour day. While they directed their arguments toward artisans and paid workers, abolitionists generally deplored labor strikes and tended to be unsympathetic to the northern labor leaders who argued that free laborers were slaves of the marketplace and suffered even more insecurity than the South's chattel slaves, who were provided for in sickness and old age.

It is also the case that the abolitionists failed to set forth specific plans to end slavery. Unlike the British, who provided financial compensation to slave owners and set up programs of apprenticeship for former slaves—though the programs quickly broke down—American abolitionists had a very different conception of their role. Their task was to awaken Americans to slavery's moral evil and to leave to politicians the job of enacting practical solutions.

But it would be a grave mistake to conclude that the abolitionists ever abandoned their campaign for civil rights. In the years following the outbreak of the Civil War in 1861, many abolitionists and their descendants responded courageously to the racial challenges that confronted the nation. During the war, abolitionists struggled intently to see that abolition became a war aim and that black troops could enlist in the Union army and receive equal pay. Many personally went to the South to take an active role in military operations and educational and relief efforts and helped support secondary schools and colleges for black Americans. Abolitionists not only advocated creation of the Freedmen's Bureau and enacting the postwar constitutional amendments that abolished slavery, guaranteed citizenship rights, and extended suffrage to black men. They also favored land grants to former slaves, government assistance for freedmen's education, and adoption and enforcement of civil rights laws. To take just one example, Lewis Tappan, the New York evangelical, helped establish Berea College, Fisk and Howard Universities, and other schools for African Americans. If the piety and the fervor of the original abolitionists receded, it is also true that in the early twentieth century their descendants were founders of the National Association for the Advancement of Colored People and other organizations for racial justice.

The Birth of Feminism

The women's rights movement was a major legacy of radical reform. At the outset of the nineteenth century, women experienced political, social, and legal discrimination. Women were prohibited from voting or holding office in every state (except New Jersey, where unmarried female property holders were allowed to vote); they had no access to higher education and were excluded from professional occupations. American law was guided by the principle that a wife had no legal identity apart from her husband. She could not be sued, nor could she bring a legal suit, make a contract, or own property. She was not permitted to control her own wages or gain custody of her children after separation or divorce, and under many circumstances she was even deemed incapable of committing crimes.

The decades stretching from the eighteenth century to the Civil War witnessed a dramatic transformation of women's social and economic position. In some respects, women's status and opportunities clearly improved. Instead of bearing children at two-year intervals after marriage, as was the case throughout the colonial era, early-nineteenth-century women bore fewer children and ceased childbearing at younger ages. During these decades the first women's college was established, and some men's colleges first opened their doors to women students. More women were postponing marriage or not marrying at all; unmarried women could now work as "mill girls" and elementary school teachers; and a growing number of women achieved prominence as novelists, editors, teachers, and leaders of church and philanthropic societies.

While there were many improvements in women's positions they still lost political and economic status when compared with men. The franchise was extended to more white males, including large groups of recent immigrants, widening the gap in political power between women and men. Even though women made up a core of supporters for many reform movements, men excluded them from positions of decision making and relegated them to separate female auxiliaries. Women also lost economic status as production shifted away from the household to the factory and the workshop. During the late eighteenth century, the need for a cash income led women and older children to engage in a variety of household industries, such as weaving and spinning. Increasingly, however, these tasks were performed in factories and mills.

The fact that changes in the economy tended to confine women to a sphere separate from men had important implications for reform. Since women were believed to be uncontaminated by the competitive struggle for wealth and power, many argued that they had a duty—and the capacity—to exert an uplifting moral influence on American society.

Catharine Beecher (1800–1878) and Sarah J. Hale (1788–1879) helped lead the effort to expand women's roles through moral influence. Beecher, the eldest sister of Harriet Beecher Stowe, was one of the nation's most prominent educators before the Civil War. A woman of many talents and strong leadership, she wrote a highly regarded book on domestic science and spearheaded the campaign to convince school boards that women were suited to serve as teachers. Hale edited the nation's most popular women's magazines, the *Ladies Magazine* and *Godey's Lady's Book*. She led the successful campaign to make Thanksgiving a national holiday, and she also composed the famous nursery rhyme "Mary Had a Little Lamb."

Both Beecher and Hale worked tirelessly for women's education (Hale helped found Vassar College) and gave voice to the grievances of women—the abysmally low wages paid in the needle trades (twelve and a half cents a day for a fourteen-hour workday), the physical hardships endured by female operatives in the nation's shops and mills (they were awakened at five, required to work fourteen hours a day by lamplight, standing all the while, breathing particles thrown off by the spindles and looms), and the lack of educational and professional opportunities. Even though neither woman supported full equal rights, they were important transitional figures in the emergence of feminism. Each significantly broadened society's definition of "woman's sphere" and assigned women vital social responsibilities: to shape the character of children, to morally uplift husbands, and to promote causes of "practical benevolence," including Sunday schools, playgrounds, and seamen's aid societies (which aided not sailors but abandoned wives, widows, and orphans). Convinced of women's moral superiority and their distinctive capacity for nurturance, both Beecher and Hale argued that women had a special mission to reform American society.

Other women broke down barriers and forged new opportunities in a more dramatic fashion. Frances Wright (1795–1852), a Scottish-born reformer and lecturer, received the nickname, the Great Red Harlot of Infidelity, because of her radical attacks against slavery, religion, and traditional marriage. A brilliant orator, she publicly advocated birth control, liberalized divorce laws, and legal rights for married women—making Fanny Wrightism a synonym for radicalism. In 1849, Elizabeth Blackwell (1821–1910) became the first woman to receive a degree in medicine.

Catalyst for Women's Rights

A public debate over the proper role of women in the antislavery movement, especially their right to lecture to audiences composed of both sexes, led to the first organized movement for women's rights. By 1838, more than one hundred female antislavery societies had been created, and women abolitionists were circulating petitions, editing tracts, and organizing conventions. A key question was whether they would be permitted to lecture to "mixed" audiences of men and women. In 1837, a national women's antislavery convention in New York resolved that women should overcome this taboo: "The time has come for woman to move in that sphere which providence has assigned her, and no longer remain satisfied with the circumscribed limits which corrupt custom and a perverted application of Scripture have encircled her."

Angelina Grimké (1805–79) and her sister Sarah (1792–1873)—from a wealthy Charleston, South Carolina, slaveholding family—were the first women to break the restrictions and widen "woman's sphere" through their writings and their lectures before mixed audiences. In 1837, Angelina gained national notoriety by lecturing against slavery to audiences that included men as well as women. Shocked at Grimké's breach of the separate sexual spheres ordained by God, ministers in Massachusetts called on their fellow clergy to forbid women the right to speak from church pulpits.

Sarah Grimké responded in 1838 with a pamphlet entitled *Letters on the Condition of Women and the Equality of the Sexes,* one of the first modern statements of feminist principles. Declaring that "Men and Women were CREATED EQUAL" and that both sexes were created in the image of God, she denounced the injustice of lower pay and denial of equal educational opportunities for women. Her pamphlet expressed outrage that women were "regarded by men, as pretty toys or as mere instruments of pleasure" and were taught to believe that marriage is "the *sine qua non* [indispensable element] of human happiness and human existence." Men and women, she concluded, should not be treated differently, since both were endowed with inherent natural rights.

After two years of intense public criticism, the Grimké sisters ceased public advocacy of abolition and feminism following Angelina's marriage to abolitionist orator Theodore Weld. But other women proved willing to endure "scorn, contempt, and ridicule" to further the causes of antislavery and women's rights. One of the most notable was Abby Kelley (1811–86). Educated at a Quaker boarding school in Rhode Island, Kelley became a schoolteacher in Lynn, Massachusetts, and joined that town's Female Anti-Slavery Society. In 1839, she became an antislavery lecturer, crisscrossing the North and arguing on behalf of "the holy cause of human rights." Although she was denounced as a "Jezebel" and an "infidel," her lecture tours continued in the 1850s. During Reconstruction, Kelley was a staunch advocate of the Fifteenth Amendment to the Constitution, which enfranchised black men.

In 1840, Kelley's appointment to the business committee of the American Anti-Slavery Society precipitated a major split in abolitionist ranks and sparked the emergence of the modern movement for women's rights. Many evangelical abolitionists, upset by the society's concern for women's rights, left the organization, which was then in the hands of the Garrisonians. They proceeded to name two female delegates to the World Anti-Slavery Convention, which would be held in London later that year. There, these women were denied participation—on the grounds that their involvement would offend British public opinion. The convention relegated them to seats in a balcony.

Eight years later, Lucretia Mott, who had been denied the right to serve as a delegate to the World Anti-Slavery Convention, Elizabeth Cady Stanton, Jane Hunt, Mary Ann M'Clintock, and Martha Wright organized the first women's rights convention in history. The convention was held in July 1848 at Seneca Falls, New York. Three hundred women and men crowded into Wesleyan Methodist Chapel, and for two days debate raged. The convention drew up a Declaration of Sentiments, modeled on the Declaration of Independence, declaring, "All men and women are created equal." The document specified fifteen inequities suffered by women. After detailing "a history of repeated injuries and usurpations on the part of men toward woman," it concluded that "he has endeavored, in every way that he could, to destroy her confidence in her own powers, to lessen her self-respect, and to make her willing to lead a dependent and abject life."

Among the resolutions adopted by the convention, only one was not ratified unanimously—that women be granted the right to vote. Of the sixty-six women and thirty-four men who signed the Declaration of Sentiments at the convention (including black abolitionist Frederick Douglass), only two lived to see the ratification of the women's suffrage amendment to the Constitution seventy-two years later.

By mid-century, women's rights conventions had been held in every northern state. Despite ridicule from the public press—the *Worcester (Massachusetts) Telegraph* denounced women's rights advocates as "Amazons"—female reformers contributed to important, if limited, advances against discrimination. They succeeded in gaining passage of married women's property laws in a number of states, granting married women control over their income and property. A New York law passed in 1860 gave women joint custody of children and the right to sue and be sued, and in several states women's rights reformers secured passage of permissive divorce laws. A Connecticut law, for example, granted divorce for any "misconduct" that "permanently destroys the happiness of the petitioner and defeats the purposes of the marriage relationship."

Utopian Socialism

In 1776, when the outlook for the future seemed bleakest, Tom Paine wrote words that have long inspired Americans: "We have it in our power to begin the world over again." This fervent belief in the attainability of a just social and economic order is a cornerstone of the American creed. But at no time was this spirit stronger than between the 1820s and 1840s, when literally hundreds of utopian communities were founded in Indiana, Massachusetts, New York, Ohio, Tennessee, and elsewhere.

These experimental communal societies were called "utopian communities" because they provided blueprints for a perfectionist vision of an ideal society. Karl Marx referred to the communal impulse as "utopian socialism," because utopians sought to create socialism in a capitalist society.

The thousands who flocked to these communities were inspired by a belief that all social evils and the weaknesses of human nature could be eliminated. If people were not perfect, this was solely because the existing society and its institutions were flawed. In the utopians' view, a competitive economy encouraged people's acquisitiveness; marriage and the family distracted individuals from their obligations to humanity as a whole; conventional notions of sex roles stultified women's intellect and constricted their development; children needed contact with more than two adults; and organized religions spread prejudice. Liberated from oppressive customs and institutions, individuals would at last be rational and virtuous.

These communities varied widely. Some were rooted in a religious faith that Christ's return was imminent and that the righteous should prepare for God's reign by living in accordance with biblical principles. Others were the product of an Enlightenment faith in the shaping influence of environment. Most emphasized economic cooperation; many engaged in radical experiments with diet, clothing, and family and sexual arrangements.

Many communities tried to emancipate women from traditional household and child-rearing responsibilities and to elevate them to positions of equality with men. Some societies, such as the Shakers, the Rappites, and, for a time, the Separatists at Zoar, practiced celibacy; others retained nuclear families while lessening restrictions on divorce and establishing communal child-rearing; still others (like the sexual anarchists at Josiah Warren's Modern Times community or the free-love practitioners in Berlin Heights, Ohio) experimented with different forms of marriage and sexuality, such as polygamy, complex marriage, eugenics, and free love.

The utopians are often treated as harmless eccentrics who advocated such things as frequent cold-water baths, whole wheat bread, vegetarianism, loose-fitting clothing, celibacy, and free love. But in retrospect, what is most striking about these communities is their challenge to the prevailing belief that antebellum American society had found the proper way to live.

Two of the most important early models for utopian experiments were the Shaker communities and Robert Owen's New Harmony. The Shaker communities reflected the religious roots of the utopian impulse, that is, the command in the Book of Revelation to "make all things new." Shaker communities were founded on the religious teachings of Mother Ann Lee, the English-born wife of a blacksmith who believed that the millennium was at hand and that the time had come for people to renounce sin. Accused of blasphemy for preaching that God had both male and female aspects and that sexual intercourse was the basic cause of human sin, she emigrated to America in 1774.

In 1776, two years after her arrival in New York City, she established the first Shaker settlement north of Albany, New York. By 1800, there were twelve Shaker colonies, and at its peak, during the 1830s, the Shaker population reached five to six thousand. These extended "families" placed Shaker men and women on a level of sexual equality and permitted both sexes to serve as elders and deacons. Shakers considered Ann Lee the incarnation of the female half of the bisexual Godhead, just as Jesus was the incarnation of God's male aspects. Critics denounced the Shakers as a "species of Roman Catholicism," because of the emphasis on women in Shaker theology and practice (which antebellum Protestants considered similar to many Catholics' regard for the Virgin Mary).

Aspiring to live like the early Christians, the Shakers adopted communal ownership of property and a way of life built on simplicity, discipline, and asceticism. Their diet included no raw fruit or fresh-baked bread, which were thought to be overly stimulating. Shaker architecture, dress, and furniture were kept simple, functional, and pure. Their communities were devoid of ornament—there were no curtains on windows, carpets, or pictures on the walls. In addition, Shakers invented many practical devices, including the clothespin, the flat broom, and the rotary saw.

The two most striking characteristics of the Shaker communities were their dances and their abstinence from sexual relations. The Shakers believed that religious fervor should be expressed through the head, heart, and mind—dancing and "shaking and singing, hopping and turning . . . groaning and laughing," giving rise to their nickname, the Shakers or the Shaking Quakers.

The Shakers also adopted strict rules concerning celibacy. One member said that his conversion involved "becoming an Eunuch for the kingdom of heaven's sake." All traces of sexuality were eliminated. Men and women were strictly separated (even using separate stairways, so that they would not inadvertently touch one another). Shaker women wore plain and simple dark dresses and white bonnets. They replenished their membership by admitting volunteers and taking in orphans and neglected and abused children; detractors accused the Shakers of kidnapping young children. It is one of the longest-lasting of all utopian societies—nine Shakers remain alive in the early 1990s.

Robert Owen's experimental community at New Harmony, Indiana, presents a striking contrast to the Shaker communities. It reflected the influence of Enlightenment ideas, notably, the importance of reason and environment. Owen, a paternalistic Scottish industrialist, found deeply troubling the social consequences of the Industrial Revolution. Inspired by the idea that environments shape people, Owen purchased a site in Indiana where he sought to establish common ownership of property and abolish religion. At New Harmony, the marriage ceremony became a single sentence, and children were raised outside of their natural parents' home. The community lasted just three years, from 1825 to 1828.

Between 1841 and 1846, there were twenty-five utopian communities, in Massachusetts, New York, Wisconsin, and Iowa, inspired by the French theorist Charles Fourier, who hoped to eliminate poverty and alienation through the establishment of scientifically organized cooperative communities called "phalansteries." During the 1850s, new communities arose in New Jersey, Texas, and elsewhere. Between seven thousand and eight thousand Americans lived for a time at a Fourierist phalanstery. The most famous was Brook Farm, which was converted into a phalanstery in 1841; the largest was La Réunion in Dallas County, Texas, which had 2,240 residents (including many French Fourierists) at its peak.

The Fourier movement offered a radical social critique of the new industrial order that was emerging during the mid-nineteenth century. At a time when older hierarchical structures were giving way to new forms of social stratification, when a market economy was supplanting agricultural self-sufficiency, Fourier sought to restore a sense of community and social harmony. As an alternative to the competitive wage-labor system, Fourier proposed that each phalanstery be set up as a "joint stock company," in which profits were divided according to the amount of money members had invested, their skill, and their labor. To make work more fulfilling, he sought to provide rich offerings of aesthetic and intellectual activities. To redress sexual inequalities, Fourier coined the term *feminism,* and in the phalansteries, women received equal job opportunities and equal pay, equal participation in decision making, and the right to speak in public assemblies. Fourier also sought radical changes in sexual relationships (Ralph Waldo Emerson thought that his goal was "to secure the greatest amount of kissing that the infirmity of the human condition admitted").

Although one Fourier community lasted for eighteen years, most were unsuccessful. Among the factors that contributed to the movement's demise, perhaps the most important were the phalansteries' internal weaknesses. These included a shortage of capable leadership and a membership that lacked the agricultural and business skills necessary to make the communities thrive. Most members were skilled artisans; few were farmers or business proprietors. Promising prosperity and large profits to its members, the phalansteries failed to demand sufficient sacrifice from participants. In 1858, a disillusioned Fourierite named Warren Chase quipped in verse:

> Shut up the book; talk not of brotherhood;
> Man lives for self, not the common good.

The Fourier movement quickly declined, but its influence lingered on in post–Civil War spiritualist, free-love, and anarchist movements. The influence of Fourierite ideas was apparent in the radical notions of sexuality and marriage popularized by Stephen Pearl Andrews, Thomas Low Nichols, and Mary Gove Nichols, as well as postbellum efforts to establish workers' co-operatives.

Among the best-known utopian experiments were Brook Farm, a community located near Boston, and Fruitlands, located near Harvard, Massachusetts. These communities were founded by American transcendentalists, a group of young New Englanders, mostly of Unitarian background, who thought liberal religion too rationalistic to meet their spiritual and emotional needs. Brook Farm and Fruitlands represented an attempt to apply transcendentalist principles to everyday life.

The transcendentalists believed that each person contained infinite and godlike potentialities; that intuition provided the deepest insights into the mysteries of human existence; and that nature was a creative, dynamic force in which people could discover their true selves and commune with the supernatural. Appalled by the complacency, provincialism, and materialism of Boston's elite, highly critical of the alienation and social fragmentation that accompanied the growth of cities and industry, the transcendentalists, led by Ralph Waldo Emerson, called on Americans to strive for true individuality in the face of intense social pressures for conformity.

In 1841, George Ripley, a former Unitarian minister, established Brook Farm in an attempt to substitute "brotherly cooperation" for "selfish competition." One community member declared, "Our ulterior aim is nothing less than Heaven on Earth." Brook Farm's residents, who never numbered more than two hundred, supported themselves by farming, teaching, and manufacturing clothing. The best-known member was Nathaniel Hawthorne, who based his novel *The Blithedale Romance* (1852) on his experiences there. The community lasted in its original form for just three years.

In 1843, Bronson Alcott, another key figure in the transcendentalist circle and a pioneer in child development and education, formed Fruitlands, a community that sought to achieve human perfection through high thinking, manual labor, and dress and diet reform. Practices at Fruitlands included communal ownership of property, frequent cold-water baths, and a diet based entirely on native grains, fruits, and herbs. Community members only ate "aspiring" vegetables, ones that grew upward; potatoes and beets, which grew downward, were prohibited. Residents wore canvas shoes and tunics, and thus did not kill animals for leather or use slave-grown cotton. Sex roles, however, remained unchanged. Responsibility for housekeeping and food preparation fell to Alcott's wife, Abba. Asked by a visitor if there were any beasts of burden at Fruitlands, she replied: "There is one woman."

Between 1820 and 1860, some thirty-five hundred to five thousand African Americans participated in organized black utopias in the upper South, the Midwest, and Canada. Some were founded by white philanthropists; in many cases, the leadership came from blacks. What was most important about these communities was that they offered a degree of freedom and opportunity rarely available in the dominant American society. Here, wrote Horace Mann in 1851, "the whites do not obtrude, and thrust aside the blacks, and seize upon all the posts of honor, and all the eligible and lucrative branches of business."

The most famous interracial utopian community was Nashoba, a product of radical antislavery thought. Frances Wright, a fervent Scottish abolitionist, founded Nashoba Colony in 1826, near Memphis, Tennessee, as a racially integrated cooperative community in which slaves were to receive an education and earn enough money to purchase their own freedom. Unfortunately, publicity about Fanny Wright's desire to abolish the nuclear family, religion, private property, and slavery created a furor, and the community dissolved after only four years.

Other notable antebellum black communities included Wilberforce, in western Ontario, founded in 1829 and settled by many free blacks from Cincinnati; Carthagena, in western Ohio, founded by a white abolitionist named Augustus Wattles in 1835, which lasted for more than a decade; and Dawn, an Ontario community established in the 1840s around a manual labor school. The most successful black community, Elgin, was founded in 1849 near Chatham, Ontario, by William King, the Irish-born abolitionist (and former slaveholder). By the late 1850s, at least two hundred black families lived at Elgin, supporting themselves as farmers and craftsmen.

Perhaps the most notorious and successful experimental colony was John Humphrey Noyes's Oneida Community. Noyes began his career as a lawyer, was converted in one of Charles Finney's revivals, and proceeded to study theology for three years at Andover Theological Seminary and Yale. Convinced that the second coming of Christ had taken place in 70 A.D., Noyes believed that the final millennium would only occur when people strove to become perfect through an "immediate and total cessation from sin."

In Putney, Vermont, in 1835 and in Oneida, New York, in 1848, he established perfectionist communities in which he sought to extend the intimacy of the family to a wider range of social relationships. Rejecting the larger society's notions of exclusive ownership or possession, the communities practiced communal ownership of property, communal child-rearing, and "complex marriage." Complex marriage involved the marriage of each person in the community to every person of the opposite sex.

Exclusive emotional or sexual attachments were forbidden, and sexual relations were arranged through an intermediary in order to protect a woman's individuality. Men were required to practice "male continence"—sexual intercourse without ejaculation—both as a method of birth control and also as a means of ensuring that sexuality was characterized by mutuality and caring rather than lust. After the Civil War, the community conducted experiments in "stirpiculture" or eugenics, the selective control of mating in order to improve the hereditary traits of children. Other notable features of the community were mutual criticism sessions, modeled on the practice in Benedictine monasteries and convents, where priests and nuns followed St. Paul's injunction to "admonish," "rebuke," and "reprove" one another. Oneida flourished in its original form until 1880.

The utopian impulse that was so strong during the first half of the nineteenth century never completely died out. During the second half of the nineteenth century, there were well over one hundred major utopian communities, ranging from Spirit Fruit, a free-love community in Ohio and Illinois, to the all-female Women's Commonwealth in Texas, and the anarchist Equality community in Washington State.

A Cycle of Reform Ends

A series of events that took place in the late 1860s brought the era of radical reform to a symbolic end. In 1865, the abolitionist William Lloyd Garrison suspended publication of his militant newspaper *The Liberator* and called upon the American Anti-Slavery Society to disband. The passage of the Thirteenth Amendment, abolishing slavery, he argued, meant that the society's mission had been accomplished.

Others disagreed. The majority of the antislavery society's members, led by abolitionist Wendell Phillips, argued that full emancipation required education, economic independence, suffrage, and full civil rights for the freedmen. The organization persisted in its efforts until 1870, when the Fifteenth Amendment, extending the vote to black men, was ratified. And even then, many former abolitionists and their children continued to support southern schools and the enactment and enforcement of civil rights legislation.

At the same time that the issue of aid to the freedmen split the ranks of the abolitionists, the controversy over extending political rights to black men brought bitter division to the women's movement. During the Civil War, women's rights advocates Susan B. Anthony and Elizabeth Cady Stanton led a large-scale petition campaign, which gathered three hundred thousand signatures demanding the immediate abolition of slavery. When the war was over, they could not agree on whether women's rights or black rights took priority. While many women's rights advocates—among them, Abby Kelley, Julia Ward Howe, Lucretia Mott, and Lucy Stone—were staunch supporters of the Fifteenth Amendment, others including Anthony and Stanton regarded the amendment, which ignored women, as a defeat and a betrayal. Stanton denounced the amendment with bitter words that would haunt the suffrage movement in the future: "Are we to stand aside and see Sambo walk into the kingdom first?" It would not be until the 1890s that women's rights supporters would reunite in a single organization.

The Civil War left many legacies to reformers, but perhaps the most important was a growing commitment to the use of state power to enforce reform goals. The grim violence of the war shattered the reformers' confidence in the "perfectibility of man" and sparked a reaction against the emotionalism and utopian idealism of pre–Civil War reform. Postwar reform, in general, was more secular and less sentimental, more likely to emphasize professionalism and a scientific analysis of social issues, and more willing to seek the support of the state.

During a period of retrenchment in the 1870s and 1880s, counterreformers reversed many of the accomplishments of prewar reformers by restoring capital punishment and making divorce laws more stringent. The postwar reformers also made uninhibited use of the state to enforce purity and morality by reenacting blue laws (forbidding the sale of goods on Sundays), censoring art, outlawing gambling and lotteries, suppressing the use of narcotics, criminalizing abortion, prohibiting the distribution of contraceptive information, and seeking to make Christianity the state religion.

Still, many of the dreams of the antebellum reformers would live on. The pre–Civil War reformers' spirit of hope and willingness to question established customs and institutions would survive as a source of inspiration for postbellum proponents of labor unions, settlement houses, penal reform, and societies to protect children and women from domestic violence.

Epilogue

Antebellum Reform and
the American Liberal Tradition

Antebellum reform has been characterized in many ways. In positive terms, it was an effort to alleviate suffering and improve the conditions of the unfortunate; to eradicate problems long considered inevitable parts of the human condition—poverty, ignorance, slavery, and gender inequality. And in the more negative description, it was a class-based instrument of social control; an effort to create modern institutions of confinement—including prisons, asylums, and workhouses; to reshape the behavior of deviant groups; and to divert attention from more fundamental problems, such as the growth of economic inequality in the North. There is, however, a term that better defines the antebellum reform impulse and better encompasses its dualities and contradictions: *liberalism.*

Liberalism is, of course, a term with diverse meanings. It can refer to an economic commitment to free competition and self-regulating markets; a religious commitment to tolerance and reason; or a political commitment to greater individual participation in government. Here, however, the term refers to an impulse to ameliorate the harsher aspects of capitalism through collective efforts at reform and a willingness to use the government as an instrument of social betterment. In the American context, liberal reformers have been those people who believed in universal moral standards, who sought to remove arbitrary barriers that stifled individual responsibility and fulfillment, and who refused to acquiesce to social injustices in the name of laissez-faire economics and the free market.

Certainly, not all antebellum reformers were liberals, at least as that term is usually defined. Some, like the abolitionist Beriah Green, were theological conservatives who believed in human depravity. Others, like William Lloyd Garrison and John Humphrey Noyes, were, for a time, genuine radicals who challenged established political and religious institutions, beliefs, and practices. Yet whether their reform philosophy was rooted in evangelical Protestantism, religious liberalism, American transcendentalism, or some other set of beliefs, the aspirations of most antebellum American reformers ultimately tended to be liberal: to broaden individual rights, foster the fulfillment or the salvation of the individual, and eradicate those institutions and customs that obstructed individual self-determination and improvement. Their goals—to extend the meaning of the "inalienable rights" with which all Americans are endowed and adopt a more inclusive definition of those who were "created equal"—were firmly based in the American liberal tradition.

Antebellum American reformers were quite dissimilar from their Tory Radical counterparts in England. The latter—such as Thomas Carlyle— condemned the abuses of capitalism, but also questioned the value of personal liberty and equality (in the name of supposedly higher communitarian values). Most American reformers maintained a liberal faith in individualism, technology, and industry, as long as these forces for material progress were balanced by moral improvement, mass education, religion, and humanitarian reform. American reformers, unlike the Tory Radicals, were not merely social critics; they were themselves modernizers, consolidators, and systematizers and were responsible for creating such social institutions as the modern criminal justice system, the public school system, and the mental health system. Thus, they played a pivotal role in constructing the modern state. Unlike their more provincial adversaries, antebellum reformers tended to be cosmopolitan, highly attuned to European ideas and innovations, and committed to creating a unified moral and political culture based on a common set of institutions and the values of refinement, self-control, and individual self-improvement.

In their belief in education and the essential fairness of a free-labor system, and their sense that social injustices were essentially extraneous to the American economy and polity, antebellum reformers shared many of the strengths and weaknesses of later American liberalism. They had an exaggerated faith that the ills of American society could be solved by a combination of social engineering, moral uplift, professional expertise, and the reshaping of moral character. And, like other liberal reformers, they were often blind to the more coercive, paternalistic aspects and the class and ethnic biases of their reform program.

Today, liberalism is a term in disrepute, and many doubt whether the American liberal tradition, rooted in the individualistic, egalitarian ideals of the late eighteenth century, is capable of addressing contemporary problems of poverty, racial inequality, and environmental degradation. Nevertheless, the liberal aspirations of pre–Civil War reform remain relevant. The antebellum reformers' goals—to place limits on acquisitiveness and exploitation, establish basic standards of human dignity and justice, and renew the ideals of the Declaration of Independence—offer an example and an inspiration to those who seek to solve the present-day problems of poverty, violence, education, and the natural environment.

Bibliographical Essay

For more than half a century, antebellum reform has been a major historiographical battleground. Since the 1920s, historians have repeatedly asked what manner of women and men the reformers were. Were they high-minded idealists, who sought to improve the conditions of the unfortunate and extend the boundaries of compassion to people regardless of race and gender? Or were they social controllers, eager to discipline the poor and the deviant and advance their own class and professional interests? Were they psychological misfits and eccentrics, whose moralistic visions were totally impractical and unrealistic? Or were they practical and pragmatic women and men, creative and flexible in their responses to social evil? Anyone who studies antebellum reform necessarily enters a minefield of conflicting conclusions and contradictory interpretations.

Half a century of controversy has not quieted these debates. Indeed, new disputes have piled atop the older disagreements. Today, some scholars regard antebellum reformers as moral conservatives, eager to reestablish older patterns of deference in the face of such disruptive transformations as the growth of cities and industry and the spread of political democracy. Others reject this view and regard the antebellum reformers as modernizers and consolidators who created our modern bureaucratic systems of public education, criminal justice, and social welfare and who disseminated a distinctly modern set of middle-class values and norms, emphasizing thrift, industriousness, and deferral of gratification. Antebellum reform remains an intellectual arena as exciting as any in American history.

General Works

Most studies of pre–Civil War reform focus on specific movements, such as abolition or women's rights. Since Alice Felt Tyler published *Freedom's Ferment,* her popular survey of pre–Civil War reform, in 1944, only a handful of scholars have offered overviews and interpretations of the antebellum reform impulse as a whole. The most recent general study, Robert H. Abzug, *Cosmos Crumbling: American Reform and the Religious Imagination* (1994), assesses the religious roots of the antebellum reform movement through a series of profiles of reformers who sought to remake society in sacred terms. Ronald Walters, *American Reformers, 1815–1860* (1978), also offers a highly readable account of the lives and ideas of reform activists. For an older but still valuable overview of major interpretations of pre–Civil War reform, see David Brion Davis, ed., *Antebellum Reform* (1967). Of the many collections of primary source materials on the early national period, David Brion Davis, ed., *Antebellum American Culture* (1979), offers a particularly rich sampling of documents of the period.

Chapter 1

During the past quarter century, the roots of the reform impulse have been subjected to intense scrutiny. A number of important recent studies have stressed reform's social and economic origins. One of the most notable is Gordon S. Wood's *The Radicalism of the American Revolution* (1992), which argues that a revolution in social relations coincided with the political revolution that severed America's ties with Britain: a shift from a hierarchical, patriarchal, monarchical social order to an increasingly democratic order. Wood suggests that the period from the Revolution to the election of Andrew Jackson, until recently the most neglected period in American history, was an era of vast social transformations in women's roles, family structure, labor relations, and commerce.

A number of broad interpretations have linked the rise of the reform impulse to the kinds of social and economic dislocations that Wood refers to in his book. Paul Boyer, *Urban Masses and Moral Order in America, 1820–1920* (1978), argues that reform emerged in response to fears about urbanization, industrialization, immigration, family disruption, and deepening class divisions. David Rothman, *The Discovery of the Asylum: Social Order and Disorder in the New Republic* (1971), maintains that such reforms as prisons and insane asylums represented an attempt to reestablish order in a society buffeted by the rise of a market economy, the disintegration of an older patriarchal and hierarchical social order, and the growth of democratic individualism.

The transformations that took place in American politics and society in the late eighteenth century were accompanied by a profound shift in sensibility. A new moral sensibility—acutely sensitive to disorder, cruelty, and physical coercion—emerged alongside a new "middle-class" code of behavior emphasizing gentility, character, and self-control. These developments are acutely analyzed in Richard L. Bushman, *The Refinement of America* (1992); Karen Halttunen, *Confidence Men and Painted Women* (1982); John F. Kasson, *Rudeness and Civility* (1990); and Daniel T. Rodgers, *The Work Ethic in Industrial America, 1850–1920* (1978).

Chapter 2

If reform was related to large-scale social and economic transformations, it also drew moral and intellectual nourishment from such cultural sources as the nation's revolutionary heritage, the philosophy of the Enlightenment, the Scottish common sense philosophy, and, above all, from religion. The late eighteenth and early nineteenth centuries witnessed momentous changes in American religion, ranging from the disestablishment of the remaining churches to evangelical revivalism and the astonishing growth of new religious denominations and sects. A valuable reference work that contains essays on major topics in American religious history is Charles H. Lippy and Peter W. Williams, eds., *Encyclopedia of the American Religious Experience* (3 vols., 1988). Two penetrating and provocative interpretations of American religion prior to the Civil War are John Butler, *Awash in a Sea of Faith* (1990), and Nathan O. Hatch, *The Democratization of American Christianity* (1989). Useful one-volume surveys of American religious history include Sidney Ahlstrom, *A Religious History of the American People* (1972), and George M. Marsden, *Religion and American Culture* (1990). Gordon S. Wood, "Evangelical America and Early Mormonism," *New York History* (October 1980): 359–86, offers a brief and highly informative introduction to the religious ferment that followed the American Revolution.

Religious historians have differed sharply in their assessment of the meaning of antebellum evangelical Protestantism. One group of scholars has argued that the evangelical impulse was essentially conservative, seeking to tame violence, refine manners, impose the Protestant work ethic, and rescue American society from barbarism and savagery. A second group of historians has looked at evangelical religion from a diametrically opposite point of view, describing it as a force for social betterment and moral improvement. According to this group, evangelical revivalists contributed to the reform impulse by defining sin in concrete terms, linking personal piety to social activism, and stimulating millennial expectations. In practice, antebellum evangelical religion had two sides. It sought to restrain licentiousness and greed and restore the government of God on earth by spreading a code of personal piety and self-restraint. But it also stimulated social reform by upholding millennial and perfectionist ideals and demanding that society conform to God's moral law.

The literature on antebellum religion is so vast that I can only suggest a few of the most important sources. On southern and western revivalism, see John B. Boles, *The Great Revival, 1782–1805* (1972); Anne C. Loveland, *Southern Evangelicals and the Social Order* (1980); and Donald G. Mathews, *Religion in the Old South* (1977). Religious ferment in western New York is examined in Michael Barkum, *Crucible of the Millennium* (1986); Whitney Cross, *The Burned-Over District* (1950); and David Rowe, *Thunder and Trumpets* (1985). Keith J. Hardman's *Charles Grandison Finney* (1987) is the most recent biography of the leading northern revivalist. The fate of revivalism following the Civil War is examined in fascinating detail in William C. Martin, *A Prophet with Honor: The Billy Graham Story* (1991).

A number of studies have sought to uncover evangelical religion's social roots. William McLoughlin, *Modern Revivalism* (1959), and Bernard Weisberger, *They Gathered at the River* (1958), link the rise of revivalism to status anxieties and resentments. Whitney Cross, *The Burned Over-District* (1950), and T. Scott Miyakawa, *Protestants and Pioneers* (1964), emphasize social instability and denominational competition as sources of revivalism. Joseph F. Kett, *Rites of Passage* (1977), and Nancy F. Cott, *Bonds of Womanhood*, tie the decision of young people to take part in revivals to the challenge of establishing an adult identity in a rapidly changing society. Paul E. Johnson, *A Shopkeeper's Millennium* (1978), argues that revivalism attracted the more ambitious, upwardly mobile citizens in Rochester, New York.

The Panic of 1837 ushered in independent evangelical movements among the urban working class, a subject examined in Bruce Laurie, *Working People of Philadelphia* (1980), and Paul Faler, *Mechanics and Manufacturers in the Early Industrial Revolution* (1981). Paul Goodman, *Toward a Christian Republic* (1988), links the rise of the anti-Masonic movement to anxieties about the rise of secularism, denominationalism, and religious fragmentation.

The Quakers stood at the forefront of many pre–Civil War reform movements. The origins of Quaker benevolence are examined in Hugh Barbour and J. William Frost, *The Quakers* (1988), and Jack D. Marietta, *The Reformation of American Quakerism* (1984). Like the Quakers, Unitarians contributed disproportionately to the cause of reform. See Daniel Walker Howe, *The Unitarian Conscience* (1970), and Anne C. Rose, *Transcendentalism as a Social Movement* (1981). Basic introductions to the history of the Mormon church include Leonard J. Arrington and Davis Bitton, *The Mormon Experience* (1979); Richard L. Bushman, *Joseph Smith and the Beginnings of Mormonism* (1984); Klaus I. Hansen, *Mormonism and the American Experience* (1981); and Jan Shipps, *Mormonism* (1985).

On African American religion, see John B. Boles, ed., *Masters and Slaves in the House of the Lord* (1988); Lawrence W. Levine, *Black Culture and Black Consciousness* (1977); and Albert J. Raboteau, *Slave Religion* (1978). On American Catholicism, see Jay P. Nolan, *The American Catholic Church* (1985), *Catholic Revivalism* (1978), and *The Immigrant Church* (1983); James E. Prest, *American Catholic History* (1991); and Timothy Walch, *Catholicism in America* (1989). Highly informative histories of American Judaism are Eli Faber, *A Time for Planting, 1654–1820* (1992); Hasia R. Diner, *A Time for Gathering, 1820–1880* (1992); and Howard M. Sachar, *A History of the Jews in America* (1992). For the important role played by women in antebellum religion, see Amanda Porterfield, *Feminine Spirituality in America* (1980).

Chapter 3

A number of books have dissected the connections between religion and secular reform, including Charles I. Foster, *An Errand of Mercy: The Evangelical United Front* (1960); Clifford S. Griffin, *Their Brothers' Keepers: Moral Stewardship in the United States* (1960); William G. McLoughlin Jr., *Revivals, Awakenings, and Reform* (1980); Randolph A. Roth, *The Democratic Dilemma: Religion, Reform, and the Social Order in the Connecticut River Valley of Vermont, 1791–1850* (1987); and Timothy L. Smith, *Revivalism and Social Reform* (1957). For the special role of religious women in organized benevolent activities, Anne M. Boylan, "Women in Groups: An Analysis of Women's Benevolent Organizations in New York and Boston, 1797–1840," *Journal of American History* 71 (1984): 497–523; Lori D. Ginzberg, *Women and the Work of Benevolence: Morality, Politics, and Class in the Nineteenth-Century United States* (1990); Nancy A. Hewitt, *Women's Activism and Social Change: Rochester, New York, 1822–1872* (1984); and Mary P. Ryan, *Cradle of the Middle Class: The Family in Oneida County, New York, 1790–1865* (1981).

The emergence of urban missions, industrial training schools, medical dispensaries, and orphanages is examined in Carroll Smith-Rosenberg, *Religion and the Rise of the American City: The New York City Mission Movement, 1812–1870* (1971). On foreign missions, see Charles L. Chaney, *The Birth of Missions in America* (1976); Patricia R. Hill, *The World Their Household: The American Woman's Foreign Mission Movement and Cultural Transformation, 1870–1920* (1985); Jane Hunter, *The Gospel of Gentility: American Women Missionaries in Turn-of-the-Century China* (1984); and William R. Hutchison, *Errand to the World: American Protestant Thought and Foreign Missions* (1987). Black participation in foreign missions is analyzed in David W. Wills and Richard Newman, eds., *Black Apostles at Home and Abroad* (1982). On missionary activity among Native Americans, see John Andrew III, *From Revivals to Removal* (1992); Henry Warner Bow, *American Indians and Christian Missions: Studies in Cultural Conflict* (1981); William G. McLoughlin, *Cherokees and Missionaries* (1984); and Herman J. Viola, *Thomas L. McKenney: Architect of America's Early Indian Policy* (1974).

The origins and changing functions of the Sunday school are imaginatively explored in Anne M. Boylan, *Sunday School: The Formation of an American Institution, 1790–1880* (1988). For a transatlantic perspective, see Thomas Walter Laqueur, *Religion and Respectability: Sunday Schools and Working Class Culture, 1780–1850* (1976).

Fresh and highly original studies of prostitution are Timothy J. Gilfoyle, *City of Eros: New York City, Prostitution and the Commercialization of Sex, 1790–1920* (1992); Barbara Meil Hobson, *Uneasy Virtue: The Politics of Prostitution and the American Reform Tradition* (1987); and Carroll Smith-Rosenberg, *Disorderly Conduct: Visions of Gender in Victorian America* (1985).

On Sabbatarianism, see Bertram Wyatt-Brown, "Prelude to Abolitionism: Sabbatarian Politics and the Rise of the Second Party System," *Journal of American History* 63 (1971): 316–41; Winton U. Solberg, *Redeem the Time: The Puritan Sabbath in Early America* (1977); and John Wigley, *The Rise and Fall of the Victorian Sunday* (1980).

The temperance movement has produced a remarkably rich and contentious literature. Many recent works have sought to rebut the argument advanced by sociologist Joseph R. Gusfield in *Symbolic Crusade* (1963) that temperance was a conservative effort by the middle class and the clergy, threatened by the growing power of industry, to reassert their moral authority; by nativists to control the growing immigrant population; and by factory owners to produce a sober, efficient labor force.

Norman H. Clark, *Deliver Us from Evil: An Interpretation of American Prohibition* (1976), argues that temperance reformers, far from being conservative, sought to promote a "bourgeois" morality, emphasizing domesticity, industry, and progress, and viewed temperance as a solution to the pressing problems of poverty, crime, vice, and violence. Ian R. Tyrrell, *Sobering Up: From Temperance to Prohibition in Antebellum America, 1800–1860* (1979), maintains that the antebellum temperance movement evolved in stages, each with its own distinct ideology, leadership, base of support, and tactics.

W. J. Rorabaugh, *The Alcoholic Republic* (1979), contends that the temperance movement represented a response to an actual upsurge in drinking, which, in turn, reflected the growth of a market economy. This development increased the availability of cheap whiskey and caused a loss of social cohesion, leading many men to drink. Barbara Leslie Epstein, *The Politics of Domesticity: Women, Evangelism, and Temperance in Nineteenth-Century America* (1981), analyzes the prominent role of women in the temperance crusade. A superb overview of the temperance and prohibition movements is James Kirby Martin and Mark Lender, *Drinking in America* (rev. ed., 1987).

Chapter 4

Scholars have presented a variety of explanations for the sudden proliferation in the early nineteenth century of asylums for paupers, criminals, juvenile delinquents, the mentally ill, and the handicapped. David J. Rothman's enormously influential *The Discovery of the Asylum: Social Order and Disorder in the New Republic* (1971) offers a structural-functional argument that antebellum Americans constructed those specialized institutions to promote social stability by inculcating discipline, order, and restraint in the poor and the criminal.

Other recent works link the emergence of the asylum to the new understanding about dependency and deviance and to the growth of cities, which made such problems more visible. Emphasizing the environmental causes of poverty, crime, and other social ills, reformers sought to remove individuals from the conditions producing pauperism, delinquency, and debility. At the same time, reformers struggled to employ rational, humane, and individualized methods of prevention and rehabilitation, free of superstition. Gerald N. Grob has offered particularly powerful expressions of this perspective in such works as *The State and the Mentally Ill: A History of Worcester State Hospital in Massachusetts, 1830–1920* (1966) and *Mental Institutions in America: Social Policy to 1875* (1973).

More skeptical assessments of the asylum founders' motives have reflected Michel Foucault's contention that such institutions gave expression to a "bourgeois" preoccupation with isolating and stigmatizing deviants and dependents and instilling order, conformity, and self-discipline. A sophisticated example of this line of argument can be found in Mary Ann Jimenez, *Changing Faces of Madness: Early American Attitudes and Treatment of the Insane* (1987).

The failure of asylums to fulfill the grandiose hopes of their founders has also stimulated debate. Some works, like Rothman's, attribute the failure and the persistence of the asylum model to the mixture of motives that lay behind the "mask of benevolence": the desire of families and communities to relieve themselves of the costs of caring for the handicapped and the impulse to incarcerate criminals and delinquents. Other works, stressing the genuine humanitarianism of the asylum founders, tend to attribute the failures to factors outside the institutions' control: public ignorance and indifference; the unwillingness of authorities to ensure decent funding and adequate staff; and the difficulty of recruiting and retaining competent caretakers.

The discovery of poverty and the growing public awareness of urban slums are examined in Robert Bremner, *From the Depths: The Discovery of Poverty in the United States* (1956); Raymond A. Mohl, *Poverty in New York, 1783–1825* (1971); and David Ward, *Poverty, Ethnicity, and the American City, 1840–1925: Changing Conceptions of the Slum and the Ghetto* (1989). Public responses to poverty are analyzed in John K. Alexander, *Render Them Submissive: Responses to Poverty in Philadelphia, 1760–1800* (1980); Michael B. Katz, *In the Shadow of the Poorhouse: A Social History of Welfare in America* (1986); and Gertrude Himmelfarb, *The Idea of Poverty: England in the Early Industrial Age* (1984).

The best general introductions to antebellum prison reform are W. David Lewis, *From Newgate to Dannemora: The Rise of the Penitentiary in New York, 1796–1848* (1965), and Blake McKelvey, *American Prisons: A Study in American Social History prior to 1915* (1936). Fascinating studies of women prisoners are Estelle B. Freedman, *Their Sisters' Keepers: Women's Prison Reform in America, 1830–1930* (1981), and Nicole Hahn Rafter, *Partial Justice: Women in State Prisons, 1800–1935* (1985). Two brilliant attempts to understand regional differences in crime and criminal justice are Edward L. Ayres, *Vengeance and Justice: Crime and Punishment in the 19th-Century American South* (1984), and Michael Stephen

Hindus, *Prison and Plantation: Crime, Justice, and Authority in Massachusetts and South Carolina, 1767–1878* (1980).

Organized efforts to address the problems of orphaned, destitute, delinquent, abused, and neglected children are examined in Joseph M. Hawes, *Children in Urban Society: Juvenile Delinquency in Nineteenth-Century America* (1971); Peter C. Holloran, *Boston's Wayward Children: Social Services for Homeless Children, 1830–1930* (1989); Robert M. Mennel, *Thorns and Thistles: Juvenile Delinquents in the United States, 1825–1940* (1973); Robert S. Pickett, *House of Refuge: Origins of Juvenile Reform in New York State, 1815–1857* (1969); Eric C. Schneider, *In the Web of Class: Delinquents and Reformers in Boston, 1810–1930s* (1992); Steven L. Schloss-man, *Love and the American Delinquent: The Theory and Practice of "Progressive" Juvenile Justice, 1825–1920* (1977); and John R. Sutton, *Stubborn Children: Controlling Delinquency in the United States, 1640–1981* (1988). Barbara M. Brenzel, *Daughters of the State: A Social Portrait of the First Reform School for Girls in North America, 1856–1905* (1983), focuses on the special problems faced by neglected or "wayward" girls. Anthony M. Platt, *The Child Savers: The Invention of Delinquency* (1969), questions the benevolence of the proponents of refuges and reformatories.

Myra C. Glenn, *Campaigns against Corporal Punishment: Prisoners, Sailors, Women, and Children in Antebellum America* (1984), examines antebellum contro-versies over the use of physical punishment in homes, schools, prisons, asylums, and the navy. On the movement to abolish capital punishment, see Louis P. Masur, *Rites of Execution: Capital Punishment and the Transformation of American Culture, 1776–1865* (1989). The best study of the abolition of imprisonment for debt is Peter J. Coleman, *Debtors and Creditors in America: Insolvency, Imprisonment for Debt, and Bankruptcy* (1974).

The classic studies of psychiatry and mental institutions are Norman Dain, *Concepts of Insanity in the United States, 1789–1865* (1964), and Gerald N. Grob, *Mental Institutions in America: Social Policy to 1875* (1973). Changing social defini-tions of madness, theories of insanity and appropriate treatment, and the motives of reformers are illuminated by Norman Dain, *Disordered Minds: The First Cen-tury of Eastern State Hospital in Williamsburg, Virginia, 1766–1866* (1971); Gerald N. Grob, *Edward Jarvis and the Medical World of Nineteenth-Century America* (1978) and *The State and the Mentally Ill: A History of Worcester State Hospital in Massa-chusetts, 1830–1920* (1966); Mary Ann Jimenez, *Changing Faces of Madness: Early American Attitudes and Treatment of the Insane* (1987); and Nancy Tomes, *A Generous Confidence: Thomas Story Kirkbride and the Art of Asylum-Building, 1840–1883* (1984). On the internal dynamics of nineteenth-century asylums, see Ellen Dwyer's brilliant *Homes for the Mad: Life inside Two Nineteenth-Century Asylums* (1987). A pioneering study of the treatment of mental retardation is Peter L. Tyor and Leland V. Bell, *Caring for the Retarded in America: A History* (1984).

A bold and provocative literature has appeared on the history of deaf people, including John Vickrey Van Cleve and Barry A. Crouch, *A Place of Their Own:*

Creating the Deaf Community in America (1989); and Harlan Lane, *The Mask of Benevolence: Disabling the Deaf Community* (1992) and *When the Mind Hears: A History of the Deaf* (1984). The best works on the history of blind people are Gabriel Farrell, *The Story of Blindness* (1956); Frances A. Koestler, *The Unseen Minority: A Social History of Blindness in America* (1976); and Isabel Ross, *Journey into Light: The Story of the Education of the Blind* (1951).

The literature on the history of education is vast. Excellent surveys of the history of American education are Lawrence A. Cremin, *American Education: The National Experience, 1783–1876* (1980); David Nasaw, *Schooled to Order: A Social History of Public Schooling in the United States* (1979); and David B. Tyack, *The One Best System: A History of American Urban Education* (1974). The best brief account of antebellum school reform is Carl F. Kaestle, *Pillars of the Republic: Common Schools and American Society, 1780–1860* (1983). On coeducation, see David B. Tyack and Elisabeth Hansot, *Learning Together: A History of Coeducation in American Public Schools* (1990).

James Axtell, *The School upon a Hill: Education and Society in Colonial New England* (1974), and Kenneth A. Lockridge, *Literacy in Colonial New England: An Enquiry into the Social Context of Literacy in the Early Modern West* (1974), challenge older assumptions about the inadequacy of American education prior to the creation of common schools.

Charles Leslie Glenn Jr., *The Myth of the Common School* (1988), traces the development of the idea that the state should sponsor public education in order to mold common loyalties and values among its citizens. Carl F. Kaestle, *The Evolution of an Urban School System: New York City, 1750–1850* (1973), and Stanley K. Schultz, *The Culture Factory: Boston Public Schools, 1789–1860* (1973), analyze the consolidation of schools into single systems amenable to uniform policy decisions. Carl F. Kaestle and Maris A. Vinovskis, *Education and Social Change in Nineteenth-Century Massachusetts* (1980), examine schooling patterns in small towns and rural areas.

A fine study of antebellum America's leading educational reformer is Jonathan Messerli, *Horace Mann: A Biography* (1972). Diane Ravitch, *The Great School Wars: New York City, 1805–1973* (1974), describes the role of ethnic conflict in shaping school policies, while David Tyack and Elisabeth Hansot, *Managers of Virtue: School Leadership in America, 1820–1980* (1982), examine the individuals who ran public schools. For critical perspectives on the class, religious, and ethnic biases of public schools, see Samuel Bowles and Herbert Gintis, *Schooling in Capitalist America: Educational Reform and the Contradictions of Economic Life* (1976); and Michael B. Katz, *Class, Bureaucracy, and Schools: The Illusion of Educational Change in America* (1971) and *The Irony of Early School Reform: Educational Innovation in Mid-Nineteenth Century Massachusetts* (1968). For Prudence Crandall and the struggle for black education, see Philip S. Foner and Josephine F. Pacheco, *Three Who Dared: Prudence Crandall, Margaret Douglass,*

Myrtilla Miner—Champions of Antebellum Black Education (1984), and Susan Strane, *"A Whole-Souled Woman": Prudence Crandall and the Education of Black Women* (1990).

Chapter 5

No field of history has aroused more bitter debate or provoked more radical revision than antislavery. Since the 1920s and 1930s, historians have vigorously debated abolitionists' motives, tactics, and responsibility for bringing on the Civil War. The earliest writings on antislavery—by former New England abolitionists such as Wendell Phillips and Parker Pillsbury—pictured abolition as essentially a New England movement under the leadership of William Lloyd Garrison. During the 1930s, two historians from the Midwest, Dwight L. Dumond and Gilbert H. Barnes, challenged this view. Their accounts emphasized the role of evangelical religion in the rise of abolitionism, disputed Garrison's preeminence in the movement, and drew a sharp distinction between radical New England abolition and a supposedly more pragmatic and responsible midwestern sort.

Also, beginning in the 1930s, a number of influential southern historians, including Avery Craven, Frank L. Owsley, Charles W. Ramsdell, and James G. Randall, raised doubts about the abolitionists' motives and methods. These so-called revisionist historians and their successors traced the roots of abolition to psychological maladjustments and status anxieties and considered the abolitionists to be irresponsible fanatics whose extremism and uncompromising moralism created an atmosphere of hysteria and pushed the nation toward civil war.

During the 1950s, the influence of the social sciences, especially the fields of sociology and social psychology, encouraged historians to study antislavery from new directions. One new approach, suggested by two influential American historians, David Donald and Stanley Elkins, was essentially sociological and attempted to relate abolition to the amorphousness of antebellum America's social structure, which lacked institutional channels to moderate dissent. A second new approach, suggested by a British historian, Frank Thistlethwaite, was comparative and cross-cultural. This approach, which regarded American abolition as part of a larger transatlantic movement, indicated the need for comparative studies to reveal the differences between antislavery movements in distinct national contexts. The civil rights movement also provoked fresh thinking. During the 1960s, a number of influential New Left historians rejected the argument that the abolitionists were irresponsible agitators and fanatics, and regarded them instead as the conscience of an immoral society. Other New Left historians, however, charged that many white abolitionists shared the racism—and the middle-class values—of antebellum society.

Today, many of the issues raised by earlier generations of historians still rage:

Whether abolitionist protests undermined slavery and racial prejudice or merely reinforced resistance to change; whether abolitionists offered realistic and practical solutions to the nation's racial problems or whether their emphasis on the superiority of free labor diverted attention from the fundamental problems of poverty and inequality in the North; and whether abolitionists were a declining social elite, who used antislavery to protest against a new industrial order, or represented rising social classes, challenging the power of entrenched elites.

The best brief surveys and interpretations of antislavery are Merton L. Dillon, *Slavery Attacked: Southern Slaves and Their Allies, 1619–1865* (1990); Gerald Sorin, *Abolitionism: A New Perspective* (1972); and James Brewer Stewart, *Holy Warriors: The Abolitionists and American Slavery* (1986). Recent directions in the study of abolitionism are presented in Lewis Perry and Michael Fellman, eds., *Antislavery Reconsidered: New Perspectives on the Abolitionists* (1979).

The sources of antislavery thought are examined in David Brion Davis, *The Problem of Slavery in Western Culture* (1967) and *The Problem of Slavery in the Age of Revolution, 1770–1823* (1975). James D. Essig, *The Bonds of Wickedness: American Evangelicals against Slavery, 1770–1808* (1982); Jean R. Soderlund, *Quakers and Slavery: A Divided Spirit* (1985); and Arthur Zilversmit, *The First Emancipation: The Abolition of Negro Slavery in the North* (1967), are superb studies of early abolitionists. Betty Fladeland, *Men and Brothers: Anglo-American Antislavery Cooperation* (1972), places abolitionism in a transatlantic perspective. The most insightful books on the colonization movement are Sheldon Harris, *Paul Cuffe: Black America and the African Return* (1972); Floyd J. Miller, *The Search for a Black Nationality: Black Emigration and Colonization, 1787–1863* (1975); and Philip J. Staudenraus, *The African Colonization Movement, 1816–1865* (1961).

A large number of important recent books analyze the perceptions, attitudes, values, goals, and tactics of those northern blacks who struggled against slavery and racial discrimination inside and outside the abolitionist movement. These include Leonard P. Curry, *The Free Black in Urban America, 1800–1850* (1981); James Oliver Horton and Lois E. Horton, *Black Bostonians: Family Life and Community Struggle in the Antebellum North* (1979); Roger Lane, *William Dorsey's Philadelphia and Ours* (1991); Leon Litwack and August Meier, eds., *Black Leaders of the Nineteenth Century* (1988); Gary B. Nash, *Forging Freedom: The Formation of Philadelphia's Black Community* (1988) and *Race, Class, and Politics: Essays on American Colonial and Revolutionary Society* (1986); Gary B. Nash and Jean R. Soderlund, *Freedom by Degrees: Emancipation in Pennsylvania and Its Aftermath* (1991); Jane H. Pease and William H. Pease, *They Who Would Be Free: Blacks' Search for Freedom, 1830–1861* (1974); Dorothy Sterling, ed., *We Are Your Sisters: Black Women in the Nineteenth Century* (1984); Sterling Stuckey, *Slave Culture: Nationalist Theory and the Foundations of Black America* (1987); Shane White, *Somewhat More Independent: The End of Slavery in New York City, 1770–1810* (1991); Charles M. Wiltse, ed., *David Walker's Appeal to the Coloured Citizens of the World*

(1965); and Julie Winch, *Philadelphia's Black Elite: Activism, Accommodation, and the Struggle for Autonomy, 1787–1848* (1988).

Important studies of black abolitionists are R. J. M. Blackett, *Building an Antislavery Wall: Black Americans in the Atlantic Abolitionist Movement, 1830–1860* (1983); Milton C. Sernett, *Abolition's Axe: Beriah Green, Oneida Institute, and the Black Freedom Struggle* (1986); Benjamin Quarles, *Black Abolitionists* (1969); and Shirley J. Yee, *Black Women Abolitionists* (1992). On the black convention movement, see Howard H. Bell, *A Survey of the Negro Convention Movement, 1830–1861* (1969). On African Americans and the Underground Railroad, see Henrietta Buckmaster, *Let My People Go: The Story of the Underground Railroad and the Growth of the Abolition Movement* (1992). Significant biographies are Jacqueline Bernard, *Journey toward Freedom: The Story of Sojourner Truth* (1967); Cyril E. Griffith, *The African Dream: Martin R. Delany and the Emergence of Pan-African Thought* (1975); William McFeely, *Frederick Douglass* (1991); Hertha Pauli, *Her Name Was Sojourner Truth* (1962); and Dickson J. Preston, *Young Frederick Douglass: The Maryland Years* (1980).

Louis S. Gerteis, *Morality and Utility in American Antislavery Reform* (1987), and Ronald G. Walters, *The Antislavery Appeal* (1976), present highly original interpretations of the abolitionist arguments against slavery. Edward Magdol, *The Antislavery Rank and File: A Social Profile of the Abolitionists' Constituency* (1986), carefully examines the social composition of the abolitionist movement. The racial attitudes of abolitionists and their adversaries are covered by Eugene H. Berwanger, *The Frontier against Slavery: Western Anti-Negro Prejudice and the Slavery Extension Controversy* (1967); George M. Fredrickson, *The Arrogance of Race: Historical Perspectives on Slavery, Racism, and Social Inequality* (1988); Leon F. Litwack, *North of Slavery: The Negro in the Free States, 1790–1860* (1961); and V. Jacques Voegeli, *Free But Not Equal: The Midwest and the Negro during the Civil War* (1967). Anti-abolitionist violence is imaginatively explored by Leonard Richard, *"Gentlemen of Property and Standing": Anti-Abolition Mobs in Jacksonian America* (1970).

Blanche Glassman Hirsch, *The Slavery of Sex: Feminist-Abolitionists in America* (1978), and Jean Fagan Yellin, *Women and Sisters: The Antislavery Feminists in American Culture* (1989), offer insightful studies of the experience of women within abolitionism. Lawrence Friedman, *Gregarious Saints: Self and Community in American Abolitionism, 1830–1870* (1982), examines the internal dynamics of the abolitionist movement. The radical wing of abolition is illuminated by Aileen S. Kraditor, *Means and Ends in American Abolitionism: Garrison and His Critics on Strategy and Tactics* (1969), and Lewis Perry, *Radical Abolitionism: Anarchy and the Government of God in Antislavery Thought* (1973).

For an incisive discussion of abolitionist criticism of the established churches, see John R. McKivigan, *The War against Proslavery Religion: Abolitionism and the Northern Churches, 1830–1865* (1984). On the legal and constitutional struggles over slavery, see Robert Cover, *Justice Accused: Antislavery and the Judicial Process* (1975); Howard Jones, *Mutiny on the Amistad* (1986); Thomas O. Morris, *Free Men All: The Personal Liberty Laws of the North, 1780–1861* (1974); Russel B. Nye, *Fettered Freedom: Civil Liberties and the Slavery Controversy* (1963); and William M. Wiecek, *The Sources of Antislavery Constitutionalism in America, 1760–1848* (1977).

For political antislavery, see Frederick J. Blue, *The Free Soilers: Third Party Politics, 1848–54* (1973); Alan M. Kraut, ed., *Crusaders and Compromisers: Essays on the Relationship of the Antislavery Struggle to the Antebellum Party System* (1983); and Richard H. Sewell, *Ballots for Freedom: Antislavery Politics in the United States, 1837–1860* (1976). Tyler Anbinder, *Nativism and Slavery: The Northern Know Nothings and the Politics of the 1850s* (1992), and Robert William Fogel, *Without Consent or Contract: The Rise and Fall of American Slavery* (1989), analyze the ideological and political struggle to abolish slavery, placing particular emphasis on the connections between antislavery and nativism. James M. McPherson, *The Abolitionist Legacy: From Reconstruction to the NAACP* (1976), examines the fate of abolition during and after the Civil War.

Many illuminating studies of abolitionism have taken the form of biographies. Among the most insightful are Robert H. Abzug, *Passionate Liberator: Theodore Dwight Weld and the Dilemma of Reform* (1980); Margaret Hope Bacon, *Valiant Friend: The Life of Lucretia Mott* (1980); Hugh Davis, *Joshua Leavitt: Evangelical Abolitionist* (1990); Betty Fladeland, *James Gillespie Birney: Slaveholder to Abolitionist* (1955); Lawrence B. Goodheart, *Abolitionist, Actuary, Atheist: Elizur Wright and the Reform Impulse* (1990); Gerda Lerner, *The Grimké Sisters from South Carolina: Rebels against Slavery* (1967); Stephen B. Oates, *To Purge This Land with Blood: A Biography of John Brown* (1970); Jane H. Pease and William H. Pease, *Bound with Them in Chains: A Biographical History of the American Antislavery Movement* (1972); Lewis Perry, *Childhood, Marriage, and Reform: Henry Clarke Wright, 1797–1870* (1980); Benjamin Quarles, *Allies for Freedom: Blacks and John Brown* (1974); Richard H. Sewell, *John B. Hale and the Politics of Abolition* (1965); James Brewer Stewart, *Joshua R. Giddings and the Tactics of Radical Politics* (1970), *Liberty's Hero: Wendell Phillips* (1986), and *William Lloyd Garrison and the Challenge of Emancipation* (1991); and Bertram Wyatt-Brown, *Lewis Tappan and the Evangelical War against Slavery* (1969).

The best introductions to the peace movement are Peter Brock, *Pacificism in the United States: From the Colonial Era to the First World War* (1968); Merle Curti, *The American Peace Crusade, 1815–1860* (1929); Charles DeBenedetti, *The Peace Reform in American History* (1980); and Valerie H. Ziegler, *The Advocates of Peace in Antebellum America* (1992).

Two highly readable and informative general histories of American women are Sara Evans, *Born for Liberty: A History of Women in America* (1989), and Nancy Woloch, *Women and the American Experience* (1984). The changing status of

American women during the late eighteenth and early nineteenth centuries is brilliantly analyzed in Nancy F. Cott, *The Bonds of Womanhood: "Woman's Sphere" in New England, 1780–1835* (1977). Barbara I. Berg, *The Remembered Gate: Origins of American Feminism—The Woman and the City, 1800–1860* (1978); Lori D. Ginzberg, *Women and the Work of Benevolence: Morality, Politics, and Class in the Nineteenth-Century United States* (1990); Nancy A. Hewitt, *Women's Activism and Social Change: Rochester, New York, 1822–1872* (1984); and Mary P. Ryan, *Cradle of the Middle Class: The Family in Oneida County, New York, 1790–1865* (1981), imaginatively trace the links between secular benevolence and the origins of modern feminism. Christine Stansell's *City of Women: Sex and Class in New York, 1789–1860* (1986) is a brilliant study of the world of working-class women. For the history of female volunteerism, see Anne Firor Scott, *Natural Allies: Women's Associations in American History* (1992).

Norma Basch, *In the Eyes of the Law: Women, Marriage, and Property in Nineteenth-Century New York* (1982), and Peggy A. Rabkin, *Fathers to Daughters: The Legal Foundations of Female Emancipation* (1980), analyze changes in women's legal rights. For post–Civil War feminism, see Ellen Carol DuBois, *Feminism and Suffrage: The Emergence of an Independent Women's Movement in America, 1848–1869* (1978). Informative biographies include Celia Morris Eckhardt, *Fanny Wright: Rebel in America* (1984); Elisabeth Griffith, *In Her Own Right: The Life of Elizabeth Cady Stanton* (1984); Kathryn Kish Sklar, *Catharine Beecher: A Study in Domesticity* (1976); Dorothy Sterling, *Ahead of Her Time: Abby Kelley and the Politics of Antislavery* (1992); and Joyce W. Warren, *Fanny Fern: An Independent Woman* (1992).

The best general introductions to utopian socialism are Arthur Bestor, *Backwoods Utopias: The Sectarian and Owenite Phases of Communitarian Socialism in America, 1663–1829* (1950); Donald D. Egbert and Stow Persons, *Socialism and American Life* (1952); and Mark Halloway, *Heavens on Earth: Utopian Communities in America, 1680–1880* (2d ed., 1966). Innovative interpretations of the communitarian impulse are Michael Fellman, *The Unbounded Frame: Freedom and Community in Nineteenth Century American Utopianism* (1973); Lawrence Foster, *Religion and Sexuality: The Shakers, the Mormons, and the Oneida Community* (1981); Rosabeth Moss Kanter, *Commitment and Community: Communes and Utopias in Sociological Perspective* (1972); Raymond Lee Muncy, *Sex and Marriage in Utopian Communities: Nineteenth-Century America* (1973); and Laurence Veysey, *The Communal Experience: Anarchist and Mystical Counter-Cultures in America* (1973).

For the Shakers, see Henri Deroches, *The American Shakers from Neo-Christianity to Pre-Socialism* (1971); Marguerite Fellows Mecher, *The Shaker Adventure* (1986); Robert L. Peters, *The Gift to Be Simple: A Garland for Ann Lee* (1975) and *Shaker Light: Mother Ann Lee in America* (1987); and Stephen J. Stein, *The Shaker Experience in America: A History of the United Society of Believers* (1992). On New Harmony and the Owenite phase of communitarianism, see William Wilson, *The*

Angel and the Serpent (1964), and J. F. C. Harrison, *Quest for the New Moral World: Robert Owen and the Owenites in Britain and America* (1969). On Charles Fourier and the communities he inspired, see Jonathan Beecher, *Charles Fourier* (1987); Carl J. Guarneri, *The Utopian Alternative: Fourierism in Nineteenth Century America* (1991); and M. C. Spencer, *Charles Fourier* (1981).

For African American utopian communities, see William H. Pease, *Black Utopia: Negro Communal Experiments in America* (1963). For John Humphrey Noyes and his Oneida community, see Maren L. Carden, *Oneida: Utopian Community to Modern Corporation* (1969), and Robert David Thomas, *The Man Who Would Be Perfect: John Humphrey Noyes and the Utopian Impulse* (1977). For communitarian experiments after 1860, see Robert S. Fogarty, *All Things New: American Communes and Utopian Movements, 1860–1914* (1990).

Essential works for understanding the fate of reform following the Civil War are Aaron I. Abell, *The Urban Impact on American Protestantism, 1865–1900* (1962); LeRoy Ashby, *Saving the Waifs: Reformers and Dependent Children, 1890–1917* (1984); Dominick Cavallo, *Muscles and Morals: Organized Playgrounds and Urban Reform, 1880–1920* (1981); George Fredrickson, *The Inner Civil War: Northern Intellectuals and the Crisis of the Union* (1965); Nathan Huggins, *Protestants against Poverty: Boston's Charities, 1870–1900* (1971); Roy Lubove, *The Professional Altruist: The Emergence of Social Work as a Career, 1880–1930* (1975); David I. Macleod, *Building Character in the American Boy: The Boy Scouts, YMCA, and Their Forerunners* (1983); Arthur Mann, *Yankee Reformers in the Urban Age: Social Reform in Boston, 1880–1900* (1954); Henry F. May, *Protestant Churches and Industrial America* (1949); David J. Pivar, *Purity Crusade: Sexual Morality and Social Control, 1868–1900* (1973); and Susan Tiffin, *In Whose Best Interest? Child Welfare Reform in the Progressive Era* (1982).

Index

Library of Congress Cataloging-in-Publication Data

Mintz, Steven, 1953–
    Moralists and modernizers : America's pre–Civil War
reformers / Steven Mintz.
        p.   cm. — (The American moment)
    Includes bibliographical references and index.
    ISBN 0-8018-5080-0 (acid-free paper).—ISBN 0-8018-5081-9
(pbk. : acid-free paper)
    1. United States—Social conditions—To 1865.   2. United
States—Economic conditions—To 1865.   3. Social reformers—
United States—History.   I. Title.   II. Series.
HN57.M56   1995
306'.0973—dc20   94-43690